"Travels with a Sad Man"

Or

"Around the World in 75 Days with a Depressed Husband"

For the anxious adventurer

– VIVIENNE KING –

An environmentally friendly book printed and bound in England by
www.printondemand-worldwide.com

Mixed Sources
Product group from well-managed
forests, and other controlled sources
www.fsc.org Cert no. TT-COC-002641
FSC © 1996 Forest Stewardship Council

PEFC
PEFC/16-33-415

PEFC Certified
This product is
from sustainably
managed forests
and controlled
sources
www.pefc.org

This book is made entirely of chain-of-custody materials

www.fast-print.net/store.php

"Travels with a Sad Man"
Copyright © Vivienne King 2011

Cover

Harrison Gates and Eddie Jackson

defydesign@live.com

ISBN 978-178035-218-3

First published 2011 by
FASTPRINT PUBLISHING
Peterborough, England.

"The Sad Facts"

Roo had a privileged childhood. His mother Mavis was a kind and gentle lady, who stayed at home to look after everyone and his father now in his eighties, was a Director of the wider family business. His brother is four years his junior.

He was an anxious scholar and suffered from spells of digestive problems while at school – especially during what we used to call 'O' Levels, but since no real diagnosis had been made this was never treated and the problem actually improved when he went to college to study for a Diploma in Business and Finance. On successful completion of the Diploma Roo entered the family business on the bottom rung – sweeping up.

The relationship with his father was not as good as it should have been, but it would have been difficult not to get on with his mother as she was such a lovely person. *"The last of the real Ladies"*, I always said. Mavis loved everyone and everyone adored her.

It was a surprise when Roo asked me to marry him during a very romantic scene with us sitting on the bench overlooking the sunken garden at his parents' house. This part of their garden being quite ancient, it was dominated by an enormous stone fountain …. *it was the sort of place you might see fairies dancing about…* Anyway - the sound of the water and the cool breeze on that summers' evening must have had some sort of mesmerising affect on me because I said, *"Yes"*.

We were married a short while later and seemed to be on a constant honeymoon, until less than a year later, my 16 year old nephew – my sister's only child was killed in an accident. This had a huge impact on our marriage as Roo tried hard to support me through my bereavement and I struggled to accept what had happened, knowing that my sister's acceptance – *to this day* - would never come.

These testing times were about to get testier when we discovered a baby was well on the way to us. Neither of us was sure about being parents but when our firstborn came eight weeks early he turned out to be just the distraction we needed and in spite of the bereavement on the one hand, the love we felt for that little boy on the other gave us a sort of balance. We had become our own family.

I somehow knew though that I was never going to be very good at carrying offspring, so it was hardly surprising when four years on and after only nineteen weeks of pregnancy, I began to lose our second baby. The consensus of opinion from everyone medical, sensible and practical was unanimous; nature must be allowed to take its course because *'it wasn't meant to be'*. But in a typical Taurean way (having been born under that sign) I stubbornly spent the next eleven weeks in bed determined to have a go at keeping the tiny scrap inside me long enough for him to survive. Every day was a bonus and I would have hung on much longer, but he was so eager to see the world that one day he made an entrance ten weeks too soon. He was the ugliest thing you've ever seen and I was quite shocked that I could have bred something so ghastly. But several months and thousands of religiously-administered two-hourly tube feeds later, he turned into the most *beautiful* thing you've ever seen.

In 1987 came more devastating news. Mavis had been diagnosed with breast cancer.

It was difficult to comprehend that someone so gentle and good-natured could be attacked by something so ugly and foul. Surgery was quickly organised followed by an exhausting regime of chemo and radiotherapy, which was to last seven years.

Meantime, our lives continued with a few more significant events. 1987 was also the year we began to build a new home in a rural village. It was a vast undertaking even though we weren't actually doing the building ourselves and a very stressful time for us both with disasters and traumas like no other. Dear Mavis rolled on with such good humour and perseverance, determined not to be a bother to anyone and like us watched excitedly as the house grew. It was obvious to me though that she was fighting a losing battle and I wished the shell-of-a-building could be a house sooner rather than later, so she would get to see the finished product.

Our eldest became a weekly boarder at school and as if that wasn't enough to take in and cope with, Roo began experiencing big problems at work. He realised he was being squeezed out of the company by the more senior members of the family and even worse felt he had no support from his dad.

He was often tearful and unsure of himself and the negative attitude towards him in the office simply fuelled the fire knocking his confidence even further. Mentally exhausted with the strain and sometimes so sad, he said he couldn't bear it any longer and admitted to having suicidal thoughts.

Bombshell after bombshell exploded. Another came when, in the same year – and without warning, my step-father died at the age of 66. With this additional heartache, came the inevitable responsibility of comforting my mum as well as my sister and Roo, who was slowly sinking into the depths of despair. He lost weight so fast you could almost see it disappearing, but when I realised nearly forty pounds had gone I knew it couldn't be ignored any longer and marched him off to our GP.

"Depression".

"Feelings of inadequacy and low self-esteem – that's Depression", the doctor said.

"There's a brand new drug on the market. It's marvellous – a real wonder-drug. This'll soft you out".

So Roo started popping pills. He had a shaky start with a high dose, but settled into a regime slowly beginning to feel – *not better* – but 'different'. This difference saw him through the hiccups and traumas of our building project and the triumphant move into our new home, which Mavis, I'm glad to say was there to see.

But to call the road we trod the following year *'rocky'* would have been an understatement. The paint hadn't even begun to dry in our new house before our littlest man fell ill. He collapsed without warning and was whisked off in an ambulance with a blue light and a siren. A three year old on a stretcher looks so tiny and as I held his hot little hand on the way to the hospital all sorts of things went through my mind. In one irrational moment even wondering if we shouldn't have moved into the house for some reason.

Well, it would be difficult for me to go through all the gory details – it was all a big blur anyway - so I won't try, but even though he was diagnosed with Kawasaki Syndrome – something quite different to the normal type of childhood illnesses, he made a full recovery and was cross when he was told he'd been in ambulance with a siren and hadn't known about it.

Our darling Mavis could not be saved though and Roo was with her when she peacefully slipped away. All those who had known her were distraught and more than a few hundred people attended her Memorial Service. Even now, family and friends talk of her charming personality and ability to see only the good side of someone.

As we coped with our huge loss and the weeks went by, it dawned on us that Roo was definitely hooked on this drug and experiencing every single symptom that went with it. The sadness he felt had been replaced by a growing list of evils, each one giving off their own destructive force.

He was irritable, restless and twitchy. Sometimes he was so tired, he couldn't stop yawning, but when he fell asleep intense nightmares woke him up. Uncontrollable sweating caused red, itchy skin all over his body and his mouth was constantly dry. His susceptible digestive system was turned upside down and anything 'physical' that had existed between us had flown out the window.

The worst thing for me though, was dealing with his aggression. He'd become a hostile zombie and at times he looked at me with such hate in his eyes, I should have dropped dead.

The only good thing was that he'd put on weight – a lot of weight!

Looking at it logically and accepting the fact that this drug was not doing Roo, or the rest of us any good, a sensible person would simply have stopped taking it, but thinking we'd better run this past our GP we returned to see him expecting a positive answer. *"Yes, come off it now. I'm sure you don't need it".* Something on those lines.

But the actual answer was a surprise. Roo was told that he couldn't just stop taking the drug, but must come off it gradually. 'Gradually', meant lowering the dose over a considerable period of time to wean him off avoiding the more severe symptoms of withdrawal. I found it hard to imagine what symptoms could possibly be more severe than the ones he'd already experienced, but trusting the Professional – *as you do*, we did as we were told.

More weeks went by and our struggle intensified the more we tried to 'wean'. It was as though the drug had actually altered him and he was stuck inside another person. He snapped at the boys for the slightest little thing and I found myself staying close to them, not knowing what he might do next. They were confused too. Where had their nice daddy gone? Who was this angry one?

Each day, we dragged ourselves along and on the way made appointments to see anyone and everyone we thought might be able to help us. Gastroenterologists, Neuro-Psychologists, Psychiatrists – we saw them all, here and abroad. But not one expert could give me my husband back. It seemed as soon as they heard about the effects Roo had experienced from the drug prescribed they backed off sending us away with no answers, or solutions. It was as though they all shared a secretive cause for concern, but weren't prepared to do anything about it.

The business-side of things hadn't improved for Roo and we both knew that his days at the company were numbered. Unable to accept the fact that this was a real illness, his father was baffled when he couldn't pull himself together and told him so, which did nothing to help Roo's feelings of utter uselessness.

It was about this time that his dad announced he was to re-marry. I really thought this would tip Roo over the edge and he would go off somewhere never to be seen again, but he attended the wedding and although the relationship with his dad and new wife could be better - with a bit of cajoling from me, Roo does at least maintain contact.

All this time, Roo's mood swung from one end of the spectrum to the other. He was on a low dose of the drug by now, but it seemed that the damage it had done couldn't be reversed. His rages and emotional outbursts continued, reaching a peak at one time when he had his hands around my throat. He didn't strangle me of course, otherwise I wouldn't be writing this, but it was witnessed by both our children and was a very unpleasant experience for us all – even for Roo, when he realised what he'd done.

Roo was finding the journey to work more difficult each time he did it and I was secretly pleased when he stopped going completely, but this meant that he had no purpose at all - no reason to get up in the morning and be somewhere important making him feel even more inadequate. In spite of the more relaxed lifestyle he continued to look and feel ill, suffering with crushing tiredness and huge weight loss all over again. He was in a constant state of anxiousness and one morning woke up looking as though his face had been painted in a delicate shade of 'Tiger Mustard', but without the whiskers; or the enjoyment of the village fete.

We repeated the march to the GP for blood work and a chest X Ray, which turned out to be as clear as a bell, but the minute the blood test results were back at the surgery our GP was alarmed enough to ring us immediately. He didn't mince his words; the results were sinister. As if Roo's mental state wasn't enough to cope with he was told that the test to look at his liver function showed that he had Hepatitis "of unknown origin" and would need to see a liver Specialist as soon as possible.

Roo wasn't particularly fazed by this news, saying he didn't know why I was panicking and was surprised when I sprang into action to find the best person available. He listened with amusement to the telephone conversations as I rang my contacts for any recommendations they had, but I didn't put the 'phone down until I had badgered our way to a private appointment in London two days later.

The next day, I sat on the telephone again and spoke to friends to ask their opinion of the 'unknown origin' bit from the liver function test results. Drug-Induced Hepatotoxicity, which can be fatal was mentioned more than once and seemed to fit the bill.

The journey to the hospital in west London was long and arduous and Roo looked ridiculous wearing the overcoat that was now three sizes too big for him. It was a cold, grey day and we both felt cold and grey too; the only bright thing was the colour of Roo's skin. The appointments were running an hour late to make matters even worse and by the time Roo was seen he was on his knees. Eventually, the Liver Man came out to meet us apologising profusely for the wait and whisked Roo off to an examination room where he pummelled, pushed and scanned every part of his torso. He obviously knew his stuff, but couldn't make a conclusive diagnosis and when we asked if the drug Roo had been on for the past fourteen years of our lives could have caused the hepatitis, his answer was as ambiguous as the discussions on global warming. He did however suggest that Roo come off it as soon as possible, which might have been the most diplomatic way of saying it wasn't doing him any good without actually condemning it.

I went into emergency planning mode to begin weaning him off, well aware that it was going to be a very long haul. The prospect of it all was more than worrying and I still had 'toxic liver' in my mind. At the same time, I asked myself if I wanted to continue with my role as carer, counsellor and warden, knowing in my heart that the answer was a positive "No".

I felt trapped, lonely and scared. Roo was so unpredictable. His anger and emotions sometimes spilled over WITH the drug, so how would I handle him without any drugs at all? I was in a panic now, but there was no alternative. I couldn't turn and run away from my poor skinny, yellow husband in yet another hour of need.

As soon as we were home, Roo went to bed. He was exhausted. I was tired too, but my mind was in a whirl of planning and drug regimes. It was early morning before I was satisfied with a systematic plan to gradually reduce his medication and as I climbed the stairs to bed felt a little more optimistic.

We began an uphill struggle juggling the dose and trying to keep him on an even keel at the same time. Regular blood tests showed that his liver wasn't improving in the way that we'd hoped and he seemed to be on a slippery slope mentally. He felt useless and unsuccessful, that he had underachieved and had never reached a goal of any kind.

Then the 'screaming day terrors' started. He talked utter rubbish, had impaired memory, extreme anxiety with catastrophic thinking and was completely irrational, which led him to suicidal thoughts all over again. Sometimes his only comfort was to screw himself up in a ball on the floor while he sobbed. Nothing I said, or did made any difference.

We were in big trouble.

By the time he was unable to function properly in a cognitive way, I had already decided to take drastic action. It was a Saturday morning and I rang the Emergency GP Service. Miraculously, the doctor I spoke to was very kind and listened carefully to what I was saying, which was something that hadn't happened before. I poured it all out without allowing him to get a word in edgeways releasing the pent up emotions of the last few years with all the force that desperation brings.

In spite of trying to appear in control of the situation, he must have realised that I was actually on the edge myself and sounded concerned for me. So much so, that for once I felt sorry for me too and howled my eyes out.

He said the only thing I could do would be to take Roo to A & E, where he would eventually be assessed for a bed in a mental health unit.

'Eventually'. I didn't like the thought of that. We needed immediate help. There had to be something else. If the NHS wasn't the solution, perhaps there was something we could pay for. I scoured the Internet for a safe haven – even an expensive one. I found it in the shape of a specialist clinic in London and after a lengthy discussion over the 'phone with the nurse in charge and then one of the Psychiatrists, we were offered a bed. The boys were home that weekend and had been horrified and upset by their dad's behaviour. Seeing Roo in this way was bad enough for them, but to see what it was doing to me too was a double-whammy, so when I told them about the offer they both agreed that it was the best thing to do. The three of us sat down with Roo to persuade him to go, because the clinic would only take him if that was what he wanted. He would be able to walk out at any time, so it was imperative that he understood the need for help and stay there for as long as it took to improve his condition. More than an hour of tears, terror and passionate arguments passed and the boys were at breaking point before he finally agreed to go. I went upstairs to collect a few things for him and found myself sobbing over his toothbrush and by the time I had stuffed pyjamas and other bits and pieces into a bag, I certainly wasn't in a fit state to drive, so we called a cab. Bundling Roo into the back seat after emotional 'goodbyes' from the boys, I hung on to him all the way there in case he tried to leap out. The two hour journey was as painful as if I were taking our beloved cat to be put down and several times I found myself on the verge of asking the driver to turn around and go home again; but ages later it seemed we arrived at our destination.

They were expecting us when we stopped outside the enormous white building and an ordinary-looking person came to the car. Roo looked terrified and I felt giddy with the emotion of it all, but once inside we didn't have to wait long before my credit card was discretely swiped and the ordinary-looking person led us upstairs to a stark, barren room. I was surprised. I thought it would be a bit more plush.

It really was as simple as that. All I had to do was say goodbye and walk away.

"Please don't leave me here", he begged, looking like a forlorn, bedraggled little boy being dumped in an alley

by a wicked stepmother. My throat was closing up and I couldn't swallow. Quickly, I went to the window and tried to open it just for something to do with my hands. Of course, the bloody thing wouldn't open and it was then I realised he was in a room for patients with suicide on their minds.

Silly me.

A plane bound for Heathrow flew slowly over the building and I looked up, following it through the air. Not because I was interested in the aircraft, but to keep the tears inside my eyes.

If I didn't abandon him in that sad, bleak room right there and then, we'd be leaving together and then where would we be? So with my head ready to explode any second, I gave him a quick kiss on his forehead and left the room without looking back. Stumbling into the brightness of the day, almost in disbelief at what I'd just done, I howled all the way home in the back of the cab. I'd never been so cruel to anyone in my entire life, but I did it for us both and felt such a sense of relief that the responsibility of looking after him had been passed to someone else.

Standing alone in the kitchen back at home ...*finally*, I was able to take a deep breath; something I hadn't been able to do for a long time.

Even though he wanted to leave every day and nearly did on a couple of occasions, Roo stayed there for a whole month. Of course I missed him. Of course I felt guilty for leaving him there. But without him, it became crystal clear just how bad things had become. It was impossible to live a normal life for that month, but it did give me time to regain my strength and plan meticulously for his return home. At night, alone with my deepest, darkest and most saddest thoughts, I accepted the fact that I had no idea if I would be able to stand the strain and be strong enough to survive a future with this other person. I knew I might have to admit defeat, but not until after I had tried even harder to find the man I once loved and make him better.

DAY ONE: "Bye-Bye"

The evidence of my headfirst descent downstairs the week before was still very obvious. Norman Wisdom would have been proud of me and couldn't have done it better. But it wasn't a choreographed fall and I wasn't pushed either – *if that's what you were thinking.* It was the skiing accident in my late twenties that had left me with an unpredictable left knee. I was sure it had a mind of its own now, just like 'Thing', the disembodied forearm in the Addams Family television series and seemed to delight in giving way, tipping me off balance at the most perilous of moments.

My very own 'Thing'- although attached to the rest of me was the reason I was limping so badly, but I knew I had to be grateful that although it was painful and swollen and exhibited an amazing band of colours, it wouldn't prevent us taking the trip of a lifetime.

Easing myself into the car I began to adjust my left leg for the journey ahead, but was still making the adjustments when the car began to move off. In sudden panic, I looked round quickly to catch a last glimpse of our lovely house and wanted to tell the driver that I wasn't quite ready to go, but before I knew it, it was too late and we were on the main road. There was only enough time for a massive-huge-enormous prayer before we left the village on that unusually sunny day in February and when the last bastions of security were out of sight, I felt as though I'd left something behind. We hadn't been able to find our big white and tan cat, Moje to say goodbye, but had given the tabby, Fred some attention and of course, it wasn't worth trying to find *'Ginger-the-mad'*; she'd be squeezed into some corner somewhere, hiding from her own tail.

We drove past brown fields and trees without leaves, which I supposed would be green on our return. We'd miss the daffs; but not the tulips or bluebells and although the first lambs would soon be born, they usually kept coming well into spring, so fortunately, we'd see some in April. The journey on the motorway to Heathrow was even more laborious than usual giving us a clear uninterrupted view of the ugly rubbish along the hard shoulder and all over the banks. Bloody people.

I kept an eye on Roo at the same time and was glad I'd decided to give him a tranquillizer before we'd left - although secretly I was much more jittery than him and needed one myself.

Coming to a slow halt on the M25, I fixed my gaze on a particularly large amount of litter and between identifying the coke cans from the Mc Donald's bags, asked myself why were we doing this? Why were we leaving hearth and home?

Oh yes. It was something to do with a snowball.

Roo had been terribly ill – *to put it mildly*. We'd both retired from paid employment and with Roo's illness in mind had a hankering to see New Zealand sooner, rather than later. The rest just sort of snowballed somehow.

The initial plan was to be away at the same time as our youngest son, Lukey. (He hates being called his childhood name and reminds us constantly that we named him Lucas).

Anyway, Lukey's Ski Instructor course in Canada would coincide date-wise and I suppose we thought if we were going as far as New Zealand, we might as well see Fiji and getting from there to Hawaii, we'd pass the Cook Islands ... and Tahiti ... *and so the snowball progressed.*

Roo sat in front in a stupefied state, looking as though he didn't have a care in the world, but the truth of the matter was that his liver was shot to bits and he was very unstable mentally. I knew he was feeling dreadful and he certainly looked awful, with a yellow streak radiating across each side of his face - a tell-tale sign that his liver wasn't at all right.

I must have been mad to take him away from his home where he felt safe and only a few hours' drive from the clinic - that wonderful sanctuary with the kind and knowledgeable people who saved him from himself six months ago.

"Too late now", I thought.

But was it? We weren't being forced onto a plane. We weren't being deported under armed guard. We could do what we liked.

Staring out of the window in the back of the car, I pictured the relief on my sister's face when we turned up on her doorstep, shouting, *"SURPRISE!"* and the cats lovingly weaving themselves in and out of our legs as we stood with our suitcases in the hall.

We wouldn't go. We mustn't go.

These thoughts must have helped to pass the time though, because suddenly we arrived at the mayhem of Terminal 3 Departures and Diane and the cats instantly disappeared from my mind.

Since no one except the Queen, or Jamie Oliver would be allowed to linger around this hallowed ground for longer than three minutes, our time here was very brief. With a quick goodbye to Dennis, our intrepid driver from the 'good old days' of the once family-run business and an even faster removal of our luggage from the car, the deal was sealed … we *were* leaving the country and everyone and everything we loved for seventy-five days.

Standing on the pavement with our belongings feeling like a displaced refugee, I watched Roo fill a trolley with the two enormous suitcases that had taken me weeks to pack and we rushed from the chaos outside into the relative calm of the new terminal.

I tried to be excited, but felt too nauseous and wanted to shout, *"No, no, we won't go!"* And had to remind myself that we were going on a wonderful holiday and weren't to be interned behind barbed wire on the Isle of Man.

Roo actually had a smile on his face for a change. It was a yellow one, but it was definitely a smile as we headed towards the automatic doors. I followed on behind like a devoted middle-eastern wife – minus the burka and *without* a smile on my face, wondering what on earth we were doing and also wondering what might go wrong first. I didn't have to wait long to find out as hiccup number one occurred immediately.

Literally sliding up with the trolley to the tall Virgin Atlantic desk on the slippery polished floor, we were greeted by a divine, smiling creature (how do they find these slim and beautiful girls?) who beckoned us to a more senior divine creature standing beside her. I'd checked in 'on line' for our flight so we should have simply dropped off our bags and sailed into the lounge, but instead the senior divine creature took one look at our paperwork and was instantly suspicious of our motives.

She couldn't understand how we could be leaving England without the return flight printed on the same piece of paper and that we weren't returning to the UK for nearly three months.

"But where will you be all that time?" she asked.

"Here we go", I thought. *"We won't be allowed to go, because the Forger from Stalag Luft III has made a mistake with our papers – I told him that crest wasn't right ...."*

Alongside the nutty things going on in mind, I thought it would be easier to show her each and every ticket for the flights we would be taking (all fifteen), but halfway through this marathon of a paper exercise, another divine creature appeared. Obviously more experienced, she seemed satisfied that we weren't International Art Thieves and adjusting her purple neckerchief in an official sort of way, nodded to her colleague to let us pass through Virgin Atlantic's version of "Checkpoint Charlie".

Was this an omen? Should we turn tail and run for home?

Had Roo gone to pieces at this point, I might have been at the exit by this time, but he appeared to be in complete control and was still smiling, charming the girls with small-talk and keen to go on up to the Lounge.

Onwards and upwards via the lift we went.

Security came next and I was sure our feet were glowing after our shoes had been X-Ray'd to search for explosives (crazy, eh?) And don't you just HATE walking across a grubby carpet barefoot? I must have looked ridiculous impersonating a ballerina, as I tried to walk on tiptoe; but anything to avoid fungal infections.

With difficulty, we found the Virgin Atlantic Lounge, which had been totally revamped since we were last there. Looking very posh and such a perfect haven for a long haul flight, I decided Sir Richard must have consulted a plethora of Psychologists to design it. It was such a relaxing space, with armchairs and sofas for sitting in and day beds for snoozing in, I could have been pampered, pummelled or even had a swim! Quiet areas were plentiful for those pondering their destiny, or destination - well away from noisy areas where the kids could let off steam.

It was quite something, but it was also seriously busy with all sorts of travellers wearing all kinds of travel-wear from one extreme to the other. Some wore jeans and tee shirts, while a lot of the women looked as if they were going to a wedding. You wear whatever you're comfortable in, or what you imagine you *should* be wearing I suppose, but I felt a bit under-dressed, compared to some.

Amongst the melee, I think I spotted a footballer/minor soap star, or two – they could have been either. They all look the same to me and as I must be the only person in the whole country who doesn't watch East Enders, what do I know?

We headed for the very swish restaurant where we could have eaten pretty much anything we wanted, but with such a long flight ahead of us, thought not only of our digestive systems and the possible outcome, but also the comfort of our fellow passengers (let's hope they were also thinking of us) and chose a freshly-cooked piece of tuna and salad, which was not only beautifully served, but also tasted as good as it looked.

Refreshed with fab food, fizzy water and the usual first class care and attention from the Virgins, we started to relax a bit.

Roo insisted he would be okay to go alone to have his hair cut at 'The Cowshed', the complimentary salon in the lounge and off he went.

I was too concerned for his welfare to leave him to his own devices (let alone loose amongst all those pretty girls) so nonchalantly wandered after him pretending to look for another footballer; although as I said, I didn't know what I was actually looking for.

No-one remotely resembling a footballer I decided, but I couldn't help noticing a simply gorgeous American businessman standing at the bar talking to a beautiful slender Virgin. This must be a great place to work. Lucky her... and so slim.

I tried to remember being that slim and convinced myself that I had been once – in the dark ages.

Losing my concentration for a while, I panicked when I came upon the salon and couldn't see Roo there. Looking left as far as my eyes would let me without moving my head, a tap on my right shoulder made me spin round to see him beside me – minus quite a lot of hair.

Unfazed by the experience, he was almost jolly.

I really wished I had taken one of his tranquilizers......

Having been fed, watered and pampered, it was soon time to board the huge airbus with those cosy 'suites' on board - good enough for business people and the like (and me, with me dodgy knee) Roo and I settled down into our 'nests'.

As comfortable as I was, I desperately wanted to find a good enough reason *not* be seated and strapped into this Upper Class seat waiting on the tarmac at Heathrow for the flight to China, but although my head told me to make a run for the door, the rest of me said *"stay put"*.

"Perhaps", I thought, wishing hard *"a late passenger will cause a delay, I'll quickly scoop Roo up with me on the way out and we'll watch the plane leave without us at the last minute"*.

(Now those of you who received a postcard from Hong Kong know that this didn't happen).

Pondering this manoeuvre while the other passengers and crew made ready, I sat there staring at the door with a 'flight or fight' feeling.

My gaze was interrupted though when I realised that we were at the point of no return and any last-minute withdrawal became impossible as a pretty, 5.7", size 12 Virgin in her tight red skirt and see-through white blouse closed the door, said *"A Okay"* to the driver and sat down. Then swiftly, silently and without any effort at all it seemed, the large piece of steel with us in it, hurtled along the runway and somehow lifted into the air.

All 250 tons of it.

So we'd left the ground and had climbed high above acres and acres of tightly-packed, fluffy cotton wool.

We were in a silver tube flying in the sky seven miles above the ground at a speed of 450miles per hour, with 338 other passengers of unknown creed, religion or origin, heading for another part of the world.

No problem there then.

Might as well sit back and relax.

Go to plan 'B'.

I'd missed 'Atonement' when it was on general release and was pleased to see that it was one of the fifty-two films available.

I'd make that "number one".

However, due to the fact that the best laid plans of mice, men and Vivienne are often scuppered I only saw three quarters of it because my darn screen-console-thingy played up so much (no-one else's of course) it was unwatchable.

The hugely-apologetic-on-board-Technician was unable to fix it. I could have moved to an empty seat further back up the plane, but that would have meant being too far away from Roo, so I stayed put and watched a bit of TV and then bought my journal up-to-date.

The cabin crew were as delightful as ever and although we were both offered treatments by 'The Flying Beautician' that Virgin had at the time, the turbulence was so bad it was impossible for her to work safely and actually none of the girls moved from their seats for quite a long time.

With so much entertainment to choose from, none of us up front seemed to mind the absence of food and drink, but I did wonder how the others squeezed into the cabins behind us were faring and tried hard not to feel guilty. Right on cue though, I felt such a ghastly stabbing pain in my left knee that my guilt disappeared and I was grateful to be able to stretch my leg out resting it on the ottoman in front of my seat.

Peeping over the top of the suite behind me, I had a good view of my patient who was busy flicking through the myriad of channels, oblivious to the motion of the plane.

He looked up at me with the sort of smile you'd get from a naughty schoolboy hiding a matchbox full of earwigs in his pocket and I suddenly came over all 'maternal' – you know that sort of feeling which makes your eyes feel soft and warm.

Bless his heart.

I was dragging him to another part of the world on a whim and a fancy.

What a wicked wife I was.

No turning back now, though. I'll just have to look after him.

Changing into a Virgin sleep suit, he turned his seat into 'bed' mode and tucked up.

As soon as I thought he was settled, I did the same, laying cosily cocooned 37,000 feet above the ground.

How peculiar.

I tried hard to sleep, but found it difficult to switch my brain off.

It was annoying that I'd had a marvellous opportunity for a movie-marathon allowing me to screen-overdose during the longest of all our flights and hadn't done so.

Of course, not the most serious of dilemmas and I told myself off for thinking it was.

Had I been able to watch loads of films, it might have taken my mind off other things. Instead, I tossed and turned until I sat bolt upright with such a loud irritable sigh, that I wondered if anyone else had heard it.

I looked around the cabin with the same interest a mother has when she gingerly opens the door where her child is sleeping, but everyone, (including the crew, probably??!) had drifted off into the Land of Nod.

Yawning uncontrollably now, I pulled the duvet up to my chin and must have switched off at last.

The sound of the engines roaring was what stirred me first and looking at my watch and then at the motionless Roo, I realised that he'd slept for about five hours and I must have had at least four.

Good. A bit of rest, at least.

With the Airbus slicing its' way through the air and away from any turbulence, each passenger was gently woken up with breakfast in bed by the Virgins who looked as fresh as daisies.

I certainly didn't look like a daisy, more like a dandelion that had been picked the day before and a starving one at that. A bowl of fresh fruit salad with crème fraiche was delivered to my seat - and how could I resist a bacon butty with brown sauce? (Blow the joint pain it would cause me over the next few days - I was on holiday). A glass of fresh orange juice and a cup of good hot coffee, a wash and brush up with all the lovely Virgin stuff in the loo and I was ready to face Hong Kong.

Roo wasn't quite so ready and needed a bit of encouragement to get organised. Since his illness began, he no longer sees urgency of a situation and leaves everything to the last minute. The inevitable rush doesn't help his anxiety one bit, so I was keen to pre-empt anything I could. He'd had his breakfast, so it was just a case of fussing and cajoling him until he too was washed and brushed up and ready to land.

The plane glided onto the tarmac as if it was made of paper and as soon as we came to a stop there was *'action stations'*, with everyone ducking and diving for their things, desperately hoping to be first off.

(Why?)

It doesn't matter what airline you fly, in whatever class, or who you've been sitting next to for an eternity, there's always a mad dash to get off when the journey is over. Do we all suddenly catch claustrophobia?

The assumption was that the middle door would be opened to let us out, but one should never assume anything and to our surprise the door at the front was opened, which meant that the passengers in our cabin turned circle and made a dash for that door in an 'Abandon Ship' sort of way.

My training at jumble sales during my former years always pays off and I jostled my way out with Roo close behind. (He's still in training).

Our exit was, of course conducted in a very orderly – albeit swift – manner, but I always wonder what it would be like in an emergency.

I hoped never to find out.

DAY TWO: Lantau Island, Hong Kong (+8 GMT)

Misty and growing dark, it was difficult to decide on the air temperature because we stepped straight out into an air-conditioned tunnel leading to the massive International Terminal. With flowers and huge potted plants in abundance, the Arrivals Hall was spotlessly clean and tidy and awash with ground staff wearing smart uniforms and bright smiles. All very ship-shape and Chinese-fashion. The Immigration Officer was efficient and friendly and didn't intimidate us the way they do in the US – you know how they can make you feel like a convicted criminal trying to get in through the back door with a suitcase full of British flags.(*As if*…) They don't seem to like us 'Brits', but the Chinese think we're quite nice. Obviously - with such a large amount of takeaways in England. I remember someone saying once, that with so many of these wonderful establishments popping up all over the country, one day the front windows of all the "Wunhung Lows" and "Ho Hums" will open up and tanks will roll out. Then they'll take over. I won't mind too much – I love Chinese food, but I'm not wearing khaki shorts for anyone.

Anyway, back to Hong Kong.

The transportation liaison chap was where he said he would be, holding a card with our name on it and we followed him outside to the hotel car. It was here we almost witnessed our first Chinese road traffic accident, when one limo reversed into another, missing it by a rat's whisker and much shouting of *"Ying Tong"* ensued before we left the airport. This incident made me feel even more protective towards Roo and I sat with him in the back seat holding his hand tightly all the way. The friendly, chatty driver spoke reasonable English, which was much better than our Chinese (but then I doubted I'd ever get to use the phrase, *"Horses mainly like to eat apples"*, which had taken me five weeks to learn - courtesy of the Daily Mirror free CD) and he whisked us off to the Marriott, about half an hour away across the bridge connecting Lantau and Hong Kong Islands.

It was Chinese New Year (Rat) and everything seemed to be painted, or covered in something red – the Chinese celebration colour. The skyscraper-of-a-hotel, gleaming in the nightlight was no exception and it too was draped in red. Both inside and out tall, willowy Weeping Fig trees stood in enormous planters with branches covered in oranges - very festive apparently, with gold Chinese letters dangling from the ceiling, which we decided were saying, *"Happy New Rat"*.

The Bell Boys wearing uniforms and box hats straight out of an Agatha Christie novel fell over themselves to help us with our luggage (if you see what I mean) and after a quick zip in a lift that the Star Ship Enterprise would have been proud of, we were in our interconnecting rooms (necessary due to Roo's Vesuvius-like snoring) where a marvellous night-time view of the harbour and city greeted us from behind the huge expanse of windows.

Towering office blocks with movie screen billboards and their flashing advertisements hung in the maze of streets below with wide roads criss-crossing each other and going off in every direction. It was all very futuristic and much-like a scene from the film 'Blade Runner'.

There was a gentle knock at the door. China Tea in a white handle-less pot and a dish of powdered sweets were delivered on a tray by a terribly polite waiter and we sat on the comfy chairs at the window to enjoy them. I didn't know whether I was supposed to let the tea 'draw', but began to pour anyway and just as I did a New Year firework display began out in the harbour.

The noise was amazing – even through the double-glazing – and it went on for at least fifteen minutes while we sipped the refreshing, strongly perfumed tea and chomped our way through the unusual sweets until the finale came with several massive fireworks that shaped Chinese Dogs in the night sky. The Chinese invented fireworks so they should have been good, but it was an incredible spectacle and like nothing we'd seen before - even at the New Years' Eve display  on the Thames and coupled with the tea, we felt as though we'd been personally welcomed to China.

I rang mum and text'd the boys. All okay. So was Roo. But how was he okay?

Perhaps I'd imagined the almost unbearable time we'd had over the last year and the four weeks he'd spent in the clinic.

No, I couldn't have imagined anything as bad as that.

"Well we're here now", I thought – *"We've come this far. Push on and deal with anything if it occurs. Try to be positive".*

With the smell of those fireworks permeating throughout the hotel, we were too excited to sleep yet and despite the adequate Virgin meals somehow thought we were starving hungry so went off to explore the hotel a bit and find some food.

Strangely enough, it was full of Chinese families enjoying the New Year festivities with hardly a Westerner in sight and at the Buffet were mums, dads, grannies, granddads and lots of delightful little ones dashing to and fro, their plates laden with food as if it were their last meal.

I'd never seen this sort of fare at the local take-away and I was a bit worried when there was no sign of a 'number 24', so I stuck to the seafood.

Crab, lobster, prawns, noodles – all pretty safe and very yummy-looking, but I steered clear of the colourful pots of steaming 'soup' containing interesting-looking floating things, some of which, were obviously still alive and moving around in the shimmering pots.

It was a treat to see real Chinese people, eating real Chinese food from bowls held under their chins, scooping dinner into their mouths with their chopsticks and was probably the closest I'd ever come to seeing Chinese family life – albeit in the confines of a five star hotel.

Our stomachs must have been almost full to overflowing when we returned to our rooms and we should both have sat up for a while, but it wasn't long before Roo had drifted off into a deep sleep.

There was no way I could lay down without having digested at least some of my dinner, so trying to forget the pan of 'moving' items, I sat opposite Roo watching Hong Kong in the dark.

A sweeping view of night time Kowloon was just visible behind the lingering mist from the fireworks and lights flashed and sparkled from an array of fishing boats bobbing about on the vast expanse of black water in the bay.

The realisation of our location in the world suddenly hit me and I had an overwhelming feeling of excitement and optimism that things would improve and we'd have a marvellous time away.

I found the low hum from the traffic below almost comforting and sat watching Hong Kong prepare for night, until I couldn't keep my eyes open any longer and I too hit the hay.

DAY THREE: "The Old Colony"

I woke several times and finally by 4am had given up all attempts at sleeping and carried on with my journal. I made a cup of PG to keep me company (never leave home without it) and watched the dawn creep slowly over the Kowloon hills.

The sun brightened the sky. With it, my sleepiness brightened too and I was suddenly wide-awake. Poor Roo could have slept on but I wasn't going to waste a second and by 7am almost dragged him out of bed.

Back to another buffet - this time for breakfast - although it was really the middle of the night for us. Fruit, yoghurt, scrambled eggs, smoked salmon – oh and a glass of Champagne.

Bliss!

We'd never been to Hong Kong before, so to get our bearings took a cab to the other (south) side of the island, which is mainly residential. More amazing sky- scrapers, but some Victorian buildings remain from British occupation, in roads with very English names - Connaught, Harcourt, Queensway – all evidence of British rule.

The day was sunny and warm.

We were actually enjoying the start of our adventure and Roo seemed quite content to go along with my suggestion.

So far, so good.

Hong Kong had to clean up following the 'SARS' epidemic, otherwise tourism would have been in trouble and now it's so clean it's almost clinical. There are huge fines for dropping litter, chewing gum, smoking, or drinking on the streets. Consequently, there's no rubbish anywhere. What a pleasant change!

A visit to Stanley Market (fake Designer labels and 'toot') was really interesting, with the sights, sounds and smells being so different to the markets I'd been used to in London's East End. We bought a couple of things, but I didn't want to drag Roo around the shops on our first day and what with jetlag making us feel a bit jaded we didn't stay long.

Hong Konger's seem desperate to try out their language skills and we found them keen to help in any way, replying sometimes in perfect English. Tiny Chinese children are delightful and the smallest look like cute painted dolls.

I was just beginning to enjoy myself and was getting all philosophical, when out of the blue Roo's mood altered dramatically. He said he felt as though his head was being slowly shrunk and had feelings of impending doom. This is nothing unusual for him - he calls it his 'crushing syndrome' and although it might sound funny to you, it terrifies him.

Instantly soaked through with perspiration caused not only by anxiety, but incredible fear, we needed to leave quickly before we were in real trouble. I began to get annoyed with myself again. Why had I brought him to Hong Kong? This was all my fault.

I grabbed his hand and headed back the way we'd come, dragging him through the stalls and alleys like a little boy hoping that with every turn we'd reach the main road. I tried not to look panic-stricken myself and stay in control, but the peculiar sights and sounds were confusing me now and I wasn't sure we were going the right way.

In our haste, one turn was a dead end and we had to go all the way back to where we started. Then 'out of the blue' we came to the water's edge, which for a moment really threw me, but here on a sort of promenade was a map of the area on a large notice board.

"Thank you, God." I whispered,

Roo looked dreadful and hadn't said a word since we left the market. He was totally spaced-out and oblivious to what I was saying as I pointed on the map the route we needed to take. With an idea of where we were I calmed down and noticing that the sea wall was wide enough to sit on, headed for it to take a breather.

There we sat for a few minutes while I talked a load of rubbish about the beauty of the water and the junks floating on it. The breeze cooled us down and gave us enough of a boost to carry on. We'd actually gone round in a huge circle and I realised we were just beside the main road. *"Please, please",* I thought, *"Let there be a cab".*

I was physically holding Roo up by now and didn't know how much longer I would last, but as if someone from above had witnessed this, an empty cab materialised beside us and I bundled him in. He was in a terrible state - visibly shaking, unable to speak coherently and wide-eyed. It was too difficult to strap him in and he rocked around with me on the back seat during the twenty minute drive, which seemed like twenty hours until we reached the relative safety of The Marriott. I hoped he didn't look like a drunk clinging on to me for dear life as we made for the lift.

It was a great relief to feel the calm and quiet of our rooms. The interconnecting door between the two sides was wide open, but Roo migrated to the room I was using and just pulling off his trousers and shoes sank beneath the duvet instantly falling asleep.

With this episode, my worries returned and I was thankful that we were at least only a quarter of the way round the world. I could arrange to go home tomorrow and by the look of Roo we needed to do just that. I watched him for a while. He was so thin and obviously ill. I'd been an idiot to think that this would work, but at least we hadn't unpacked. Everyone at home would want to say, "*I told you so*", but would be too kind to actually say it. I tried to convince myself that the trip didn't matter really, but it did.

With so much going on outside the window it was difficult for me to be bored while Roo slept and I watched the Chinese goings-on in the daylight this time while listening to his deep breathing. Reflecting on the attack he'd had at the market I thought about the way I would have handled it at home. He seems to recover more quickly when he feels safe in a bolt-hole – he's curled up into a ball on the floor before now, which is very upsetting to see and also embarrassing for him.

I dug deep into the side of one suitcase to find the flat bedside travel tray, clipped the poppers together to convert it for use and placed it on the nightstand in his room. Then positioned the hotel slippers and bathrobe in a homely sort of way and arranged his toiletries nicely. Only little things, but I hoped familiar touches might help him to feel safe.

He looked much better when he woke, with just a slight yellow streak on his right cheek; the earlier panic and terror thankfully had subsided. The nap had done the trick for the time-being and after a shower he was calm and able to talk, so I made us both a cup of PG and chatted about ordinary things while we drank it. I decided not to mention plans to go home until after dinner.

We should have gone to a restaurant in Aberdeen that night, but cancelled the table in favour of a more laid-back meal in the hotel and while we ate, I casually suggested we ring Virgin Atlantic to see if we could get seats to London as soon as possible. He wouldn't even discuss it and we went to bed with differing views about what would come next.

DAY FOUR:

"More Hong Kong"

Sheer exhaustion must have helped us get a reasonable nights' sleep. I felt optimistic again and quite different when the alarm went off, but gingerly eyed-up Roo up to see how he was. It was amazing that he could have an episode as bad as that one minute and the next be right as ninepence. I was still very wary though and felt that literally anything could happen.

Amazingly, he'd chosen to forget the fun and games we had yesterday and showered and dressed as if he had not a care in the world. I would try to do the same; although I knew where to lay my hands on the telephone number for Virgin Atlantic in a hurry and stuffed a tranquilizer into my purse. I wasn't sure if it was for him, or me.

A nice breakfast gave us the energy and inclination for doing as much as Roo felt able and after a quick discussion, we decided to see the island from the highest point, Victoria Peak and left the hotel walking in this direction.

Roo started off quite well, but we hadn't gone very far when without warning he began to have one of his 'angry' moments. His behaviour is quite frightening when he has these. In an ordinary way to begin with, he tried to get his point across and convince me that I wouldn't be able to walk up the steep hill with my dodgy knee. But in the blink of an eye, the next second he was totally out of control.

He stood absolutely straight – almost to 'attention' with his arms beside him and hands clenched into pure white fists. He had his 'mad' look too with saucer-like eyes staring straight at me on a long pale face; his thin lips screaming loudly between clenched teeth.

I try very hard not to let him see that I'm really alarmed when he does this, but it's rather difficult. You have no idea what he might do next so need to tread carefully. Talking calmly and slowly in an authoritative voice usually does the trick and the moment will then pass; but not before you think you'll throw-up. I agreed to catch a cab to the Victoria Peak tram instead and by the time we reached the station he was different again.

The sinking feeling in the pit of my stomach remained the same though.

There was no way I could stand this away from home for the next seventy-four days, but I wasn't sure what to do about it. Obviously there was nothing to be done right then so my plan was to plod on and not make him unnecessarily agitated.

The queue for the tram wasn't enormous, but big enough to worry Roo and while we waited I could feel his anxiety level rising so I rambled on about something-or-other, which passed the time and pretty soon we reached the turnstile.

The tram isn't a tram actually it's a sort of funicular railway straight up to the peak – about 45 degrees in places, which means that for some of the journey you're almost laying flat. It must have helped my blood pressure, which would have been sky-high by that time. When we reached the top we were disappointed as we couldn't see the view - a mist completely covered the harbour so we bought a postcard of the view instead, showing us what it should have looked like with a beautiful blue sky over a sparkling South China Sea.

Roo had recovered from his outburst by this time and couldn't apologise enough. I can handle these episodes, as long as they don't get any worse. They're upsetting more than anything else and I feel like running away, I don't know about him!

We wandered around the viewing area, but the scene was the same from every angle – thick cloudy mist so we ended up looking around the shops there instead. I fell in love with a figurine of a lady in Chinese dress and bought it for the drawing room at home.

Home seemed a million miles away at that moment.

Following the sound of drums and cymbals, we were led outside to the open air where we saw a magnificent troupe of Dragon Dancers doing the whole dragon dance thing. It was quite exciting and very colourful and the Chinese watching were all going bananas. However, I was desperately trying to conceal my disappointment. After only a few days away I knew I'd been kidding myself. I had to accept the fact that Roo was ill and going on a trip of any kind wasn't going to help – it might even make things worse. I tried to appear like an interested tourist until mid-afternoon, but really wanted to cry. On the tram again we had a nice lay down – quite welcoming after all the walking we'd done and I had time to recover from Roo's angry moment and have a think. After the 'think' though, I hadn't made any decisions, or come to any new conclusions, but by the time we made it back to the hotel and had several cups of strong PG I felt revived and my optimism returned. Perhaps if I gave it a bit longer he'd settle down.

Back in England, we'd arranged to see Roo's cousin and his family who've lived in Hong Kong for eighteen years. We were both really looking forward to seeing them and I kept my fingers crossed for an uneventful evening Roo-wise. A cab took us out of the city to the Hong Kong Cricket Club (how British) where we had an emotional meeting with the delightful Giles's. We would be eating at the Foreign Correspondent's Club and drove back down into the city to this historic building. It was obvious that Roo felt safe amongst a true extension of his mum's side and looked relaxed the whole time. Will and Julie are great company and their children delightful. Ollie is sixteen and 6'4"!! Alice is 6 (going on 26) and the twins, Guy and Harriet are fourteen. Harriet is a real beauty, with copper-coloured hair falling in ringlets around an amazing freckled face. It's difficult to believe she's a keen Rugby player.

We had a smashing evening and hoped it wouldn't be too long before we saw them again. Roo didn't stop talking – even when we returned to the hotel and still had a smile on his face when he was asleep.

In spite of the nice evening the memory of his earlier agitation kept me awake for a long time, but at least he hadn't tried to strangle me.

DAY FIVE:

"Bladder-Freezing Weather"

Roo = 6 out of 10 this morning. I haven't brought up the subject of going home again (yet), so we'll still make the trip to Po Lin on Lantau Island today, to see the world's largest Buddha.

The 'fast' ferry took us from Hong Kong Central Pier, across to Lantau, the largest outlying island, where it's very different from Hong Kong Island. There are six prisons there! The experience of the taxi ride from the ferry up the mountain to see the statue will remain in my memory forever. It made us realise how precious life is!! The 100` Buddha, built in 1993 weighs as much as an Airbus and can be seen for miles. To reach it in person means climbing more than two hundred stairs, which I declined – not only because of me knees, but it was so cold! In spite of wearing raincoats over jumpers we were both chilled to the bone.

The howling wind suddenly reached my bladder and I required a loo quite urgently (how Menopausal). Roo, of course, being a bloke had no problem and disappeared into the men's room, but typically the queue for the ladies was a mile long. As if that wasn't bad enough, when I did eventually get inside there were four loos – three of which, were simply holes in the floor.

The fourth was a raised water closet in a cubicle with a door and this had another queue of Western ladies all waiting in an orderly fashion, but with strange looks on their faces. I couldn't help smiling when I realised they were desperately trying not to breathe in the pungent odours. I'd been a nurse for a very long time, but the job teaches you much more than how to nurse and it was quite early on in my training that I learnt how to handle this sort of situation. The toothy smile on my face wasn't due to the joy of seeing the giant Buddha, or for the queue of ladies, it was to allow me to breathe without enduring the pong. Much to the amusement of the Chinese, who with their slim, lithe legs were able to perch over the holes and perform without embarrassment, or spilling a drop, the westerners and I waited patiently for the more civilized private loo. Still grinning, I stood praying that the *'older-lady-nether-region-muscle-exercises'* I had practiced over the years would finally pay off and I'd be able to hang on. When the water closet became available, it took me longer to sanitise and make safe the area with my '4711' wipes, than it did to pee, but at least the young girl from Ruislip using it after me would be pleasantly surprised. She probably raves about the cleanliness of the sweet-smelling loo in Lantau even now.

We decided to leave the giant Buddha to the adoring Chinese and hailed a taxi and an equally, if not more scary ride down the mountain reminded me to look at our Life Insurance when we returned home. The 'slow' ferry back to Hong Kong sailed on a very congested sea. A mixture of enormous cargo ships piled high with a mish-mash of containers, odd-looking rusty junks and passenger ferries literally jostled for the waterway. It made the English

Channel look like the boating lake in Newquay in comparison and all this with the weather closing in again. It was quite frightening and I was glad to get off. Fortunately, the hotel was within walking distance of the ferry, so it wasn't long before we were back there. Roo laughed his head off (for a change), when I reiterated the story of the loo and I made a point of sitting down to put it in writing before I forgot the story.

With a cold, damp mist covering the island visibility was so poor, that there wasn't much point in going to the scenic tower with the revolving restaurant at the top where we'd reserved a table. Instead, we ordered Room Service. A good, hot pumpkin soup and a funny film on TV finally warmed us up after a very chilly day and all in all, in spite of the weather and a few worrying moments, Roo had been fine.

PS: Ladies = If you're hoping to see the giant Buddha sometime, go with an empty bladder, or get catheterised beforehand.

DAY SIX: "Panda-Wanda's"

Roo woke to another of his irrational mornings. He was muttering something about 'numbers' and said he wasn't actually here. I told him that of course he was, but he was so mixed up he couldn't get his words out slowly enough to make any sense and I'm not sure he even knew what he wanted to say.

He really had to think hard to construct what he thought was a sentence, but when he did it was a load of rubbish. I didn't muck about and gave him a tranquilizer.

This was an ideal opportunity to get home. Instead of continuing the flight to Sydney, we'd reverse and head back to England. There was no choice, we had to be sensible and at least we had seen some of Hong Kong.

But Roo didn't want to be sensible and when, half-an-hour later I broached the subject he was horrified that I could even suggest going home insisting that it was probably jetlag making him a bit 'up the pole' and he would improve the further we went on.

I wasn't so sure.

Anyway, whatever our destination, we wouldn't let it ruin our last day in Hong Kong, which was quite sunny and warm and after about forty-five minutes of quiet time he'd calmed down enough for us to dash off for a late breakfast. Eating something always helps his mood. Back at home, I'd been suspicious about this and had his blood sugar tested to see if he was Diabetic. He's not.

The hotel was allowing us to checkout later than their usual time and as I'd only unpacked enough for Hong Kong, could deal with the suitcases when we'd been out for the day. I was so excited, because we were going to Ocean Park where they have Giant Pandas. In the cab on our way there, Roo seemed oblivious to the earlier problem so I didn't mention it; but he looked ghastly.

Ocean Park was packed to the gunnels with Chinese. It was a bit like a gone wrong Disneyland in a bad dream. High-pitched Chinese music played loudly through massive speakers, while tiddly Chinese ran around screaming with delight being chased by bigger versions of themselves. It was all very Chinese and made worse with everything being red for their New Year. Poor Roo was terrified.

I was desperate to see the Pandas, but had made up my mind that if there was a huge queue of potty Chinese waiting to see them I'd have to forego the visit. Fortunately reaching the enclosure, we found no queue and not too many inside. Thank You, God!

There are four Pandas there and I'm happy to say that they are living in extremely good conditions. Two adults - Jia-Jia and An-An and two babies. These are truly delightful creatures – great big, living, cuddly teddy bears. The babies were both asleep, lying upside down and looked comically-gorgeous. The experience for me was one I'll never forget and was right up there with seeing whales in Hawaii for the first time.

Roo being spaced out with the tranquilizer wasn't as bowled over as I was, so we didn't spend a vast amount of time there. But at least I'd been within a few feet of them and saw them living happily in the closest thing to their real habitat. I bought a crystal Panda from the 'Everything Panda' shop and suggesting we get out of the crush of Chinese headed for the cable car lifting you up and over the China Sea to Aberdeen, which of course is nothing like the one in Scotland. The cable cars were big enough to take six people and I decided that if we had to share with others, I'd chuck them out as soon as we reached a decent height. However, this experience was obviously not on the 'Chinese List of Things-To-Do' and fortunately for the Chinese found we had a car to ourselves. With a magnificent view of the sea and Aberdeen beyond, we felt quite soporific by the time we got off and made our way back to the hotel.

With a long flight ahead of us (in whatever direction), I was concerned that Roo might not be in a fit state to take it, so I packed fast and we spent the last two hours 'chilling' beside the pool. The sun was so hot Roo burnt the bald bit of his head. Soon though, sunburn and all, it was time to be collected and driven to the airport where Chinese efficiency continued with an easy entry into the terminal.

It was time to make a decision one way or the other (literally), but with Roo behaving like a completely normal human 'bean', there seemed little contest.

We would carry on to Sydney after all.

Checked in. Bags taken away. Up to the Lounge. Roo fine.

The Hong Kong Virgin Lounge was very nice, but quite small and not a patch on the Heathrow version. It was a tranquil space though and the loos were spotlessly clean enough for Roo to stay in one of them for twenty minutes. After an hour or so, there was another Airbus to board where more charming cabin crew served a yummy seafood dinner. Right up my street.

I watched the last part of 'Atonement', but it was all disjointed, so I need to see it properly one day, but I did see all of 'Elizabeth', which was brilliant. (I love what's-his-name, who's in it).

The nine hour flight seemed to go on and on with lots of turbulence again, but I must have dozed off until there was such an amazing shake somewhere over Outer Mongolia, I woke up from a deep sleep in a state of panic.

Thankfully, courtesy of the tranquilizer, 'Alprazalan', Roo slept on in glorious oblivion.

DAY SEVEN: "Oz" (+ 11 GMT)

No sooner had I dozed off again, 'El Capitano' announced that we would shortly be landing in Sydney.

Torrential rain welcomed us to Australia - and I mean – torrential! But then we hadn't come for a tan. (It's dangerous to get one here and anyway by the look of things, all we might get is a serious case of rust).

We'd heard various horror stories about getting things through Australian Immigration and especially Customs, so had meticulously rehearsed our story to cover the 2,000, or so PG Tips Tea Bags stashed in Roo's carry-on. (If challenged, we would say that I had to have them for 'medical' reasons). We'd get them through, by hook, or by crook!

Immigration was a doddle – the Officer even cracked a joke (we reckon he was new), but the queue to get through Customs was at least one hundred people deep. I was jittery and in my mind's eye, could see the PG Tips burning a hole in the side of the carry-on – just as the crate the Ark of the Covenant did, in 'Raiders of the Lost Ark' – although without such serious consequences. The loss of my teabags would be a bitter blow if they were confiscated and it would mean I would have to settle for 'Lipton's' Tea each morning, with PG hard to find. Unacceptable.

We thought we'd be waiting for hours, but at the last minute instead of joining the queue on the left, we jumped to the one on the right. This was most fortuitous, as the bored Customs chappie who met us at the end of the line simply asked if we had any fresh food secreted about our person. *"Certainly not"*, I said, *"But we do have an illicit bar of Cadbury's chocolate in a spongebag, which we're happy to sacrifice"*.

For some reason, he found this rather amusing and waved us through. In the booth beside us though, we saw a poor soul whose luggage was being taken apart by an Officer with a sickly grin on his face. Our PG was safe. Hallelujah!! I was also grateful that the mobile hospital and Chemist store lurking in one of the huge suitcases had also made it through.

In Arrivals, another nice man holding yet another card with our name on it led us to the airport car park and drove us to the harbour. Our first impressions were that Australia wasn't as clean and tidy as Hong Kong. More like the US, or a bigger England. Arriving at Quay West at an area known as The Rocks, our apartment was huge, clean and with windows all around giving us a breathtaking view of the Opera House and the harbour bridge. I would have been quite happy to have done nothing else, but sit looking at them both for the next five days.

It was mind-blowing. We were actually on the other side of the world in Australia.

Roo was done-in and needed to sleep. He'd been so good and had managed the journey from Hong Kong without going wrong once. I rang mum and hoped to speak to Di too, but she wasn't home. Perhaps, next time. Harry, back in Bristol and Lukey in Canada were both fine and I felt relaxed enough to join Roo for a short nap.

It really was short and I woke with a start, but that view was something else and I had to tear myself away from the window to walk to the shops for supplies. I was too tired to cook that evening, so Roo popped out for a Pizza – rather novel after all the posh, rich food we'd been having lately. He seemed as excited as me and still hadn't gone wrong since Hong Kong. Perhaps this was a turning point.

We watched a bit of Australian TV and then forced ourselves to get ready for bed and after brushing my teeth, took one more look at the Opera House magically lit up just a few hundred yards away. While we'd been dozing, a cruise ship had docked opposite, adding to the amazing scene. I still couldn't believe we were in Australia. But we were – *really!*

DAY EIGHT: "Darling and Beyond"

Roo felt well enough to begin exploring and our first thought was to make our way to the ferry terminal at Circular Quay. Being so water-orientated, Sydney is dominated by the ferry system and it's all run very efficiently and as eco-friendly as possible; a comfortable, human place where we felt very at home. Being a relatively new city (compared to London) and designed with people in mind, the quay was easy to walk to and it was simple to buy the tickets allowing you to hop on and off the Darling Harbour ferry. The trip, although quite short blew away any cobwebs we had hanging around and it was great fun speeding through the water passing the Opera House and zooming under the bridge to Darling. Everything looked so colourful and big and much more 'Australian' than I expected it to be. I thought it would be like a newer England, but there's no comparison really.

When we arrived at Darling Harbour – literally round the bend in the river we visited the Aquarium first. You can never overdose on Aquariums and as it was the hottest time of the day, we both needed to get out of the sun. Roo's bald patch was glistening and I could hear my hairdresser reminding me that my hair colour was not my own.

The Aquarium was definitely worth seeing and had some amazing fishy things, but as we'd been spoilt by at least three visits to the best one in the whole world in Monterey, California (in our opinion), we didn't linger. After a cup of tea and a spot of people-watching, Roo and I wandered along the deck running alongside the water looking for a nice place for lunch. It reminded me of my Grandmother, Ethel. She had liked to holiday in Southend and her way of finding the most suitable accommodation was to walk up and down 'the front' until she decided which Guest House had the cleanest net curtains.

I knew Roo should have worn his hat. His skin is over-sensitive due to his medication and with the different climate in mind he'd begun to grow a beard for our time way. It was probably a good idea, but it already resembled a dead badger stuck to his face. It really was blisteringly hot and wouldn't be a good idea to stay out in it much longer, so after eyeing-up five restaurants we reversed back to open-air restaurant number four and found a table with a parasol quite close to the waters' edge. The menu at the restaurant was marvellous and not overpriced and our waitress was a pretty young thing from England on a Gap Year. We couldn't resist bombarding her with questions and discovered that she lived two villages away from us! What a small world it is.

After lunch, we caught the ferry back to Circular Quay and looked around the shops there. I like to buy a Christmas tree decoration from wherever we might be and found one with the inevitable 'Sydney' on it and on our way back to the apartment, we stopped to listen to a busker playing a didgeridoo. In his 60's and dressed in full outback regalia, he was such a character and so good at playing that crazy-looking instrument that we bought a CD of his music.

It was a relief to get back to the air-conditioning in the apartment as Roo was flagging fast and had had enough for one day. He'd been pretty good. We listened to the CD, while I cooked him a couple of lamb chops and some pasta for me and we ate at the dining table beside the window. Below us in the harbour opposite the majestic Opera House, we realised it was P & O's beautiful ship the 'Aurora' that had recently docked and I wondered if our ships would be as lovely. It was a very romantic scene and I would have been quite happy to sit and gaze, but had the luggage to sort out. I had to decide which of it would be stored in Sydney while we spent time in northern Australia and anyway, we needed to get to bed as soon as we could as we had to be up at the crack of dawn for our trip to the Blue Mountains.

Roo = 7 out of 10 today.

Hurrah !!!

DAY NINE: "Blue, blue Mountains"

We managed to get up in time to be collected for our day trip. Although not too enthusiastic and suffering from the usual 'morning blues', Roo gathered himself up for the day out. Armed with hats this time, we waited outside our apartment building for the 4 x 4 and then transferred to a sixteen seat 'HINO' – a large, all-terrain bus, with a gorgeous driver called Jedd. Our companions for the day were a mixture of English, American and German and it wasn't long before we left the city behind us and made our first stop at a wildlife park.

There were koalas, kangaroos and wallabies galore. Most of them were available for petting and didn't seem to mind being pushed and pummelled at all. The wallabies fur felt just as I thought it would – flat and silky, but the koala I stroked was quite different. I will, however, save my comments on the koalas until I tell you about the sanctuary we visited in Brisbane – when I actually _held_ a koala!

The park never turns away an orphaned animal. Most of them are survivors of natural disasters (mainly fires), but also road accidents, where the mother is killed and the baby survives in the pouch and some kind person brings them in; thank goodness.

The young animals were hilarious.

Koalas sleep twenty hours a day and eat the other four. The little ones here though, seemed to spend their waking hours scooting around chasing each other. One of them was bashing a playmate over the head with a branch from a eucalyptus tree like something from a Laurel and Hardy film. I could have watched them for the whole four hours.

The free-roaming wallabies and kangaroos were in seventh heaven and only annoyed slightly when someone stepped on their tail. Visitors were encouraged to feed them ice cream cones from a box at the entrance (just the cone - no ice cream).

No wonder they all looked tubby!

Wherever you go, do you encounter Japanese tourists? We seem to. There were dozens of them in the park, frantically taking photos of _everything_ rushing around and clicking at anything that moved − including their companions. They're behaviour is quite different to ours'. Perhaps we're too conservative, but the word 'bonkers' springs to mind.

One group we saw was especially hyper. The park had a covered bay where three adult koalas sat on the branches of a eucalyptus tree. We were allowed to stroke them − under supervision and after queuing sedately, took it in turns to gently touch them. However, the Japanese slant on this was quite different. One of the girls in their group stood in a sort of statuesque position and pointing with an outstretched arm screamed her head off while a picture was taken. Most odd. The docile, eucalyptus-munching koala fortunately wasn't at all fazed and simply carried on munching.

My eyes are getting worse. I told Roo to look at the dear little yellow bird sitting on a branch. It was, in fact, half an orange – a treat for the fruit bats inside the cage.

(Note: make appointment at Opticians on return).

The inmates seemed very happy and content here. It was pleasing to see the love these orphaned or injured animals receive and the care and attention available. The behaviour of 'others' though, is a mystery to me.

Roo = 7 out of 10, so far.

It was a good choice of tour, with not many people and as long as you weren't Japanese, there was no need for hurtling. By the time we left the park though, Roo was visibly shaking and in the heat that dead badger seemed to be growing fast giving him an odd, shadowy look. Our party reported back to the Hino at the allotted time and as we drove off for the next visit, Roo settled down and relaxed.

Reaching the National Park, Jedd told us that we had to go off road because the recent rains had made huge ruts and even the Hino would have trouble moving on. After half an hour of 'sea-sick' driving, we stopped deep inside the forest for a walk.

It was absolutely quiet, apart from the strange 'singing' or 'chirping' of the millions of Cicadas (large transparent-winged insects) and the reply from the birds. The Cicadas song – a sort of high-pitched humming noise is supposed to annoy the birds so much, that they won't eat them.

The trees here are mainly Eucalyptus, with 800 varieties!

Jedd was keen to see which of us could play the didgeridoo (for some reason only known to him) and we stood in a circle and some had a go. Roo managed to get something out of it (must be his trumpet-playing days that helped) but Jedd, of course, was the real star entertaining us in more ways than one! After his performance, we piled back into the Hino and carried on driving through the forest.

It was quite uncomfortable at times – and worrying, with deep gorges inches away from the wheels on one side and thick, dense forest on the other. If you broke down in a vehicle here you'd have a very long wait for help to come. Thankfully, the lunch stop loomed ahead and we were all grateful for a visit to the (conventional) loo and a wash and brush up before eating. Roo was a bit spaced out, but still managed to talk to our dining companions and after lunch, which was nice, simple and easily digestible (taking the journey into consideration) we felt honoured when Jedd asked Roo and I to sit up front with him for the rest of the journey to the canyon outlook. As the terrain opened up the nearer we drove to the mountain range, the view began to alter and we could see the Blue Mountains ahead. This is another World Heritage Site, with signs of Aboriginal life going back 22,000 years and with areas that man (or woman) still hasn't set foot.

The magnificent Blue Mountains get their name from the blue tinge seen from a distance. It's a deep blue haze given off by millions of Eucalyptus trees and is truly 'Grand Canyon', although in a more lush and densely forested way, compared to the one in America.

There are fires here often (usually caused by lightning), which sounds alarming, but this allows the sun to penetrate the ground after the heat from the fire has sparked off new growth. So as long as it doesn't get out of control, it's okay. Years ago, the fires were quickly extinguished, but then it was realised that it was a natural phenomenon and it was stopped. Hundreds of Park Rangers – who take their jobs very seriously – are required to patrol on foot and also in wooden outlooks high in the trees to keep the area safe.

The next stop was Katoomba, a deep ravine with a glass-bottomed cable car above it.

Before the cable cars were glass-bottomed and less glamorous, they were used to transport coal from a mine on the side of the mountain. Now of course, the cable car hanging more than 3,000 feet above sea level is a huge tourist attraction. Leaving Katoomba on our way back to Sydney, we passed through the village built for the Olympic Games where they were held in 2000. The houses and apartments are private homes now and all ecologically perfect, with their own water recycling units and solar power. Reluctantly, we had to leave Jedd and the Hino at this point. We'd had a glimpse of the Australian Interior and had loved every minute of the long, dusty day. The ending was perfect though, with a fabulous ride in a catamaran back to Circular Quay.

Passing dozens of beautiful water front homes with access to their boats and a fast route to Sydney, Roo was bowled over by the obviously perfect life-style. Putney, Chiswick, Woolwich – not quite the same as those areas back home, but it convinced him that this was the life for us.

I wasn't so sure.

How would we leave the lovely house we built ourselves and the Norman church in the village? Would we ever see our friends again? What is Aboriginal Dreamtime? Anyway, my sister wouldn't leave my nephew's grave behind, the boys wouldn't leave England full stop and Roo would miss Tim too much, so that's that.

I wrote the last few pages sitting at the desk in the apartment overlooking the harbour. Every now and then, I looked out of the window at the Opera House and the bridge. It was still strange to see it all there just a few yards away. In the distance, just behind the Opera House, dozens of little sails were zipping around on the horizon – yachts taking part in the weekend Regatta. I knew this would be a magical place to live, but it was too late for us now. We should have thought about it ten years ago. Perhaps if we had made the move, Roo might not have succumbed to this dreadful illness. On the other hand though, he could have been worse and we'd have blamed it on emigrating.

Who knows?

DAY TEN: "The Opera House"

A lovely warm day and an optimistic Roo.

Good all round for a walk to the Opera House, but first, Roo had to get a taxi to take the big cases to 'TCP' (not the ointment, it's a storage facility) so we didn't have to lug everything to Cairns and Brisbane.

It was a brilliant idea of mine (although I say it myself) as it would lessen the stress for the trip up north. On the downside, we'd have to buy anything extra we might need when we got there (what a nuisance that would be!).

I was worried all the time he was gone and wondered why I hadn't taken the taxi with him, but really needed the time to do some washing and ironing. He was back in under an hour and I tried not to look relieved when he walked through the door.

It had been an easy outing for him. The taxi driver had waited while he dropped the cases and the people at TCP had been kind, so it all helped to make a success of the exercise.

I hoped we see the suitcases again!

With these chores behind us, off we went.

It took only a few minutes to get to the Opera House and the closer we came, the more beautiful it looked. The building costs were set at AUS$10m, but the usual scenario prevailed and it actually cost AUS$110m. It's not surprising though, it's a fabulous building. I hate most modern things, but couldn't help loving this. The architecture is so unusual. It sits so proudly on a peninsular sticking out into the water right beside the Botanical Gardens and doesn't look real somehow.

You can't miss it – it's the first thing ships see when they round the bend from the Tasman Sea and if you didn't say, "WOW!" at first sight, there'd be something wrong with you. From the air, it's a magnificent landmark and is now quite rightly, yet another World Heritage Site. In front of the steps leading up to the entrance is an enormous expanse of paving, which is used as a meeting place. *"Meet me in front of the Opera House"* must be an often-used phrase. (You just couldn't miss your date). There are café's and restaurants in every shape and form; everything from Bistro type to terribly posh and expensive and with varying forms of clientele too. The tourists (us included) in shorts, tee shirts and sensible shoes are easy to pick out while the locals, dressed up to the nines, arrived for a performance of some kind. It was so nice to see them in their evening dresses having made a real effort – the chaps too, but it was quite funny watching some of the girls in their skimpy dresses trying to walk in stilettos. (I'm only jealous).

It was late in the afternoon now and the temperature was just right with a warm breeze and a few fluffy clouds, so after we'd had a drink in the bar nearby it was safe to wander around taking in the atmosphere.

We were just in time to watch a huge catamaran slide up to the jetty and tie up right beside the Opera House. A queue of revellers piled aboard while a band on the upper deck played loud jazz making everyone who could hear it jiggled around. It was all very jolly and Roo was enjoying every minute of it.

I secretly wished I could be aboard the cat.

Once they were all loaded, it slipped from the quay and for a while you could hear the laughter amongst the jazz and the chink of glasses until it grew softer and softer and the cat disappeared from view.

A sleek yacht took its' place and with it, some 'beautiful' people sipping champagne. They were very happy to be watched and when they sat down at a table for what looked like a sumptuous dinner, it reminded us that we needed to eat our bananas. We wandered into the Botanical Gardens and sat on a bench for a while, peeling our narnas and listening to the birdsong. With the backdrop of the Opera House it was all quite surreal.

While we sat finishing our snack, a wedding group marched past us. They must have been married somewhere in the gardens. The bride looked gorgeous and when she swept past, the air was filled with the scent of the jasmine she was holding. The groom was wearing a kilt. Not very Australian we thought, but then of course, Australia had immigrants from all over the world and it was good to see traditions being maintained.

We suddenly realised the time and finding it hard to locate a rubbish bin, began the walk back to the apartment armed with our banana skins. Eventually, we came upon a receptacle, but not before we had received several odd looks. We'd booked a table for dinner at the Marriott, where they have a seafood buffet - hence the snack on the bench – I knew we'd fill up later. It was necessary to go into 'speedy mode', changing into more suitable attire, but arrived at the hotel in good time for our table.

The buffet was a magnificent display of 'fruits de mare'. I managed to chomp my way – 'Darryl Hannah style' – through three halves of lobster and enough smoked salmon to cover my plate. Roo ate an assortment of meats, finishing with a sumptuous pud. I was glad to see him enjoying a meal, he needed to regain some of that weight he'd lost and was beginning to look much better (in spite of the dead badger) but continued to have weird moments.

Suddenly, he was having one of those moments and was more than 'spaced out'. I could kick myself for not bringing a tranquilizer with us, but deciding not to be too hasty to leave we migrated to the lounge where a very good singer and pianist were performing.

We managed to stay long enough for a cocktail each (non-alcoholic for Roo) and it would have been nice to linger, but instead bolted for the safety of the apartment.

Overall, it had been a lovely day. It was a shame it came to an abrupt end, but it could have been worse. I went to bed wondering whether Roo was concerned about tomorrow.

I'd booked a day out to a restaurant on the Hawkesbury River and the only way to reach it was by seaplane.

DAY ELEVEN: *"Flight from Rose Bay"*

I think Roo *was* nervous about the flight to the restaurant, but even so, we were in good time for the 11am ferry from Circular Quay to Rose Bay, which was the site for Australia's first airport – *with water for a runway.*

A regular service using Empire Class Flying Boats with sleeping accommodation, bathrooms, first class catering with bone china crockery and silver cutlery left Southampton, England for Rose Bay via Egypt, India and Singapore with fifteen wealthy passengers travelling in sheer luxury. It was terribly expensive and must have been very romantic, arriving in Australia nine days later, after thirty-five fuel stops. That was in the Thirties - now the flight takes less than a day. Catalina's also flew from here on internal routes and were used for search and rescue in the Pacific during the last war as well. The poor chaps left in the water after their ship had been sunk, desperately trying to avoid being eaten by sharks must have been elated to see those planes.

The day trip terminal was easy to find – right beside the original terminal building – now a restaurant called "Catalina" with a huge covered veranda hanging out over the water giving diners a sensational view of Rose Bay and the seaplanes. We checked in, but as we were early, had time to watch planes taking off and landing amongst the Pelicans doing exactly the same thing. With a good view of passengers boarding from the floating deck, I began to wonder how I would manage to get in (and out) of this miniscule aircraft seating six passengers and the pilot. The last time I had been in a small plane was on the flight to Yosemite over the Grand Canyon. I was ten years younger and three stone lighter then. I could feel panic setting in, but just as I was thinking about 'heading for the hills', our flight was called and I gingerly walked out onto the deck with Roo and the other four passengers as if I were going to be shot at dawn. I could even hear the 'dirge' being played. The seaplane looked even smaller close-up and to my horror, I realised that the door to said seaplane was only big enough for a bottom half my size.

Panic! Panic! Panic had set in!

We stood for a moment, while the pilot gave a safety talk.

The other female passenger, who was as thin as a pin laughed nervously while we donned our lifejackets, but all the time I was just thinking about the size of the door.

Having had to divulge our weight at the time of booking – *and been truthful for the sake of the other passengers and aviation history* – the pilot knew exactly where to place us inside, but of course I had no idea whether I'd be first, or last to board. The wait to know was awful and either way the outcome would be similar. Would it be best for everyone to see my enormous rear, or witness my ample front squeezing through the small gap?

Instant nausea came upon me and I hoped no one would take photographs. Sure enough, two of the other passengers were photographing the occasion for posterity. *'Posterior'*, being the word uppermost in my mind. I was finding it hard to swallow by the time the pilot made the decision to board the other four passengers first and had them ensconced inside. Then in slow-motion it seemed, he turned to me pointing towards the door. Taking a deep breath before stepping across the deck and onto the float as instructed, initial contact caused the aircraft to tip towards me and I was surprised that there were no screams of *"abandon ship"* from inside, but hanging onto the ladder for dear life,

somehow hauled myself up landing facedown and balanced on my upturned nose in a very ungainly position with arms outstretched.

My torso was aboard, but my bottom half remained on the ladder outside the aircraft. The two passengers sitting in the middle looked over the back of their seats at me with sympathetic grins and I could have sworn I heard Roo discussing contingency plans with the pilot, but I could have been wrong. I was beginning to wish I'd never seen the advert for *'Sunday lunch on the Hawkesbury River by Floatplane from Rose Bay'*. With my bottom being much bigger than my top half, I had visions of the pilot and Roo having to grab a cheek each, turn me sideways and throw me through the gap on the count of *"three!"* This gave me enough reason to make one last huge effort and with all my strength and the summoning up of emergency help from God, raised myself up on both hands 'push-up' style shifting the remainder of me aboard. I could quite easily have lay there to recuperate for the rest of the trip, but Roo squeezed past, stuffed me into my seat as best he could and told me to stop groaning. Feeling a bit light-headed and actually amazed that I was aboard, I pulled the headset on while Roo strapped me in (it's difficult for me to see me waist over me bosoms). Take-off was great and made me sit up straight. Bouncing on the water for a few moments, I hung on to the bosoms for decencies' sake until the wind caught us and we left the water. This was fantastic even with my nose squashed up against the window.

There's such a lot of Australia out there and it would appear that everyone owns a boat. (But then the rest of the world thinks that everyone in England has met the Queen). At such a reasonable height, the miles and miles of vegetation we were flying over resembled huge broccoli and the slices of long curved yellow beach bright bananas, with what looked like white cotton wool moving along it. Captain Cook's eyes must have popped out when he saw it all – although he wouldn't have flown over it in a seaplane, of course. After about fifteen minutes of flying around, we turned towards the Hawkesbury River and landed on it to let one couple off at their chosen restaurant. The next bouncy take-off had me clinging to me 'you-know-whats' again as the flight continued across lush forest repeating the process at the next venue for the other couple until our final destination came. I could have taken off and landed all day long, it was that enjoyable, but a few minutes later, landing on the part of the river beside 'Peat's Bite' the plane chugged noisily through the glistening water and dribbled to a halt about a hundred feet from the restaurant.

Staying in our seats while we bobbed-about and the plane was secured, I looked out of the window to get an idea of what the restaurant was like, but just then saw a large chap in a small boat 'putt-putting' his way out to us. It was the tender from the restaurant. Oh God! I had to manage another assault course and this time with an audience from the diners at the open-air restaurant.

I decided there was no easy, or beautiful way to do it – and anyway I was starving hungry by this time - so I launched myself into the arms of the waiting pilot (oh, I hadn't realised how nice he was until then – and he's viewed my bottom!) and with even more gusto into the even larger arms of the hunk on the boat. (I should be helpless more often).

The short trip from boat to shore revealed the restaurant in greater detail. I could see a lot of diners – more than I thought there would be, since there are only two methods of transport (plane ore boat) to reach 'Peat's Bite' – and an assortment of rough-looking dogs. Now I was worried about Roo. He wasn't too good in a crowd, but he did like dogs. Music from a guitar came lilting across the water and after we landed and had been shown to our table a singer joined the guitarist. They were a husband and wife team and very good. One of the dogs, a 'Lorgi' (cross-Korgi/Labrador) called Doris, attached herself to us as if we'd been friends for years sitting beneath our table while we ate and the attentive staff fussed around doing all they could to make our visit a pleasant one.

The surroundings were very tranquil and the food excellent, considering there was no mains electricity there and all supplies have to be brought in by boat from Sydney. We were served with five delicious courses and the time simply flew by. Bit of a pun, because we hadn't long finished eating when we heard our plane diving down to the water and landing on the river for our return to Sydney. This excited Doris and her gang enormously and they all ran around together in a sort of frenzy until the plane came to a standstill. Then when the hunky chap started up the outboard on the tender, they began the ritual all over again running around in small circles together. It was really funny and I wouldn't be surprised if this is a bit of a ritual for the 'Peat's Bite' dogs. They seem to know they're entertaining the diners. I would have been excited too, had I not remembered that I had to get in and out of the boat and onto the plane again. I refused to have nausea. I didn't know what it might lead to and wasn't going to waste all that lovely food. This time, I would try to relax and not care about the manoeuvres.

Perhaps it was the wine, perhaps I was getting the hang of it, but it didn't matter because this time it was all a lot easier and although ungainly, my entry and exit into the boat was uneventful. It might also have been the fact that the pilot hadn't collected the others yet, so the plane was empty and landing the other way round meant the door was on the other side away from the diners gaze, so it was only Roo – who'd seen it all before anyway and the pilot – who I'd never see again, who had to witness the entry of my gluteus maximus into the aircraft. I bet the pilot has them in fits of laughter down at his local every evening.

The return flight was equally as captivating, with views of more broccoli and silvery-gold beaches and as we flew nearer and nearer to Sydney, it was easy to make out the arch of the bridge and then the tell-tale tips of the Opera House roof.

Roo had been great and seemed to have enjoyed the whole day with just a small panic attack during the meal that we'd easily coped with and it soon went away. But when the pilot warned us that he had to make a tight turn over the Opera House it was a different story. The 'G Force' was unbearable and really unpleasant for what was probably only twenty seconds, but seemed like an eternity. Roo instantly broke out into a cold sweat and blood drained from his face.

It was hard to enjoy the marvellous view of the building under these circumstances, which was a shame because it would have been a great photo opportunity. Fortunately, we landed back at Rose Bay before Roo could throw up and he improved as soon as we set foot on terra firma.

All in all, we had a wonderful day, but we'd need to spend a quiet evening in for Roo to recover enough to cope with tomorrow. He'll be jittery about the move on to Cairns, where it's hot, steamy and stormy at the moment.

It sounds quite exciting though and we both have our macs.

DAY TWELVE: "Cairns and the Great Barrier Reef, NE Australia"

Early mornings find Roo at his worst and today was no exception. He was very tearful for no apparent reason, which was doubly sad when you think where we were - within touching distance almost, of the Opera House. There was more irrational thinking and terror of something he can't explain. Forgetting to take his Clomipramine last night didn't help and that made me feel bad too and he took it this morning with no idea of the consequences. There was no recollection of the incident the night before either when I'd spent more than an hour dividing the remainder of our clothes between two bags, weighing them to make sure they conformed to hand baggage rules and had stowed them ready to go. A little later, I found he'd taken it upon himself to 'relocate' the contents for no apparent reason and I had to repeat the process all over again. Even the simplest of tasks was difficult for Roo and to make things worse, he was unable to retain information the way he used to – one minute it's there, the next it's not. He gets upset insisting conversations didn't take place, or that I hadn't told him something important. It's really difficult because some things can't be organised on the spot and if at the eleventh hour we need to do just that, he becomes panicky very quickly. This is why I try to think ahead as much as possible. My list-making is endless.

A late check out helped. We should have been gone by 10am, but as our car wasn't coming until noon we asked to stay a bit longer and sat quietly for an hour, or so and by the time we left Roo was more composed. Our driver was again, the nicest of chaps and we were at the airport in no time at all.

No problems with checking in and then we joined a queue for what we supposed was the line-up for Security. Fortunately we hadn't gone very far before we discovered it was the queue for a flight to Bangkok. We had a laugh about that and managed to find the right area where our palms, feet and bags were swiped for explosives. (Well, I WAS hot stuff, once upon a time!) Having passed the test, we located the Virgin Blue Lounge just in time, because Roo was really shaky (probably with the late dose of Clomipramine). He said he was worried about going home in 58 days time – and whether, or not Harry will be happy in later life! (What?) His words were coming out upside down and back-to-front in a garbled mess and to stop him talking for a while, I made him eat something. It was a shame because he looked really well today and I think he'd put on some more weight. He'd made fantastic progress since the start of his illness. If only he'd realise it. This behaviour really wears us out though.

The three hour flight to Cairns was uneventful and we were very impressed with Virgin Blue. I must tell my friend, Sir Richard. Although it's franchised in Australia, the company has his logo and style all the way and like Virgin Atlantic has professional, courteous and smart cabin crew. The flight was one class only, but we'd paid for a bit of extra space to accommodate my knees and Roo's 'stir-craziness'.

Apparently, I was in charge of the exit door in an emergency and at one point, had an overwhelming urge to open it. Obviously I didn't, because we landed safely in more torrential rain.

The humidity hit us like opening the door to a sauna. This part of Australia is very tropical with palm trees, parrots and more tiny dickies resembling that half an orange I'd seen in the Wildlife Park.

The hire car was some sort of Fiesta-like vehicle and driving away from the airport, with the help of the map I'd 'Googled', we easily found our apartment building, which was right on the shore in front of a beach.

'Reception' had gone home, but the keys had been left in an envelope with our name on it and we let ourselves in to find a massive two bed/two bathroom ultra clean apartment. It was tastefully furnished (as they say) and had an amazing 1,200 sq ft terrace (big enough to host a wild party) looking out over the ocean. The rain was coming down in a serious way now, but in spite of it we dropped everything and donned our raincoats to walk ten minutes to an open air restaurant we'd spotted along the way. The tables were covered by a sloping roof and we sat watching the water pouring off it in torrents and bouncing off the tiled floor like 'dancing dollies'. The Coral Sea was only a few yards away behind a row of palms and we could hear the surf crashing onto the shore and pounding up the beach. It could have been a very romantic moment, but anything like that was about ninety-third on my list at that moment.

There were a few other diners who had also braved the weather and we all sat looking out towards the water without actually being able to see it, so we must have looked a bit daft. The menu was quite confusing and although we attempted surreptitiously to look at what the others were eating, we couldn't recognise anything.

The pretty young waitress suggested the 'Bugs'. Having never eaten insects before, the thought of doing so was really abhorrent. However, noting the horror on my screwed up face, I was assured that it was in fact seafood – something between prawns and crayfish, which had never set foot or claw on dry land. So I went with the 'bugs' and Roo had Mackerel and Chips (how Australian). Both the fish and 'bugs' were excellent and if you're ever in Cairns, you must try the 'bugs' – whatever they are.

'BUG'

Roo was not in the best of shape and felt tired, so without lingering over coffee, we picked our way through the puddles back to the apartment – thankful for our macs. (I heard you laughing at the end of "Day Eleven".) The rain continued and by the time we were safely inside, it had worsened into a humdinger of a storm making any attempt to make a call home to England impossible. We'd have to wait until tomorrow to speak to mum. The noise raging outside kept us both awake and even when it subsided, Roo was still restless. He was having more irrational thoughts and was mumbling before he dozed off completely.

"Don't let's go back. Let's get everyone we like to come out here" he whispered.

"Okay," I replied, knowing he'd instantly forget what he'd said.

DAY THIRTEEN:

"Cairns Exploration"

Although we didn't sleep well, we were both quick to rise to see what Cairns had to offer in daylight. The storm had moved away for the time being and the sky was a bright blue. For once, Roo was being quite reasonable and as usual, I didn't mention his 'ramblings' of the night before.

First things first though – supplies are necessary; we shouldn't keep eating out. I just can't afford the calories. After breakfast on the terrace we left to go shopping. Passing the never-ending beach and a few cute stores, we came across a small shopping mall. It was clean, tidy and had leather sofas placed along the middle of the walkway, which we thought quite novel. The best thing though, was the lack of graffiti and 'oiks' to slash the sofas. Food and other things weren't any cheaper than in England, but the choice was greater and I bought a really nice pair of spotty turquoise pyjamas. On our way back, instead of the deer we were used to seeing at home we were amazed to see kangaroos hopping in the fields beside the road. They looked quite comical, as if they were bouncing around on a huge trampoline stopping every now and then to eat the grass, or laze under a tree. We returned to the apartment with our supplies and with the weather behaving as it was it would have been criminal not to take advantage of the terrace as much as possible and we ate our lunch out there. Screeching red, green and yellow parrots in the palm trees and butterflies the size of blackbirds kept us company, while a Kookaburra cackled in the distance with a few million chirping Cicadas to accompany him. As I said, the apartment overlooked the ocean and with the terrace being on the first floor, we had a panoramic view of the Coral Sea. The water was the same colour as the sky, making it difficult to differentiate between the two. Gentle waves quietly lapped onto the beach, trickling tiny bubbles along the sand and a cool breeze interrupted the heat from the sun every now and again. What a difference from last night!

I went to clear away the lunch debris on the table, to find an army of pale green ants guarding a piece of bread. It was a bit worrying when I attempted to remove it and several of them stood on their back legs ready to attack. They were rather large for ants and for fear of them remembering me and eating me alive in my bed that night, I relented and left them to it.

Not a bad day, Roo-wise. Keeping the pressure off is the key. Trouble is, it puts more on me and I'm constantly trying to pre-empt every situation and put it right before it has a chance to go wrong. (If you see what I mean).

Still trying to relax a bit. Kuranda trip tomorrow. Should be okay – train up through the rainforest and a cable car return over it, then a visit to an Aborigine encampment of some kind. Checked the seaplane flight times to and from Green Island and the Great Barrier Reef – all okay. All we have to worry about is the weather changing.

Before I started dinner, we went for a walk along the beach – our first this trip.

There are warnings at intervals about not walking with children and dogs too close to the water, due to the large number of saltwater crocodiles finding them quite tasty. Swimming is banned too, not only because of this, but also because the jellyfish can kill you. (That is, if you haven't already been eaten by a crocodile). I couldn't see any 'crocs' (see how well I spoke the lingo already?) but could feel two of them submerged in the water eyeing me up. They were probably licking their lips and formulating a cunning plan to drag me into the water where they would feed on me for the next year, so I steered Roo up onto the safety of the bank.

Along, what we would call in England, The Esplanade, are 'STINGER POINTS', where barrels containing bottles of white vinegar are kept to treat jellyfish stings. This is the first course of action once you've been dragged out of the water, horribly covered in big, red lumps. If you're lucky enough to survive the stings and being pickled in vinegar, it's off to the hospital for three days. Those vinegar bottles wouldn't last long in England, they'd be nicked for someone's chips.

Two weeks had passed already. I knew it would fly by. At least all is well at home and the boys have nothing serious to report, although the first words Roo uttered when we eventually got through to Lukey in the Canadian Rockies were, *"You've broken what?"* My immediate vision was of him at the age of nine when he broke both arms together and had been encased in curved plaster casts from his fingers up to his shoulders. He looked like a crab, poor chap, colliding with everything and anything when he attempted to move about and suffering from bruises to his forehead from them when he wriggled about in bed. Fortunately this time, it was just his MP3 Player that was broken, but tomorrow he was going to ski a particularly hazardous terrain as part of his course. I would try not to think about it.

We went straight to bed after dinner and read a bit. Mustn't be late for the train tomorrow.

Roo = 7 out of ten

DAY FOURTEEN:

"Kuranda and Beyond"

When I saw Roo this morning, I knew he wasn't right. He said he'd had a dreadful nights' sleep because he was worried about getting up (?) He hadn't wanted to wake me in the middle of the night and lay there hour after hour in a terrible state. Tearful and frustrated with himself I thought it best not to go on the trip to the rainforest. We'd been to the one in Maui and surely all rainforests were the same. We could see Aborigines on the Discovery Channel if we were that keen, so no – we'd stay in the apartment and perhaps have a swim in the pool later.

Of course, he was horrified that he would be the reason for cancelling.

When I booked the trip, they had sent us a map and the instructions of how to reach the station; both were quite straightforward, showing it was a fifteen minute drive away in a straight line. It was as simple as that, but Roo was in total meltdown about getting there on time and in the midst of his worst episode so far.

Having planned the day in the finest of detail I wondered if I should have plotted the route in even *finer* detail, but surely we would be able to follow a simple map! I was at the end of my tether and couldn't think about anything anymore. All I wanted to do was run down to the Coral Sea and tempt the crocodiles. The only thing I was sure of was that I liked my new pyjamas (I was still in them, which shows you how the morning had gone) and gave the silky material a stroke, closely examining one of the white dots while I thought. Brainwave! Ring the station....Let him talk to a human....Confirm the directions.... A 'phone call later and he'd calmed down a bit. *"Straight down the Captain Cook Highway in a straight line to the station, the girl told me"*. Roo blurted out excitedly. *"Yes, I know"*, I said to myself in exasperation. Twice before leaving the apartment, I decided it was too dodgy to go and each time Roo said we were. So we went. We drove past more bouncing kangaroos and soon reached the station. It was a doddle and Roo once again felt like a twit. Easy (and free) parking in the station car park and a hop (ha-ha) over to the platform where the Kuranda Scenic Railway was waiting for passengers. Reminiscent of the trains we had when I was ten this one was just so twee. No steam engine, but a look-alike diesel-electric version with twenty cream-coloured carriages and two green 'Gold Class' carriages. I'd purposely booked seats in 'Gold Class', not because I'm a snob (well, only part-time) but because they carried half the amount of people and had comfy tub chairs that could be moved around. We settled down into two of the seats and realised that the two carriages were authentic and typically Victorian with mahogany doors and window frames and had a very grand Cocktail Bar. There was an impressive sparkling loo to the rear, which was also original and the ceilings were made of embossed tin in the Victorian way. These carriages had been built to last. There was no air conditioning though and I could see that

Roo was getting agitated with the heat and apprehension of the journey to come. Then at exactly 9.20am with ten minutes to go, Roo sprang to his feet and bolted for the door saying he was too hot and had to get off. Suddenly alone, I wasn't quite sure what to do and just sat to attention watching him out of the window. With the minutes ticking away, I had visions of the train going without him and anxious with the situation wondered if I should get off too. Standing on the platform with terror in his eyes, he looked like someone being suffocated; inhaling great gulps of air, wiping his face with a tissue and pulling at the neck of his tee shirt as if it were strangling him. I wouldn't have been surprised if an ambulance had been called. I had real bad vibes now and was on the edge of my seat ready to leave the carriage, when I saw a large bald-headed chap approach him and begin a conversation. I had no idea where he came from; he just appeared. He looked equally hot and uncomfortable, but whatever he said changed Roo's whole demeanour immediately. Actually smiling with his breathing returned to normal, Roo chatted to him as if they'd been best buddies for years. Then, when a hoot erupted from the engine, a laughing Roo quickly jumped back on board just making it in time as the train began to move off and the large chap vanished as quickly as he had come.

"Where'd he go?" I whispered to myself.

He wouldn't have had time to reach another carriage and the train didn't pass him on the platform as it left the station; he simply disappeared – not in a puff of smoke, but almost. Don't laugh when I say this, but I think he might have been an angel. An experience I had a few years ago with something similar convinced me that they really do exist and I must make time at a later date to tell the story, which would convince you too.

"What were you talking about with that big guy?" I asked.

"Oh, he just said he was hot too." Roo replied returning to his chair looking as if he hadn't a care in the world.

"This is all very bad for my nerves", I thought. But then a wave of calm completely overtook me. I get that sometimes. It's the feeling that someone I can't see is with me; someone supporting and assuring me in my hour of need. Corny, eh? But true for me. If I'm wrong, I'll feel a proper Charlie when I'm dead and they say there aren't any angels. We'll see, won't we?

The train rocked and rolled and my soporific feelings increased as I gazed out of the window knowing that Roo sat safely beside me. If only I could feel this like all the time instead of wondering if the cliff edge I was standing on would suddenly crumble away tipping me into a never-ending black hole.

There were eight Japanese tourists in the carriage with us, their interpreter and two Australian Hostesses making eleven in total. None of the foreigners spoke English, so it would be just the two Hostesses and the interpreter I'd have to explain to, if Roo threw a 'wobbler' on the long journey up to Kuranda. I wondered how the interpreter would put it in Japanese, but could only hope they would understand. Surely depression occurs even in

Japan! But it wasn't long before there was a commentary to listen to and drinks and canapés were served, which was enough to dispel my worries. Roo seemed more content with the windows wide open and lots of fresh air rushing in and with lots to distract him, perhaps we'd be okay as long as none of the Japanese didn't start screaming.

The train continued its journey, chugging past magnificent terrain with deep, dense gorges of rainforest vines and flowering plants including orchids, ginger and figs and waterfalls swollen to overflowing due to the excessive rainfall.

Halfway up, the train made a brief stop allowing us to get off at the Barron Gorge to witness an incredible sight – a waterfall of amazing proportions tumbling noisily hundreds of feet down the mountain and cascading into the river below. While we stood by the fence at the look-out there, I hung on to Roo tightly. I couldn't imagine him jumping over the edge, but wasn't taking any chances - although the way I held his arm, he'd probably take me with him if he did. It was almost as good as Niagara Falls and enough of a spectacle that even we *'oo'd and aahh'd'*, along with the Japanese, who are famous for their 'ooh's and 'aah's', as well as their photography. Back on the train refreshed with the spray from the waterfall, we moved off. Roo's eyes widened even more when the window he was sitting beside came within an inch of a massive spider's web complete with 'inhabitant' and a body the size of a mandarin orange.

Fortunately for Roo, we were making very slow progress up a steep incline and the train at this time wasn't causing a draft along the way. Had it done so, it was quite possible that the sudden rush of air could 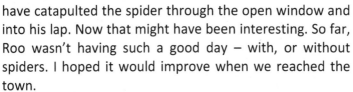 have catapulted the spider through the open window and into his lap. Now that might have been interesting. So far, Roo wasn't having such a good day – with, or without spiders. I hoped it would improve when we reached the town.

Kuranda had been home to a large clan of Aborigines for around 10,000 years. They must have thought the 'white men' were mad to establish a gold mining town around them in the late 1800's when gold didn't mean a thing to them. Hundreds of people died building the railway through accidents, insect bites, or disease and the gold soon ran out anyway. In the 70's, it became a huge hippy commune, frowned upon by the more conservative Cairns inhabitants, but when the hippies all grew old and left, it was then that some enterprising person bought the railway as a tourist attraction – saving it in fact. A cable car was built over the rainforest canopy as an alternative conveyance and now Kuranda is full of original quaint buildings and shops selling local crafts and rainforesty-things. There are nature trails with wildlife-spotting days, 'Eco' Holidays, where you sleep in a tent amongst the wildlife and insects (NOT on my list of things to do), Gap

Year Expeditions and a Butterfly Sanctuary. We visited the butterflies in an enormous glasshouse, managing not to swipe any that landed on us. That would have been awkward. You can picture the headlines ....

"BRIT ATTACKS BUTTERFLY"

"PLAN TO PROTECT WILDLIFE FROM MAD BRITS", says Minister.

Roo was still somewhere else as far as his brain was concerned, but was interested enough in a fabulous crocodile belt to buy it. (We were assured that the croc had died of old age). I bought a shopping bag with a croc on it for Diane and some useless bits and pieces tourists can never resist, which is fortunate for the shopkeepers who need to eat from time to time. We still had the 'Abo Experience' to do, so by mid-afternoon, headed to the 'Sky Rail' station for the long ride back down to civilisation.

Sailing across the rainforest canopy with 'broccoli' as far as the eye could see, the sound of kookaburras, parrots and cicadas penetrated the transparent bubble we sat in. Halfway down, we made a stop at another station and were joined by a young German student. Her English was perfect (groan). She told us that she had just spent three amazing days and nights in a tent up in the rainforest and was full of stories about insects and animals.

She didn't smell so good, but I think she was entitled to hum a bit. However, the nurse in me didn't like the look of the huge bites on her arms and neck. The insects up there must be the ones from that giant insect film, *'Starship Troopers'*.

Isn't nature wonderful? And here, thank goodness, it's all preserved.

Reaching the bottom, we headed straight for the 'Aborigine Experience'. Real, true to life *'Abo's'* (probably Solicitors, or Accountants really) talked about their ancestry and way of life as it was thousands of years ago; which for the ones who weren't Accountants, apparently hadn't changed much. They played the didgeridoo (expertly), threw spears (with amazing accuracy), made fires from nothing (seemingly) and explained their method of medicinal treatments and cures for all ills (magically). I loved it. I think Roo loved it too, because half an hour later, he'd bought a didgeridoo! How we would get the four foot piece of wood into the suitcase though, I just didn't know. Arriving back at the beachfront totally exhausted, we collapsed in a heap on the apartment sofa.

Pilchard sandwiches for tea, I thought.

DAY FIFTEEN: "Green Island"

Oh dear! Not a good start. Another mad, bad morning. Roo can't string a sentence together and is in panic mode again.

Rang the tour operator to get the low-down on today.

Pick up from the apartment … seaplane out to Green Island … boat trip out to Great Barrier Reef … Lunch … catamaran back … return to the apartment by car.

Sounds simple enough for me, but not for Roo.

Once again, I told him we would cancel, but he was determined to try and make it. I suggested he has an Alprazalan, but then we realised that we'd be on a plane in less than an hour and he'd be zonked by that time. Should there be an emergency, I might have trouble getting him out, so I took a tablet with me to give to him later on – assuming we manage to get to the island at all.

We were delivered to the seaplane office where the obligatory safety brief and the dreaded weigh-ins were done. I supposed it was necessary to distribute the weight evenly on such a small aircraft – otherwise we'd be flying round in circles if all the 'heavies' were on one side. With four Oriental co-passengers, it was off to the harbour next, where there was an assortment of boats but no sign of a seaplane. To my horror, we were expected to launch ourselves into an inflatable dinghy the size of the rug in our hall at home for the trip out to the plane.

"I can do this", I told myself. *"Try to keep calm and pray"*. (Fortunately, I had become accustomed to 'speed-praying').

Aah! The power of prayer. Seconds later, I was sitting in the dinghy. I hoped I was not giving the appearance of a white-knuckled desperado hanging on for dear life and attempted to nonchalantly perch on the side of the pink rubber vessel as if I did it every day. Quite the Seafarer, I thought, but I couldn't help noticing that my bottom was the only one making a dent in the side of the inflatable (of course, the Oriental girls were no more than six stone between them). Would my weight impair our cruise? Would we be swamped with water and have to bail it out?

I directed my gaze slowly over to Roo. (Even this, I thought, might rock the boat). He was loving the dinghy experience and would have enjoyed a longer ride in it than the minute, or two we actually had in the ruddy thing as we sped away from the dock. I could just picture him in his Captain's hat standing on the bow with one hand behind his back and the other directing a telescope towards the plane.

Oh, the plane. Yes, another flippin' plane. I still had to manoeuvre myself gracefully in and out of that. I was relieved when we 'sploshed' up to the side of it where we bobbed around waiting to be told who would sit where for the trip. I wondered if the pilot would put one Oriental girl on top of the other to make a whole one, but eventually he positioned them and their partners to the rear. I was relieved. At least I wouldn't weigh it down at the back. Loathe to abandon the last bit of safety the dinghy provided I kept contact with two fingers pinching the pink rubber until the very last moment. Perhaps it was the discovery of muscles I didn't know I had, or divine intervention, but whatever it was, something assisted my propulsion out of that dinghy and into the plane. However, I still have nightmares about pink rubber and have since replaced my washing-up gloves at home with a yellow pair.

A good, smooth take off (being an expert at seaplanes, I knew this) and then it was just a few minutes before the edge of the Great Barrier Reef loomed. Beautiful blue, green and turquoise water surrounded the coral as far as you could see.

Green Island looking extremely green appeared on the horizon and within twenty minutes we had landed about 100yards off shore. It was easier to get out of the plane and into the boat this time, because a real jetty was provided making the whole process a most civilised affair. We were ferried to within twenty yards of the beach, but needed to remove our shoes and hitch up our trousers to wade through the ocean for the short walk to reach it and while everyone else jumped into the water with gay abandon, for the sake of my knees, I sort of slid down the side of the boat as if I were crewing a Luge sled. The gloriously warm turquoise water came up to my thighs and I would have been happy to stand in it in a therapeutic way, but would have melted in the heat so followed the others to the beach. Reaching dry sand, it was so hot it burnt our feet and we headed 'hot-foot' (literally) for some shade and replaced our shoes.

Roo was down to four out of ten by this time.

Tranquilizer, eat, drink. In that order I decided and we marched off to find the buffet we'd been promised. It wasn't difficult to find – we just followed the smell of the 'barbie' and came upon it quite soon amongst the oasis of little boutique-like shops and snorkel hire amongst the swaying palm trees. Lunch was served on a circular arrangement of tables with the 'kitchen' in the middle and each dish had a transparent dome covering enormous barbequed steaks and chicken, interesting-looking fish and prawns the size of small lobsters, salads, pasta and pungent-smelling 'noodley' dishes designed for anyone with a desire for Asian fare. A colourful array of fresh fruit completed the buffet - if you thought you'd have room for anything else. I served Roo with two large pieces of meat and some salad and my plate was filled with just three of the prawns. Looking for somewhere to sit, we noticed diners sitting at tables in a large caged-off area. They looked pretty silly and we couldn't imagine why they were eating in there when there were plenty of tables outside under the trees. We thought we'd much rather sit there with the dickies.....tiny green ones, small turkey-looking ones and mean-looking ones resembling miniature Pterodactyls. Finding a table under the shade of a big tree, we made ourselves comfortable to eat. But soon, we understood the reason for the cage as we were instantly surrounded by hundreds of the flying things. They landed on our laps, on our heads, on the table, the back of our chairs, under the table and others had formed a queue, but they all had one thing on their mind - our lunch! Shooing them away in a frenzy of waving arms, feet and serviettes I managed to give Roo a tranquilizer with my third hand.

He wandered off with it to find a glass of water while I sat dutifully waiting for him (I'm a stickler for etiquette), but the moment he left, the birds returned and I dived for a handful of serviettes to cover our lunch. I must have looked like someone doing 'semaphore' while having a fit at the same time.

Then without warning and with amazing audacity, one of the Pterodactyls landed on the table, expertly speared one of Roo's steaks with his beak and made off with it. With horror and disbelief my immediate reaction was to give chase, but that would expose the remainder of our lunch to the baying hordes waiting to pounce – including my very delicious-looking prawns. Anyway, Roo would be fine with one piece of meat; birds do have to eat too you know, but the annoying thing was the Pterodactyl wasn't eating the steak at all. He was playing with it, gleefully throwing it into the air and catching it again. You could almost hear him laughing. Roo returned and probably wouldn't have missed the loss on his plate, except for the show the bird was putting on, prompting recognition of the missing steak. We ate fast.

Wishing to escape the set of the film 'The Birds', we walked back to the beach and boarded a glass-bottomed boat for the trip out to the reef. This marvellous invention revealed the bottom of the ocean while we sat in relative safety and showed us that beneath the waves, everything was in good order. It was so different to see fish swimming in their natural habitat, rather than an aquarium. Apparently, there are more fish there than anywhere else in the world. The electric blue fish were my favourite, but the little Clown Fish are cute – and we found Nemo! Reef sharks were everywhere and the boat skipper threw some food pellets into the water so we could watch them feeding like mad things – the pellets were gone in seconds - but the large chaps don't appear until nightfall at this depth, so we didn't see any. (I think I was quite glad). The coral looked as though it could have been hand crafted and just come out of a kiln and if you looked closely, there were minute little swimming things amongst the giant clams and swaying seaweed. Everything seemed to be painted in bright, luminous colours that don't exist on land. It was another world – simply magical and made you want to be there under the water with them. Diving at this particular spot wasn't allowed though and all the snorkelling and diving sites are strictly regulated.

The tranquilizer had done its job and Roo had managed to total a score of 7 out of 10. Now he was cross with himself for taking it! He needed it though. I wish he didn't, but he does sometimes. The times he needs it seem to coincide with 'activity' of any sort – even doing something nice. If I didn't push him, he'd be quite content to lay cocooned on a sofa watching TV for the rest of his life.

Great Barrier Reef seen then! Well, a tiny portion of it – it's huge and much of it is out of bounds, patrolled by Coastguards. It also gets very deep and consequently, is unsuitable for viewing by glass-bottomed boat. In fact, boats of any kind are banned from sailing on a lot of it. Good.

Back on dry land after the enlightening reef tour and with Roo in 'normal-mode', snorkelling at a permitted site was next on the agenda for him. But for me, being larger than your average size 16, I was loathe to expose myself for fear of onlookers running away screaming and as snorkelling whilst wearing a sarong is ill-advised, I volunteered to stay behind and guard our belongings.

Equipped with snorkel, mask and flippers, a thick coating of factor 50 and with no resemblance to Sean Connery in any way, Roo slapped his way down the beach and into the crystal clear water to *"view the deep at close quarters"*, he said.

I thought I would be able to keep an eye on him as the water was so clear, but when he disappeared, the TV series about Reggie Perrin and his apparent suicide sprang to mind. What was I thinking of letting him go alone?

Ages passed. And then more ages. Should I find a Green Island authority figure and ask them to contact the Coastguard?

But seconds later, he surfaced and I tried not to show my relief, although I had to bite my lips to stop me laughing at the sight of what was coming towards me. It looked like a creature escaped from the Black Lagoon. I think the green slime draped gracefully across his forehead was funny enough, but the way he walked stiff-legged in the flippers giving him the appearance of an arthritic frog was even funnier.

He was so excited and while he removed the flippers from his lily white feet with a sucking noise and emptied the water from them, he jabbered on about what he'd seen and nodding approvingly at what he was saying, I brushed away the slime from his forehead. He'd been amongst fish, fish and more fish in every sort of shape and colour imaginable and went on and on, about almost standing on what looked like a smooth rock - until it moved and he saw it was a stingray. He'd had a great time.

We lay on the beach for him to recuperate until the sun got the better of us and had to retreat to a bench in the leafy picnic area. It was a relief to be out of the heat and in the shade and we sat looking out to sea, marvelling at the day we'd had.

A young bird, one of those little 'turkeys', took a liking to us and stupidly thinking it was friendly, I encouraged it to come up to me. Suddenly, it turned into an 'attack-turkey' and before I could take evasive action, it had my toe in its beak. Flinging it off my foot and high into the air as if I were kicking a football, thankfully it flew away. What was it about the flippin' birds on this island? Would we soon bump into Alfred Hitchcock?

We were returning to mainland Australia by catamaran. Shame in a way, now that I was such a seaplane expert. The cat was the last one of the day and it was quite full, mainly with Orientals who were all asleep the minute we left the quay. Perhaps this was an Eastern tradition – perhaps they'd eaten too many noodles – I didn't know, or care. We were exhausted.

It had been quite a day, in more ways than one. A calm one tomorrow, I hoped.

DAY SIXTEEN: "A Quiet Day"

Hair appointment and pedicure today – very necessary following the unprovoked attack on my toe yesterday and I *"lah-lah'd"* cheerfully while making breakfast, pondering on the day ahead.

Roo appeared after a lengthy time in the bathroom. He was in there so long in fact, I'd been on the verge of investigating to see if he'd flushed himself down the loo, or was attempting to hack his way through his wrists with a toothbrush. I tried not to look at him too much and carried on *"lah-lahing"*. He said he'd slept until daybreak when the inevitable kookaburra chorus began. It's just the same as the cockerel crowing back home really, so I don't know why he found it so annoying.

It was a beautiful, warm and sunny day.

The salon was five minutes away and Roo left me there before going out on his own to find the Post Office, insisting he'd be able to amuse himself and that he'd be okay. The two hairdressers and one beautician were lovely and the salon clean and tidy with polished chrome and gadgets everywhere – some of which could have been mistaken for instruments of torture, but were obviously hair-beautifying things.

The Aussies are fascinated with England and the minute they realised I was British, the girls bombarded me with questions about why we were in Australia, the weather back home and the Royal family. One of the hairdressers said she would love to go to England some day, but wouldn't want to drink tea every afternoon. I thought this was quite funny at the time, but then realised just how much tea we do drink. I'd even bought some with me, hadn't I? I sat in a massage chair while my hair was being washed and actually relaxed a bit. Roo turned up twice, while I was being 'done' – I supposed just for reassurance that I hadn't run off. He was more than happy when I was finished and it was time to go back to the apartment.

My first experience of an Australian salon was a good one. Gillian, my hairdresser at home would have been in her element with a place like that, but it did seem odd being in the middle of one of the biggest nature reserves in the world, that such hi-tech was available. What did I expect them to offer me then? Aboriginal body painting and tongs heated over a flame?

Later, we went to the pool together, but didn't swim myself, as it would have ruined my freshly-painted toes and hair-do. (That was an excuse actually: there was a family from Oklahoma swimming too and I didn't want to frighten them). Roo had a good old float around and chatted to the Americans (he loves Americans), but back at the apartment he was in tears again. This time, he said he was missing Harry and Lukey (having seen the family together in the pool, I suppose) and I had to remind him that they were big boys now and they were at least meeting up with us in Hawaii. He finally agreed that this was better than not seeing them at all for months on end and rambled on about their antics as little ones.

It was our last evening in Cairns, so after we'd had dinner and packed for the morning trip to Brisbane, we went out for a drink at the place I'd eaten the 'bugs'. We listened to the waves again and talked about the reef and the stingray and the bloody birds.

We both liked Cairns. The people are nice, the terrain, sea life and (some of) the birds are wonderful. We'd recommend it – as long as you can stand the heat, but if you see anything resembling a Pterodactyl, or a turkey – run!

DAY SEVENTEEN: "Brizzy" (+10hrs GMT)

We woke up to an emotional Roo. He didn't want to leave Cairns! But then he didn't want to leave Sydney!! Everywhere we go, he has to lay down some roots to establish stability. I told him that each time we move, we're a bit closer to seeing the boys and that cheered him up enough to get him to the airport.

The flight to Brisbane was easy and without a hitch. When we landed, it was like opening the AGA door. The temperature was 38degrees - not hot and steamy this time, more like a dry Las Vegas desert heat. We sorted out the hire car and discovered that the map I'd 'Googled', showing us the location of the next hotel and specific route to take was not in our folder. It was gone. Disappeared. Caput. I could see Roo's eyes widening, which meant he was heading for mass panic, but realising our predicament the hire car chappie suggested we rent a SatNav, which miraculously led us to the Medina Suites, easy-peasy.

Phew! The wonders of science.

Another fantastic location. All that homework and investigation was worth it. This apartment, on the fifth floor of a ten storey building was only a quarter of the size of the last one, but had a fabulous view of the river snaking its way through tall office blocks and apartments. It was so different to our last location and somehow rather exciting. However, the tree branches dangling beside our balcony terrace were full of squawking parrots and rattling Cicadas, making any 'lie-in' doubtful. We also discovered that we'd missed Rod Stewart, who was there yesterday.

Roo had been reasonably okay until we arrived. In spite of the familiar things around him – slippers, bedside tray, Cornflakes and PG, he was a bit tearful and unsure of things again. He said he felt guilty that he hadn't been more involved with the arrangements for the trip making less work for me, but we had to laugh when I reminded him that at the time I made all the arrangements he wasn't even capable of dressing himself.

With the sun going down, I wrote this sitting on the balcony while I waited for Roo to shower and change.

The buildings in Brisbane are mostly new, but several Victorian buildings still stand. I'm not sure why this area was so significant, it must have been something to do with the river and transporting wool. There's a lot of high-rise, but once again, the Australians here look like they're enjoying life while they work – not just working to live. There's a huge difference.

Just as the sun disappeared, that *'plinky-plinky'* piano music that I love drifted across the river and I hurried in to change for dinner. Roo was fine now – he's always a bit better in the evenings. We wandered around the riverside, but couldn't decide where to eat and instead of a meal, ended up with mega-sandwiches at a Bistro right on the waterfront where we sat people-watching. Eventually, we ran out of people to watch and were both so tired, hailed a cab back to the apartment. It was a bit too early to go to bed, so we switched on Brisbane TV and discovered that they'd just bought *'The Vicar of Dibley'* and was showing the very first episode.

Wondering what they'd make of it, I went to bed feeling a bit homesick.

DAY EIGHTEEN:

"Brizzy by boat"

Same scenario. Roo going over and over again about his feelings of inadequacy and the need for a life raft every step, of every day. A pep-talk always helps, but I say exactly the same things and he too says the same, "*I know you're right*". He needed to get out and be busy as soon as possible and after a bowl of 'Crunchy Nut' and a nice cup of PG, or two we were off to the quayside again.

I decided that you can only live in Australia if you emigrated when you were quite young, or were born here. (My feelings could have been influenced by that episode of 'Dibley' though). It's all so obviously new and energetic. Everyone seems to be buzzing around being healthy, or doing marvellous things with jet bikes. It IS nice to be outside a lot, but I do like tucking-up in front of our log fire on a damp foggy night, or being in the garden watching for the first signs of my carrots bursting through the cold, soggy, earth. I'm sure you only need to wait 24hours to grow something in this climate and there's no sense of achievement, when you can go and buy giant-sized-everything in a supermarket. I get a real kick out of watching things happen in my vegetable garden and even while we were here, I'd made mental notes of jobs in the greenhouse for our return. So there. Stick that in yer pipe and smoke it!

One of the most relaxing ways to see any city must be by boat and the 'Kookaburra Queens' Paddle Steamer seemed like a good idea. The bonus here, was the lunch included in the price – the Carvery for Roo and a 'Seafood Platter' for me. The boat was clean and quaint in a modern sort of way and manned by the all-Australian crew, one of which looked like a white-haired Captain Pugwash.

CAP'N

He was our lunchtime 'entertainment' setting the 'Pugwash' scene further, when he began to play the accordion. *And a jolly time would be had by all.* The Carvery and buffet was really well-presented, consisting of gammon and beef and a selection of vegetables. Roo waited for my platter to arrive and when it did, it resembled a complete 'catch of the day' – enough for four people ...half a dozen oysters, prawns the size of Walls sausages, a whole lobster, half a blue crab, enough smoked salmon for two breakfasts, calamari and hot goujons of plaice, all set amongst a veritable sea of fresh fruit and salad. We both sat looking at it for a minute and then I grabbed our waiter to ask if I had the right meal. I was sure it was meant for the family of four at the next table. But when I collared him, he was carrying an even bigger platter for them. Well, you know me and seafood. I dived in, doing my Darryl Hannah impersonation and managed everything but the oysters. I had gone right off oysters, ever since the *'Black Velvet'* episode at Ascot, which I prefer not to share with you. I will only say that I ruined the suede shoes of the chap I was with that day and I never saw the chap again.

By this time, 'Captain Pugwash' had the children dancing around the restaurant hysterically and it all became a bit noisy. Roo wasn't eating very much and it was obvious he was struggling, so we went out on deck to see what we were sailing past (which was why we were there, for goodness sake). There was stark contrast between the beautiful modern new homes built on the waters' edge and the disused Victorian wool warehouses and factories, which had (surprise-surprise) .... *also* become beautiful new homes. Turning round at the bend in the river signified a return to the dock and it wasn't long before we were back at the quay. Everybody shook Captain Pugwash's hand and thanked him for his musical abilities and the mood was all very friendly. Roo, however, was still in the depths of despair and needed another distraction, so I bravely suggested we walk back to the apartment. This would also burn off a prawn or two and might even stop their inevitable descent to my thighs where they would linger and turn into cellulite. Naughty prawns – but nice!

Brisbane is another incredibly people-friendly place. You are able to walk beside the river on both sides and all along the quayside is an easy boardwalk, which makes for a very pleasant stroll. Back in the safety of the apartment, Roo had a snooze and woke an hour later feeling bright enough for a swim. It was such a beautiful evening I stood on the balcony watching him pounding backwards and forwards and waving to me after each length ..... another 'security thing'.

I couldn't sleep for thinking about the Koalas at the Sanctuary tomorrow, where if we're lucky we might be able to hold one, or was it because I'd probably overdosed on seafood?

DAY NINETEEN: "Orion"

He was anxious this morning and couldn't get his words out. When he did string a sentence together, it was garbled. At times like these he realises it would be impossible to hold a job down and that the road to recovery will be slow and long. It's a catch 22 situation because these thoughts depress him even more. Roo was perspiring so much, he looked as though he'd had a bucket of water thrown over him, but we managed to go down to the restaurant for breakfast. Fortunately, as we were so late, we were alone and the big TV was on, which took his mind off himself. His memory really wasn't so good either. I wondered if this was anything to do with his illness, or he'd have this problem anyway.

He was quite confused and mixed up, but ate a small portion of bacon and eggs and I had fruit and yoghurt. When we'd finished, we went to ask for a late checkout the next morning. As before, it would mean we didn't have to hurry to leave the relative safety of the apartment and could go straight to the airport. Less hassle, less time for Roo to get in a state and time to iron out any problems. The flight back to Sydney was only an hour and a half and the port to get the 'Sapphire Princess' was a short drive. But now I was worried about him being on the ship surrounded by all that water – or losing him on the massive boat, just like the time Lukey, at the age of five went missing when we were on a Med cruise. While I coped with the 'Death of a Thousand Knives' that every parent feels with a child lost (especially at sea) he was found playing billiards with the crew in the bowels of the ship.

We went back to the apartment to chill a bit before going out – maybe. I had resigned myself to giving the Koala Sanctuary a miss, but realising that time was marching on, Roo was adamant that we'd get there and summoned up all his strength of mind to go. It wasn't difficult to get to, but the Sat. Nav gave me extra confidence and we were soon outside pulling on our macs once again to protect us from the drizzle.

'Lone Pine' is a fifty acre park, founded in 1927, by a chap whose main concern was preserving the Koala. There are one hundred and thirty of them living here of various ages, amongst assorted Kangaroos, Ostriches (or is the plural *'Ostrie'*?), Crocodiles and other Australian animals. Millions of Koalas were killed for their fur by the early settlers. I don't know how they could have done it to such adorable creatures, which because of their gentle nature were an easy target. These Koalas were born at 'Lone Pine', so have no fear of humans, but the other animals had found there way here for various reasons. There were Koalas everywhere, but the queue to actually hold one was very long, due to the strict rules the Sanctuary staff have to abide by. Those in the queue were warned that they might not reach the end if the time that each Koala was allowed out expired. They were permitted human contact for only thirty minutes a day, with every third day off. When one is bought out for a cuddle, the exact time is logged so he or she could never be taken advantage of. It was good to see the keepers adhering to the rules and it was obvious that they all loved their 'work'. Who wouldn't? I was in seventh heaven just being there. I had no intention of queuing – that wouldn't do much for Roo at all, so we began our visit by entering the Kangaroo enclosure and stood amongst several 'bouncers' – one with a Joey in her pouch. Some Kangaroos grow to a height of 6`6" – I wouldn't want to meet one of those on a dark night (or daylight, actually).

We decided that God had lots of bits over after he'd made all the other animals and rather than waste the bits had come up with the Kangaroo, which seems to be a combination of a very big mouse, a hare, a Meerkat, a camel and a fox.

Well, what theory do you have, then?

Even stranger-looking is the Ostrich. Two young ones were in an enclosure for their own safety away from the free-roaming ones. Until around a year old, they're very inquisitive and will eat anything shiny, or coloured so their enclosure is constantly monitored for anything that might kill them if swallowed. The adults roamed around alone and one of them walked along beside us, as if it was a visitor, stopping when we did to look at something. We half-expected him, or her to make a comment, in an Australian accent like, *"Nar, this erv cars is a species indijnuss to the rajun"*, or *"Aah, isn't hay a cudey?"*

'ORION'

Roo was doing as well as he could, but would probably have preferred to lay down and go to sleep somewhere – I saw him looking longingly at the Wombat den and moved him away fast.

Drifting back to the entrance, we noticed that there was no 'cuddle queue'!! I couldn't believe it – everyone had gone, apart from the two chaps who were 'cuddling' at that moment. Was I too late? Yes, this one was ready to go back to his house, but the keeper must have seen the disappointment in my eyes and said, "O, alright then" and went to get a fresh one!! I thought my heart would stop when she put 'Orion' in my arms. He was heavier than I expected and about the size of a one year old human. He felt so good. His fur was very dense and I could feel the warmth of his podgy little body against mine. He was quite sleepy and clung with his arms round me as best he could resting his head on my bosom; which made me cuddle him even closer. He gave a big sigh and closed his eyes. I wanted to run away with him.

Usually, the cuddle lasts about three minutes before they move on to the next person, but because there was no queue now, they seemed in no hurry to take him from me. Roo sensed my utter contentment and kept the keeper talking. I held 'Orion' for fifteen minutes and it went on my list of most momentous occasions.

Roo eventually dragged me away – without Orion and we drove back to the city.

I checked in on line for the flight to Sydney the next day and also rang Auckland Airport to make sure there was a luggage store there, so we could leave the bulk of our stuff while were in the Bay of Islands and Fiji. Roo relaxed on the sofa with a cuppa.

We'd eat in the restaurant downstairs tonight: hassle-free for Roo and it would give me more time to organise for tomorrow.

While we were getting ready to go down, I noticed that Roo's face was bright red. At first, I thought he must have caught the sun - you can on a cloudy day sometimes. But then I realised that this was something that happened a lot at home. Discussing this phenomenon in great detail, we came to the conclusion that the couple of shandies Roo had drunk over the last few weeks must have had an accumulative and detrimental effect on his liver. Combined with that and the three, or four Alprazalan, it must have tipped him over the edge, liver-wise.

As well as feeling unable to cope with daily life, he feels ill as well. Great, eh? No more shandies and as few tranquillizers as possible from now on.

He didn't need much encouragement to go to bed and was asleep before his head touched the pillow.

Though just as tired, the excitement of the day kept me awake. I could still feel the warmth of Orion's body against mine and wished he was tucked up in bed with me. I would have slept like a log if he had been.

DAY TWENTY:

"Sapphire Princess"

Not too bad this morning and no red face.

We talked about the plan for leaving Brisbane today and had it all straight in our minds. It was pouring with rain again, but the temperature was very pleasant and after returning the hire car checked in for the Virgin Blue flight to Sydney, which was on time despite the bad weather. The Lounge was big and comfy and Roo was calm and content. What a relief. I went to the loo and had trouble doing my trousers up. Bugger. I must have put on pounds already and this was BEFORE the cruises, but what a stroke of luck, our flight had just come in and was boarding in twenty minutes. The one after was cancelled, due to a massive storm coming in from the Pacific Ocean. If we didn't get this flight, we would literally miss the boat in Sydney. In spite of the storm approaching, the flight was smooth and we flew all the way in the brilliant sunshine that often precedes bad weather.

Yet another luvverly limo driver met us at the terminal. I think it must be nice driving those cars, because the chaps are all so friendly and helpful and obviously enjoy driving people around. We'd arranged for this one to pick up our cases from TCP before collecting us and we were relieved when he told us that the cases were safely in the trunk. It had all gone according to plan miraculously and we had clothes to wear! Half an hour later, we were at the cruise ship passenger terminal, where there was just as much bag-screening and security as there was at the airport. I tried not to keep looking up at the ship, which looked like some giant-great-thing sitting beside us and not like a boat at all. I've always had a strange fear of 'big things'. Airships moving slowly in the air … the 'walkers' in the 'Star Wars' films. This has worried me so much over the years, that I traced it right back to the time I was living in a council-run home when I was only two, or three. You might say it's impossible to have recollections at such an early age, but I know I was frightened at the sound of big footsteps on the wooden staircase leading up to the nursery where I slept. But that's another story.

Passing, once again as an '*A OK*' British Citizen, we were allowed to board the 'Sapphire Princess' and picked our way through the massive vessel to find our suite right at the end of an incredibly long corridor. We knew it would be roomy, but we didn't realise just how roomy.

Once through the double oak doors leading to the round entrance hall, we stood on the cool white marble floor in the subtle lighting, which enhanced the appearance of Trompe L'oeil murals. The dining room came next, housing a circular glass-topped table and six chairs, floor-to-ceiling sliding doors to the deck and more murals. Further on, the lounge consisted of a four-seater sofa, two armchairs and a coffee table displaying a bowl of magnificent flowers and one of fresh fruit. The sliding doors from the dining room continued on this side, while the other side had been fitted to house a large TV, DVD, stereo, fridge – with bottle of 'bubbly', a sink, a bar – with miniature spirits, assorted glasses and chocolate, while a whole corner was taken up with a computer, fax machine and all things 'office'. The bedroom, with another wall of sliding doors onto the deck, was big enough for a king-sized bed, dressing table, chests of drawers and a dressing room. The marble bathroom was exquisite with Jacuzzi bath, a multi-jetted power shower, two beautiful scallop shell basins with cupboards and drawers beneath. The bathroom led out to a powder room with dressing table, second loo and another scallop shell basin. The sliding doors, we realised were actually the walls of one side of the suite and on the other side was a 50` deck with teak tables, chairs and sun loungers – all for just the two of us! Looking at the plan of the ship, our suite took up one half of the stern, on the starboard side. (What a Seafarer I had become – knowing all the technical terms).

It really deserved its name 'The Grand Suite'. Far from the other passengers, we could stay locked away and live on room service. Roo would feel safe and sound and I could sunbathe almost naked, but then we'd miss Melbourne, Tasmania and New Zealand.

Roo and I stood outside looking at Sydney. The sky was beginning to look more than angry and large drops of rain began to fall. When the large drops became torrents, we went inside. Our Fillipino Steward, Roger (short for Rogellio), rang the doorbell and politely told us that before formal introductions could be made, he'd have to wait for his boss to arrive, but when Roger's boss turned up, he said he'd have to wait for HIS boss. So, we chatted INformally, until the boss's boss came. The two bosses were in smart summer uniforms and the film, 'Carry on

Cruising' sprang to mind, where Liz Fraser (Glad) and Dilys Laye (Flo) were completely bowled over by the handsome crew in white.

Formal introductions complete, we were left alone until our luggage arrived. By this time, the weather had really gone downhill and the rain had turned into a raging storm. One of the suitcases was completely soaked through and the contents were sodden with rainwater. Roger didn't hesitate and removed the soggy mess to be laundered.

"I might have to take him home with me", I thought.

Leaving Sydney was a memorable experience. We stood on the covered part of the deck protected from the rain, listening to Pavarotti singing his heart out over the public address system and the sound of the ship easing its' way slowly out of the harbour in the dark. Most cities look romantic at night, but the sight of the Opera House and the bridge all lit up as we left Sydney are ones I'll never forget. I stayed on deck alone, until the Pilot's boat sounded a horn and flashed its' blue light at me. By this time, Sydney's tall buildings were mere dots and it was difficult to see where the black sky ended and the sea began. I wondered if we'd ever return.

Back in our suite with its' subtle lighting, I followed a trail of silver paper to find that Roo had already eaten the chocolates. Picking the paper up as I went, I told him off for 'littering'. His excuse was that he needed something more substantial to eat and had scoffed the chocolates in desperation. As if on cue, Roger walked in with a plate of canapés and Roo pounced on them. We had to stay put for the moment, because it would soon be time to go to our Muster Station for the 'Abandon Ship' drill, so we sat and ate the canapés with our lifejackets beside us until the claxon sounded and the whole ship went into disaster mode. I'm awful at stairs now that me knees are clapped out, but the lifts of course, were out of action and by the time we came to the third flight, I was beginning to feel a bit dizzy and wished I hadn't eaten so many canapés. At least it took my mind of my knees. Once we had done the drill and replaced our lifejackets in our suite, we found the 24 hour buffet. We didn't go mad with food. We could have – others were loading their plates as if the drill had been real, but it was very late by now and we were keen to see some of the ship before we went to bed, so after the snack and without a real plan we walked out onto the deck to have a look around. The squeaky clean inside pool was equally as lavish at the outside pool and the atrium in the middle of the ship was serviced by a brass and glass bubble lift and a sweeping 'Gone With the Wind' (won't mention 'Titanic') staircase. A pianist tinkled the ivories in a way I wish I could and teak-fronted shops with alluring sparkly things in their windows beckoned you in.

Roo was fine now. I was amazed. He seemed like the 'old' Roo from a hundred years ago. I hoped it would continue – or had we turned a corner at last?

By now, a throbbing knee told me that we'd done enough walking and should turn in. Back at the suite I wandered from room to room, examining everything in closer detail. It really was comfortable and homely and with the gentle sway of the ship in the waves, I felt almost drowsy so I thought I'd freshen up a bit. Dropping my clothes onto the bathroom floor like Lady Muck, I gingerly stepped into the shower closing the door behind me only to find that you needed a Degree in Plumbing to work out the jet-things. Examining the numerous amount of gold plated equipment on the wall, I decided that for someone used to medical flashy-lighty things, operating this unit would be a doddle. I thought I had mastered control of the water fountain above my head by turning the biggest brass knob, but instead a sudden spray Fireman's-hose-style, erupted from somewhere below, tickling my feet. Then as I bent over to try a low-lying handle rather than a knob, another gush of water wet my more unmentionable nether regions making me squeal in surprise and jump into the steamy air.

Turning knobs and pulling handles like a demented Submariner on 'speed', I expected steam to be forced out of the pipes and bells to go off any second, just like in the film, 'Torpedo Run'. Frantically looking for instructions, I wiped the steam, from the door and peered out into the bathroom, only to catch sight of myself in the mirror above the basins.

I looked ridiculous standing naked, but for the plastic hat on my head, which had slipped over one eye 'Quasimodo'-style. Exhausted, I had been wetted only intermittently and had no alternative but to evacuate the state-of-

"QUASIMODO"

the-art shower and finish off the procedure in a more conventional method. I would definitely not attempt to use the Jacuzzi. *"Did you use all the jets?"* Roo asked. *"Of course"*, I replied. Bed.

Roo carried on watching TV in the lounge, but I felt so tired and furious that I was unable to control water, that I sank under the duvet. I closed my eyes, expecting to sleep, but suddenly felt quite alone on this vast ship and called Roo in to watch TV with me in the bedroom.

Must sleep.........zzz... Have to make use of every minute on this trip..... zzzz ..... Had to sell my last remaining kidney to pay for it.........Z.

DAY TWENTY-ONE: "Get your Sealegs here" (Three weeks have passed)

Had dozed off initially, but woke several times during the night. Hope I get used to the movement of such a big ship. The only other liner I'd been on was medium sized in the Mediterranean. The Sapphire Princess houses 2,700 passengers and 1,000 crew and its sheer height makes its structure tremble as it moves across the water. The weather is much more pleasant today – almost like an English summer, with a few fluffy clouds dotted around a pale blue sky. Roo will get a tan at this rate.

A scrambled egg breakfast with accompaniments was delivered and served on the circular glass table, dead on the dot of 8.30am as promised with good, hot coffee. Roo had slept like a log for a change (his own words) and had no morning blues. Perhaps rocking him to sleep is the answer – I wonder if I can rig something up at home?

After breakfast, we sat outside on the deck, until the 'Tuxedo Steward' arrived. (They seem to have a 'Steward' for everything). The two jackets – one black, one white – which had been delivered when we first arrived didn't fit and if they couldn't be changed, we wouldn't be going to the formal evenings. It would be a shame since I'd lugged two evening dresses half way across the world, but not going for the 'fine dining' would be kinder probably to my figure. (What figure?) The Steward took the jackets away and promised to sort them out.

We had received a very posh invitation to the inevitable Captain's Cocktail Party, but the idea of mingling with dozens of other people and having to talk, filled Roo with horror and fear. Whether we went or not, depended on how he felt at the last minute. I had my doubts about going and thought it would be better not to go at all, rather than have to leave mid-cocktail. Anyway, we had a table booked for dinner, after which came the evening entertainment, not in the enormous Theatre, but in one of the many lounges with fewer people to threaten Roo. The Comedian, Kelly Monteith would be performing and that should be enough fun for one night. The poor Captain must get sick to death of having to make small-talk to passengers, so two less would be a bonus for him.

Canberra was in the distance, so we must be about halfway to Melbourne. The ocean was as flat as a pancake, with a few big cargo ships on the horizon. In perfect conditions such as these, I can see the attraction of life on the ocean wave.

1pm: Time to ring Lukey in Canada. We communicated with Harry via text message from Sydney last night – all was well in not-so-dramatic Bristol.

No signal.

Apparently, the only way to make outside contact, was to be bounced off a satellite circling somewhere over the Indian Ocean. 'They', (who know about these things), say it's an expensive way of making a call, but the thought of NOT speaking to him, made me want to speak to him even more. I would cancel my next hair appointment in lieu of the call, thus offsetting the expense. When we eventually got through to him, his voice came across quite different to his usual 'Hell-oh', with several squeaks and 'pings' in the background, you know how astronauts sound from space? But it was worth doing, just to know that all was well with him and Canada.

Two corsages had been delivered. Both were red roses, but one more pretty than the other, so I supposed that was the one for me. Roo said he'd look a plonker wearing it and I wasn't keen to pin it to my dress, so I attached then both to my handbag instead. They rather overpowered the small evening bag, but at least we showed our appreciation of the gesture.

That nice Steward returned with the jackets and assured us that these would be a perfect fit. Roo looked fab in the white one, but as I was wearing a black ensemble, we hoped we wouldn't look like the 'Black & White Minstrels' (you need to be over 45 to know what I'm talking about). I was having difficulty breathing (my outfit had obviously shrunk in that rainstorm) and the bosoms were having their own difficulties staying inside the top.

The philosophical approach to this dilemma would need to be put into operation, *'If they're looking at your bosoms, they won't notice the size of your arse'* and satisfied with this rationale, I practised taking small breaths. Time marched on and if we were going to the cocktail party, it was now, or never. Looking at Roo's pained expression, it was *'never'*. That was fine by me. I wouldn't have trouble being unsociable if it meant we had a nice evening. We would go to the Piano Bar before we ate, listen to the smooth Jazz and if we pretended to be honeymooners, we'd be left alone. We couldn't help noticing how nice we looked all 'dolled up' and off we went. I had to keep a firm grip on Roo's arm – not for his sake, but because I was wearing what I call my 'eating' contact lenses. They allow me to see things close-up – reading with them is great, for example and to be able see what I'm eating without wearing glasses is wonderful. The problem is though, that everything further than three feet away is a complete blur. Anyone spotting my cautious gait and voluminous eyes, must have thought that I HAD been to the cocktail party and downed one too many, but between us we managed to reach the bar without bumping into anyone.

It was a popular place, probably because the pianist was so good and the only empty chairs were at the bar itself. You know the very high ones, with the foot bit for resting your feet? Mmmm … a ladder would be useful ….. perhaps someone could hitch up my long skirt while I clambered up. Oh, why am I so useless at these things?

My initial attempt at a soft landing on the stool led to a dangerous moment when with the effort it took, my left bosom tried to escape completely. Rather than be arrested for exposing myself, all I could do was abandon the attempt and lean against the stool with both feet on the floor perching the lower end of my buttock against the seat and hope I looked 'cool'.

Breathing just enough to remain in the upright position, I tried to sustain an air of composure. The Martini Roo had ordered was gone in a flash as I sought

'Dutch Courage', but this only added to the dizziness caused through my lack of oxygen. I knew I would never master the stool and needed to sit down fast.

With alcohol figuring a big fat zero in Roo's life, sitting at a bar is not much fun for him, so rather than end up on the floor with blue lips, or be sozzled on my lonesome (and still end up on the floor), I suggested we go to eat. We felt like naughty children not going to the cocktail party, but knew we'd made the right decision.

The friendly staff in the sumptuous restaurant made a real fuss of us and our table was perfectly placed to carry out a conversation with the Maitre d', who gave us tips on how to make the most of our time on board and things NOT to do ashore.

We were served with sixteen 'tasting plates' of delicious food and by the time we reached the last one, I was lucky not to have burst out of my top completely. Roo was comfortable with the situation and seemed particularly at home on the ship now.

With dinner over, it was time to go and hear Kelly Monteith and although he was just a big blur as far as I was concerned, he was very funny and Roo laughed a lot, which was good to hear.

Another exhausting day not doing very much, except lounging around and eating.

Lying in bed listening to the waves hitting the ship was both romantic and creepy all at the same time. Because we were right on the stern, we could actually hear the propeller blades slicing through the water and the sound it made was a bit like hearing water boil. I could imagine the blades turning like crazy and their responsibility for pushing us over the sea, but with the thought of this in my mind's eye, I suddenly saw the bit in the film 'Titanic' when you see the propeller coming up out of the water just before it sinks.

Not a happy thought to go to sleep on really. "Night, night".

DAY TWENTY-TWO:

"Melbourne"

We didn't wake up until 9am and although I knew where we were headed, I was still surprised to see Melbourne out of the window. I hadn't arranged a shore excursion here, because I didn't want to push Roo too much to begin with, but we thought we'd catch a bus into the city after breakfast; which in spite of the marathon meal last night, still managed to find its way into our stomachs. A 'full' breakfast for Roo and pancakes for me – with not too much maple syrup, but isn't it lovely?

Roo was being quite bossy, which was a good sign. If I act all pathetic now, perhaps he'll buck up a bit. I was horrified to see that my left arm was peeling. Strangely though, it seemed to be the same colour underneath. Perhaps I was turning into something.

We disembarked, which was easy as we were docked in the harbour and caught the tram for the short journey into town, passing quaint Victorian buildings beside high rise apartments and offices, which grew larger the nearer to the centre we came.

Melbourne has a reputation for being a very lively working city, with plenty of culture and amazing beaches – what a combination! We left the tram to mingle with a mixture of office workers, tourists and locals, all of whom were hurtling around being busy. We didn't feel like being busy with them though. It was only 66 degrees and Roo felt chilly in his shorts, (oddly, as we headed further south it would get colder – the dead opposite of what we're used to in England), so we didn't stroll around too much, but just had a quick look at some of the shops spotting the original Victorian facades above some of them advertising 'old' Melbourne wares.

Roo's demeanour was less bossy and he was clearly not happy to wander around the shops, so before he reverted back into the depths of despair, we hopped on another tram and returned to the ship.

Delicious canapés delivered. Irresistible. Fortunately, I was sure these were the ones without calories. Just one or three then. It would be a shame to waste them.

We'd booked a table at the 'Savoy' Restaurant tonight. Hope it's as good as the one in London.

Roo had been marvellous ALL DAY. He'd been absolutely fine and I was frightened to mention his well-being, in case it altered his psyche. On the other hand, I thought it was important for him to know he was making progress, so I *did* mention it. He agreed that the last two days had been good and assured me that he was trying to remain optimistic. We were both looking forward to going to Tasmania and seeing the sheep-shearing, so maybe he'd be too busy to think about himself.

Waiting to move off from the dockside in Melbourne, we watched a ferry being loaded beside us in the next berth. Security here seemed all cocked-up. Every third car was being stopped and examined under the bonnet, while camper vans and trucks were waved on. We thought this was a very odd method of ensuring passenger safety. Perhaps there was something we didn't know, in spite of being old hands as far as 'security' was concerned. Maybe they were looking for something specific. Anyway, we floated away from Melbourne and while I watched the city grow smaller and smaller on the horizon, I wondered if we'd put it on our list of places to see again. Maybe we didn't see enough of Melbourne to appreciate it, apart from the huge shopping opportunities.

Washed and polished, we arrived at The Savoy for dinner and had a nice table by the window with a view of a fantastic sunset. I defy anyone to say they get tired of seeing the sun sink down into the water. It doesn't matter where you are in the world, it's always a wonderful thing to see and we weren't disappointed with the display out of the window this time. I could have got all romantic and gooey-eyed, but that wouldn't have done, at all. We talked to some Aussies on the next table. They were 'cruise junkies' and spent most of their lives on one ship, or another mainly floating around Australia. Takes all sorts, but I would miss me garden. Roo and I had a stroll around the Poop Deck, (or whatever it was called) before returning to our cabin and I kidded myself that the walk would be enough to nullify the scampi I'd just eaten. Well, it might hasten its way down to my gizzards – going to bed on a full stomach was not something I liked to do and with the Tasman Sea behaving in its usual rough manner – so we were told, it might be a good thing if it was as far down as possible.

DAY TWENTY-THREE:

"All at Sea"

We were halfway to Tasmania. The sea was a bit lively last night and I was woken up several times with what sounded like tidal waves hitting the ship. Crossing the Tasman Sea can be very dodgy apparently. I wished I could stop thinking about the 'Titanic'.

It was a beautiful morning, although the swell on the water had altered dramatically and when our delicious breakfast was delivered the plates slid around on the table like letters on a ouija board. After we'd eaten (again) we spent time out on deck watching the rise and fall of the huge waves and soon spotted the beginnings of Flinders Island, which was discovered in 1798, by a British chap called Matthew Flinders. We were about fifteen miles from Cape Portland, just on the north-east tip of Tasmania.

Flinders seemed uninhabited, but I could just see a plume of smoke away in the distance, so there must be people living there. The sea was quite empty apart from our ship and the tranquil scene peaceful, other than the sound of birds swooping around in the blue sky and the splash of the water against the hull.

I weighed myself on the scales in the powder room this morning, but the motion of the ship made it difficult to determine my mass. When we rolled to the left – I'd lost a few pounds and when we rolled to the right – the numbers were disastrous. I liked the roll to the left best and decided to be content with that.

Roo went off to the library. This gave me the opportunity to tell you secretly that he'd been bright and breezy again and felt confident enough to go right to the pointy end of the ship and up several floors alone to the quiet part. I hoped he'd find his way back okay.

We'll be at sea all day until we dock in Tasmania, so we can both be very lazy and catch some sun. I'd bought a factor 6 yesterday, which had a strong smell of coconuts reminding me that it was only four weeks before we met the boys in Hawaii. I was longing to see them both and I knew Roo missed them terribly too.

Time passed and I began to do my nervous thing again. Should I go and look for him? Had he jumped overboard?

Of course, he walked through the door a few minutes later and of course, I was my usual nonchalant-self, hiding my relief.

For once, he hadn't chosen a spy-orientated book. He reads so many of these it must be a sign of something. Perhaps it's wishful thinking that he'd once been a suave and debonair 007, but he's certainly no Mr Bond; more of a Mr Bean. But then had he been a James Bond, he would have had a Claudia Schiffer wife, not a blonde Vicar of Dibley.

We repeated the ritual for going to dinner. I had never been so clean, in spite of using only one of those damn spoutty-things in the shower. I'm sure it's not good for your skin to be without at least a few good bugs, but mine was constantly gleaming and so obviously bug-free.

As if we needed to be fed, we went to the Steakhouse. Now you know I don't eat meat, don't you? I like meat, but meat doesn't like me. If I eat it, my fingers blow up like Wall's sausages and my joints throb and moan at me, so I avoid it like the plague. The poor waiter spent ages showing us all the different steaks available and looked really disappointed, when Roo ordered a plain T Bone and I asked for some fish. He went away mumbling something about "bloody heathens".

With dinner tucked away in our ever-increasing storage facilities (I had to look at gastric-banding on our return), we hurried to the theatre, where a show was about to begin. The auditorium was enormous, seating 705 people and had a 36ft arched stage. The sets, costumes and quality of singing and dancing were all first class and of West End proportions and we were astonished that it was possible to produce something so professional on a boat. I mean, ship.

I went to bed singing one of the songs (badly) and eventually, Roo told me to shut up, or he'd put a pillow over my head, so I carried on singing to myself.

Anyway, the show had been fantastic and so had Roo.

DAY TWENTY-FOUR:

"Sheepy, Sheepy, Sheep-Sheep"

6.30am – Tasmania.

It was an early rise for our trip ashore and I thought I was hearing things, when I caught the sound of singing. Having gone to sleep with music in my ears after the extravaganza last night I had to be imagining it, but although it was just after the crack of dawn, children from one of the Hobart schools stood on the quay in their red and blue uniforms to sing us awake. It was charming and made us all smile as we trooped ashore.

The organisation to herd passengers off the ship and onto waiting coaches was perfect and soon we found ourselves leaving the dock with twenty-three assorted Americans and 'others' all looking forward to seeing some of Tasmania, or 'Tazzy' as the locals say.

As we left, we saw the kids scrambling aboard behind us for the breakfast they'd been promised as a reward for their delightful singing.

The coach trundled away from the dock and Veronica, our tour guide for the day introduced herself. She was an ex-Londoner in her 70's who had left England behind in 1958 and loved her life in Tasmania. Our driver, Michael, was a ruddy-faced true 'Tazzer', who had never felt the need to leave the island. Our first stop was at a salmon farm, which had been built amongst serene gardens and would, I imagine make it a smashing place to work. I wasn't terribly interested in the fish unless they'd suggested we eat some, but it was lovely to walk around the gardens. Moving on, our next stop was a small wildlife sanctuary where we had a close-up of several Tasmanian Devils. These cute little black things are a cross between a small dog and a furry pig. Sadly, around 80% have been wiped out in the wild by a contagious cancer peculiar to them. Consequently, there's a big breeding programme going on and a lot of research to find a cure, since they're very important to the islanders.

This sanctuary does such a wonderful job caring for sick, injured or orphaned animals that it attracts wild animals as well; simply because it's a nice place for them all to be. The sanctuary owners and their volunteers don't seem to mind how many they care for and often can't remember which animals should officially be there. A beautiful creek runs through it and the constant flow of pure, crisp water has become home to several Duck-billed Platypus. (plural: 'Platypi') ((perhaps)). For some reason after seeing one, I was looking forward to being able to say that I'd actually seen a duck-billed platypus. (Perhaps I've seen too many 'Monty Python' sketches).

Driving through the Tasmanian countryside, there was a distinct lack of people and Veronica told us that although the island is the same size as Scotland, there are more animals there than humans. Heaven to live there, if you love animals.

Lunch next, at one of the oldest Tasmanian Inns where a good, deep quiche and salad, followed by a selection of scrumptious puddings was provided. We shared a table with four Americans from Philadelphia, who were glad to be out of the heat and stayed in the cool, blue-painted room until it was time to leave, but Roo and I wandered outside. We found a herd (well, three) of Emus in the garden attached to a ramshackle house along the dust road. We patted them, which they seemed to enjoy in spite of the heat until Michael hooted the horn at us. Back on the coach, I wished I could have washed my hands before we left, as I smelt suspiciously like an old Emu and as I warmed up the smell became stronger. Fortunately, we were just a short drive away from our next stop where I was able to wash away the Emu on me. This was a rather unusual house, packed full of ancient artefacts owned by a widely-travelled elderly lady. African spears hung on the walls and below them bows and arrows.

The nursery, crammed full of china dolls and toys, was a bit creepy and after having a look at the kitchen and the original fittings there, Roo and I spent time in the garden, where we were much more at ease. A beautiful mix of an Italian design on an English theme, the garden reminded us of the one we'd left behind, which would be well on its' way to blossoming by now. I could picture the Narcissi I had lovingly planted many moons before and wondered how my other bulbs were doing.

Andrew nine out of a possible ten. We were doing well.

While everyone else seemed to be content with the house and garden, Roo and I were keen to see some sheep and were pleased when it took only twenty minutes to reach Curanga Farm and its 800 four-legged woolly things. The owner, Tim met the coach and took us straight to a shed to see the poor old sheep being sheared. To carry out this task, the young 'shearer' had to lie down in a harness, which looked quite comfortable actually while he held the sheep between his knees clipping away merrily with an electric shaver, until the sheep (who didn't seem to mind the process at all) was completely bald. Amazingly, the fleece was removed in one whole piece and the shearer proudly told us that he was able to produce one fleece every minute. Then the wool is graded, washed and spun into several different materials. Some of the fleeces were sold in the (inevitable) shop there and I bought a fabulously soft Marino wool cushion case as a memento.

While we watched this clever chap, who was no more than twenty-three, one of Tim's sheepdogs joined us. He seemed to know that he was the next star on the agenda and led us out into the sunshine again where we waited in the shade of a farm building. At a signal from Tim, the dog teamed up with two younger dogs, who had sat patiently waiting for him and suddenly they were off. The older dog was a true professional and took the lead with the others watching his every move, until the three working together showed that they were a team of expert 'rounder-upperers'. Their expertise and foresight to determine where the sheep would go and how they laid down in an instant at the sound of Tim's voice was impressive. The only thing that wasn't good was the flies.

I suppose you have to get used to them if you live on a sheep farm. When the finale came, it was a magnificent sight. Two hundred and fifty sheep standing beside the lake one minute and the next, galloping towards us at speed. I hoped they would stop when they reached us and not pin us all against the wall where we were standing, but shortly before trampling us all to death, the dogs swept in front of the herd and turned them; just like a flock of birds. Those dogs are priceless.

Tim came with us on the coach on the way out, to show off his poppy fields. He grows these pretty flowers under a strict licence and later sells them to a drug company for the production of morphine. Alongside the poppies, he grows cabbages for seed. The endless rows of cabbages looked really funny, compared to the amount I grow at home. A lucrative sideline for him is tourism and he has several cabins dotted around the lake with a couple set in more remote areas of the 800 acre farm. Tim was a smashing bloke, who obviously works hard, but insists he will never get rich from growing sheep.

It was time to head back to the ship. We were really tired, although we hadn't actually done much all day, but it had been an early start and the heat can be quite exhausting. I was even looking forward to a shower using ALL the knobs and pulleys.

At the dock, the Hobart Police Pipe Band pristinely dressed in kilts in the Fletcher of Dunans tartan and other Scottish regalia were ready to pipe us away from the quay and Australia itself. It was all a bit sad. We had enjoyed being here and would like to have seen more. There's such a lot of it to see, but we had made a good start. We resisted the urge to jump straight into the shower, choosing to wait on deck to hear the band play first.

They were as marvellous as we thought they would be and proudly marched away playing 'Auld Lang's Syne' while the ship inched itself away from the harbour. However, no sooner had we moved away, we moved back again, much to the surprise of the bystanders waving us off and whose 'goodbye' smiles on their faces turned into puzzled expressions. The Captain told us over the PA that a member of the crew was very ill and at the last minute, the ship's Doctor had decided to hospitalise him (or her). So we spent an extra half hour in Australia, until the ill one was ashore. By this time the bystanders had all gone home, but we still stood on our deck waving at an empty dock to say goodbye to Australia.

I was done in and just wanted to get clean (I was addicted to being squeaky clean by now), but Roo (still nine out of ten) wanted to eat and as his liver needs all the help it can get I encourage the eating process. Of course, he eats like a horse and doesn't put on a pound, whereas I only have to look at a slice of

< cabbage!

cucumber and you know where it ends up. So, Roo had a burger and chips and I had a glass of water.

I counted sheep. It was pretty inevitable of course, but when I started counting cabbages I was a bit worried. It could have been ampoules of morphine I suppose. Now that would have been strange.

DAY TWENTY-FIVE: "Land of the Midnight Kiwi"

Cap'n told us that we would be at sea now on route to Milford sound in New Zealand for two whole days. Roo's nine out of ten had dipped to a seven, but I've had to cope with a nought before, so couldn't complain. We can do nothing if we want. Be lazy. Be slobs.

With nothing but sea and sky – not even a bird to look at, we decided to be slobs. Staying in our suite we watched three films one after the other and then dozed off for while. We were slobs of the utmost slobbery and lost an hour off the world clock at the same time by crossing the Tasman Sea. In fact we didn't venture out until 10pm., when we hit the buffet. While I was replenishing my cellulite, I couldn't help noticing the lady sitting at the next table who resembled a very pale Twiglet. She was as thin as one of my legs, but her dinner plate was piled high with food. This is something I find most depressing and was made worse when, having eaten everything on her plate she went back to the buffet to choose not one, but TWO puddings. Ugh!! Roo remained a seven, or maybe a six.

We meant to go for a bracing, healthy walk on deck, but as it was blowing a gale and quite chilly, we somehow found ourselves watching the Line Dancing. It was great fun, even though we didn't move from our chairs and laughed so much at people making fools of themselves as we sat smugly and firmly on our barstools. Of course, we wouldn't have dreamt of making fools of ourselves too.

We'd had one of those days, where you feel guilty that nothing had been achieved. I hadn't read a serious book, been to the Gym, or done a Miss Marple by solving a mysterious murder (thank goodness), but I did feel very chilled-out, which made me sleepy. It must have been the strenuous Line Dancing.

I was looking forward to getting into bed and when I did, I pressed the button that miraculously pulled open the curtains. The plain expanse of window revealed a most beautiful sky. It was as black as pitch out there, but with a million sparkling stars twinkling amongst the blackness. Switching off the bedside lamps helped my eyes adjust further and with just a glimmer of light from the stern to pollute the effect, the more I looked the more stars I could see, until the blackness was almost white. It was extraordinary. How many stars must there be?

DAY TWENTY-SIX: "Rescue on the High Seas" (+13hrs GMT)

We'd had a ghastly night. Roo was down to four out of ten and I think I was minus four.

The ship was all over the place. The engine noise was unbearable and the superstructure was shaking and vibrating so much, that I thought we'd reached a point where we would topple into the sea. There didn't seem to be a reason for this and by 7am we'd given up trying to sleep and had a cup of PG. The Tasman Sea had an even more enormous swell on it and at 9am El Capitano came over the PA, apologising for the 'choppy' conditions.

'CHOPPY'? Ha-very-Ha. If that was 'choppy', what was 'ROUGH' like? We'd also moved on another hour on the world clock, making us thirteen hours ahead of England. But of course, that didn't make any difference to the sailing conditions. (I don't know why I said that).

It wasn't just the adverse sea causing such discomfort. The Captain told us that he had been approached by the New Zealand Coast Guard who had asked for help to locate a yacht that was in trouble. 'We' (the Royal kind) had said, *"Yes"* and had consequently increased our speed to the maximum, which was about 26 knots.

The nurse in me did see the urgency though and of course, the mother in me realised how scary it must be for the occupants, but I thought it was odd that 2,700 passengers (mainly 50+) and 1,000 crew should have had to endure the ghastly night, been thrown around dangerously for the last eight hours and diverted 100 miles off our course, to look for a tiny yacht. Obviously, I was a hard nut and certainly no seawoman. The crew though, were quite excited at the prospect of a 'rescue' and official lookouts were posted to try to locate the boat. Unofficial lookouts amongst the passengers posted themselves.

At about 1pm with the assistance of the Maritime Rescue Centre and a spotter plane, the yacht was sighted and we slowed down, which was a great relief. It was almost relaxing, as the massive ship gently bobbed around in the swell like a toy boat on a pond.

The yacht had a crew of three. Two of them were suffering from a serious case of seasickness and associated dehydration. Strange, I thought. Surely, if you were embarking on a mega sea voyage, you would know beforehand whether, or not, you had "sea legs". There I go again, a cynical hard nut. Anyway, regardless of this, they needed to be rescued and the Captain began a blow-by-blow description of what was going to happen next. Roo, in spite of being down to three out of ten now, had gone down to the boat deck to capture the event on film. However, he should have waited, because the

"HELP!"

ship - at least I think it was the ship, but it could have been the yacht - serenely swung round, giving me a wonderful view from our deck where I was able to watch the whole event in privacy; which was a good thing, since I was only wearing my dressing gown. We were close enough to see a chap standing at the helm who was obviously okay and able to shout across the water to us. 'Us' being the would-be rescuers and for the moment, it looked to me as though it was going to be a pretty simple exercise. But what did I know about these things? Suddenly, the mood changed into a flurry of excitement as an orange rescue boat manned by four valiant officers was lowered into the sea amid *"cheers"*, *"whoops"* and furious clapping from the watching passengers. The engine on 'Orange One' roared into action and the craft sped heroically towards the stricken vessel with a *'whoop'* from the (mainly American) spectators. It was all very Stephen Segal, with a hint of Mel Gibson. The rescue boat had a devil of a job getting close enough to the yacht though and now it was easy to see just how big those waves actually were.

Ooh, was I glad I was standing watching and not part of the rescue team. At one point, the whole mission seemed to be in the most perilous-of-peril, taking into consideration our location in the middle of the ocean and the skill required to conduct the rescue. The chap in charge of the rescue boat tried to position it so that the poorly ones could be hauled unceremoniously aboard. But with the waves being such an amazing size, the yacht was in danger of landing right on top of the rescuers, Wo! It was really exciting. Some of the watching passengers squealed in anticipation of a disaster and a crowd hanging over the rails of the deck above me were being very 'doom and gloom'. *"They'll never get them"*. I heard one man say. *"They'll all end up in the drink"* said another. And *"They've had it. They're not coming home to Mumma now."*

Very encouraging. A most positive attitude.

Each time the two boats were close enough for a transfer, they were bashed together by the waves. It was only the expertise of the officer driving – steering, or whatever – that all at once it was over for one of the sick people – a young woman – who was quickly plucked (grabbed actually) from the yacht. Cheers went up and I expected to see flares shot into the air in celebration, but as the rescue boat passed the stern it was easy to see this poor girl's face. She looked dreadful and so obviously in need of medical attention. Then I felt bad that I'd moaned about the mercy dash. Once she was safely aboard, the team returned for the sick man, repeating the process.

What heroes those chaps were and thank goodness we have people like them and not more like me.

The yacht would return to mainland New Zealand with just the owner, who asked for a few supplies – bread and whisky (?) and his two shipmates would continue with us for an enforced stay in a hospital on a luxury liner.

So, with the mood returning to one of joviality, the stoker threw on a shovelful of coal to start the engine and we moved away from the yacht. Of course, there WAS no stoker and not one lump of coal. The ship was propelled by diesel and/or electric turbines. When we needed the speed to reach the yacht, both were used. (This is a little bit of technical information to impress you). We must have moved across the water like a wound-up elastic band on a pencil. No wonder we were chucked around!

Well, I hoped that this was the only bit of emergency excitement we'd have – remembering that the lifejackets made you look even bigger than you really were and you just never knew who might take photo's – even in an emergency.

Roo was very yellow again. I had to get him off those ruddy tablets. He's sad again and wants to cry. I tucked him up in a lounger on our deck and he snoozed for a bit. The sun was going down slowly, but still had a lot of heat – perfect for writing, so I sat beside him as I scribbled. I felt so sorry for him.

My writing was interrupted by a knock at the door. Oh gawd! We had TWO plates of canapés and a bottle of Moet delivered. Don't they know I have a distinct lack of metabolism? I nibbled at the fishy ones and saved the others for Roo who was snoring his head off. How could I put him through the 'getting-ready-to-go-out process' when he felt so ill? Well I couldn't, could I? So I rang room service and ordered dinner in. Blue crab for me and chicken for Roo. There was nothing else to do but treat him gently when his score was low. What's the point in watching him struggle?

Dinner was amazing and Roo perked up a bit. He was sorry we had to stay in, but I really didn't mind and by the time we had finished and the Steward came to collect the crockery, Roo must have felt better because he chatted away merrily with no sign of the deep doldrums he'd had an hour before.

I was in carefree mode anyway, but so would you have been with no one to share a bottle of Moet with.

Early to bed, to catch up on last night and we had to be up at daybreak when we would reach Milford Sound, where the watery parts of 'Lord of the Rings' was filmed.

Can't miss that.

DAY TWENTY-SEVEN: "Oh Lord! What a Sound" (+13GMT)

I woke up just before dawn with a pounding headache – courtesy of Moet & Chandon. The sky was almost white with stars again, but this time with a dark blue background. Another beautiful sight. But unable to see exactly where we were I dozed off again until the motion of the ship slowing down woke me up completely.

First light, accompanied by a clear pale blue sky revealed a spectacle we'd only seen in the film. Standing on our deck in awe and still in our dressing gowns, we were totally unprepared for the magic of Milford Sound, which is one of New Zealand's fourteen Fjords surrounded by three million acres of National Park.

Apart from the sound of falling water, it was deathly quiet as we entered the Fjord. It was as if we'd gone through a portal into another dimension. Our breath showing up in the cold, crisp morning air made it even more surreal. The ship hardly made a ripple as it moved slowly along water so clear, it was easy to see myriads of fish. Dolphins raced right beside us, surfacing and diving in such a knowing and comfortable way it had to be a ritual every time a ship came in. They really seemed to be enjoying themselves.

Towering snow-capped mountains rising to nearly 4,000 feet with sheer rock faces covered in lush rainforest thrown up from the earth five hundred million years ago lined the sides of the Fjord. Excessive rain had created cascading waterfalls gushing from every possible orifice high above us falling hundreds of feet into the water below, while smaller waterfalls drifted away in the wind, never to hit the water.

The mountains were formed by intense heat and pressure deep in the earth's crust and the channel we sailed was once a glacier – 400 metres deep in some places,

which has allowed black coral to grow. The sun rose improving the scene further – *if that was possible* - and it was difficult to know where to look next, because everywhere was so beautiful and we didn't want to miss a thing. A ray of light hit the mountain tops, gradually inching its way down to the water flooding it with colour. It was more than spectacular and so heartening to be able to see this beauty without actually setting foot on it. This heavenly place was undiscovered until 1773, when good old Captain Cook fell upon it, but not realising just how marvellous it was, it didn't become a real attraction until the 20th century. The New Zealanders are very proud of the area and fiercely protect it. Roo and I felt very honoured to be there. Reaching the end of Milford Sound, the huge ship turned a complete circle from the stern, as if it were spinning on tarmac and then headed out towards Thompson Sound hugging the New Zealand coastline as we sailed. Doubtful Sound was just as beautiful, but much wider and longer with more vegetation and not so mountainous. There was more insect life here too and it was here that I was stung by a bee the size of a sparrow. It really hurt. Dusky Sound was different again. Had the vegetation been gorse rather than the 'broccoli' type, you would have thought you were floating on a Scottish Loch, but with much bigger mountains rather than hills.

Apart from the dolphins, seals and penguins, we couldn't pick out any animals in the rainforest, but we were assured that there are thousands roaming around the three million acres - 5% of the New Zealand land mass.

Roo had filmed like a mad-filming-thing and been nine out of ten all day. But had he been anything less, I would have bashed him up. I don't know how ANYONE could be depressed being here.

Everything looked so healthy and fresh. It was easy to see why so many movies are made in unspoilt New Zealand, where paradise seems to go on and on. Even after spending a whole day sailing in and out of the Fjords we weren't bored with it. But the sun eventually set and it was time to leave and head south to Dunedin. Roo suggested we have dinner at 'Vivaldi's' and then catch the performance by the ships' officers and crew at ten o'clock. The fact that he actually made a suggestion must have meant he was at least nine and a half out of ten. 'Vivaldi's' was fantastic and so was the show. One Officer's performance was so hilarious I can't remember laughing as much for years. Roo sat beside me and enjoyed it too. This time, the tears were running down his face with laughter, rather than sorrow.

We'd been away from home for a whole month. It had been good so far and I'd managed to handle Roo's bad bouts without too much trouble. It was a bit like giving birth – the bad bits pale into insignificance. I tried to remain optimistic, but with a hint of negative anticipation – just in case.

DAY TWENTY-EIGHT:

"Edinburgh of the South"

The weather was wet and windy when we arrived in Dunedin, so we dived straight into a cab after jumping ship. The cabbie was a very helpful soul and offered to give us a potted tour of the area.

Very much uphill and down dale, the terrain reminded us of Scotland (our second favourite place in the world) and of course Dunedin is the old Gaelic name for Edinburgh; in fact it's called the 'Edinburgh of the South' and maintains strong ties with the Scots who were the first to settle there and even has a 'Haggis Ceremony'.

The city has a statue of Robbie Burns outside a lovely Anglican church, which beckoned me in. I hadn't been to a service for a whole month and had visions of being ex-communicated, so I grasped the opportunity of making a bit of reparation.

I find most churches a bit of a bolthole and this one was no exception. The Scottish influence was very obvious and I sat silently with Roo absorbing the atmosphere. It was good to get a 'fix' and have time for a bit more than a speed-prayer. I hoped there would be an Easter service on the next ship – even a catholic one would do. We lit candles for the usual list of lost loved ones – my nephew being the first in line, then Mavis, then dad and left the church feeling uplifted.

Roo spotted an 'All Blacks' shop and couldn't resist a look inside. With Lukey being into Rugby we just had to buy him a shirt, but as it was so expensive he would have to wait to have it for his Birthday in May. With the shirt, came a canvas 'All Blacks' bag and ONE sock. The other could be claimed by visiting one of their other shops and waving this one in the air shouting, "*I claim my sock*". All very novel.

Roo hadn't been too bad, but had that liverish 'odour' again and I wondered if a detox supplement of some kind might help, so bought some 'Milk Thistle' in a health food shop. He was shaky and nervous and I could see where we were headed. Time for a pot of tea, I thought and perhaps start him on the 'Thistle'. No time like the present.

The tea helped initially, but my gut feeling was to get him back to the ship and I flagged down a taxi. This time, the driver took another route following the harbour round and now that the weather had improved there was much more to see.

Back in the security of the Sapphire, Roo began to feel better and after he'd showered he insisted he was alright to eat out.

The ship left Dunedin while we were eating and once again we were exhausted. Back in our suite, we tucked up in loungers on our enormous deck and star-gazed. It was all very romantic – but without any canoodling.

DAY TWENTY-NINE:

"Christchurch"

We were a dab-hand at disembarkation now and soon on the coach to take us to the 'Tranz-Alpine Express', a scenic train ride up to the southern alps - a land of ice, rock and alpine flowers. Unfortunately, the couple sitting opposite us were 'Gabblerdictums' and really put poor Roo through hell. It was impossible to get a word in edgeways, so we simply sat enduring the mindless conversation about their trip and Roo made several visits to the loo to relieve the monotony. I smiled a lot and made what I hoped were the appropriate noises in the right places, but couldn't give my undivided attention to the narrow bridges we crossed and the lush Canterbury Plains we passed on the way up. There were loads of tunnels to go through and trundling along one very long one, I imagined that when we'd reached the end of it, this pair had disappeared. The funny thing was, Roo had thought similar, but it was us who had disappeared! It would make a good film I'd call it, *"Mystery of the Disappearing Gabblerdictums on the Tranz-Alpine Express"*. But doubted I'd ever threaten Agatha Christie.

Boy, were we relieved to get off the train when we reached the Alps.

And guess what? Just for a change, our friend Captain Cook first visited the area in 1770 and the highest peak is

153

named after him. This is the longest and highest mountain range in New Zealand and once again, most of the area is National Park. The Southern Alps area is also a ski resort, which we found particularly interesting and were impressed with the dramatic geology. It wasn't hard to imagine the scene in the winter months between June and September when the area becomes piste and is descended upon by skiers. Once we'd had our fill of the peaks and the wonderful fresh air we hopped on a coach, which drove us back to the bottom. It was quicker than the train somehow and would also give us a quick look at Christchurch itself.

We stopped at a place called Castle Hill Rocks on the way down.

It was this area that was used for one of the locations in 'The Lion, the Witch and the Wardrobe' (remember the battle at the end?) It was easy to pick out certain parts from the film and I could have

sworn I saw a lion sitting on that flat rock; but every visitor says the same thing, apparently.

The tour meandered its way down, passing deserted hamlets for winter sports and lakes that were remnants of glaciers, until we'd descended four thousand feet to the bottom – the top being twelve thousand feet.

Roo got the shakes for no apparent reason and I was glad that the next stop was for afternoon tea at a ramshackle 1850's Homestead. The owners had a dear little cat, not much more than a kitten and we watched him squirreling around chasing imaginary mice entertaining us, while we sat in the garden drinking our tea and eating homemade apricot cookies.

There was more sheep shearing and herding if you wanted it, but instead, I had a chat with the lady in the shop there about her many life-threatening operations following a near-death accident. Have I always been morbid? Or do I simply attract this sort of people? It is a bit worrying though, because I do find conversations about blood, guts and gore really interesting.

The Homestead wasn't very far from Christchurch and this was our last stop before joining the ship again. Called the 'Garden City', Christchurch is a delightful and popular place to live, (so our driver told us), but wasn't inhabited properly until 1815. Around a thousand years before that, several different Maori tribes lived there from time to time, but it was whaling that really got things going at the turn of the nineteenth century. Fortunately, tourists go to see the whales swimming around now, rather than killing them.

One of the things I like about cruising is that you know there'll be a nice dinner of whatever you fancy waiting for you. I was pigging out most days on the kind of seafood you just don't find in England and tried not to think too much about my cholesterol, which must have been sky-high by now. I was really looking forward to being clean, fed and watered and as Roo had been a bit dodgy all day, we chose one of the less formal restaurants. In spite of having to 'Feed the 5,000' (3,700 with crew) none of the restaurants were ever crowded and the standard of food and the choice available was terrific. The crew could not have been more professional and helpful and every single one of them seemed to be a cheerful, happy soul. With a ship the size of a small Third World Country, I'd hate to have to do the shopping, peel potatoes, or do the washing up – in that order.

DAY THIRTY: "Being Formal, again"

We were all at sea again. The sun was shining, but at the sharp end, not the blunt end where our suite was. So, unless we became ante-snobs and joined the sunbathing hoards 'atop', we would be in the shade until later in the day; or if we altered course. We wouldn't alter course unless we had to rescue someone again, which we hoped and prayed would not be necessary, so resigned ourselves to the fact that we'd be in the shade. Not a bad thing. It would encourage me to start packing, because believe it, or not, we were coming to the end of the first cruise. It had flown by and as you can see, we'd already had thirty days away.

Sitting on the bed, I reflected on those thirty days as I smoothed body lotion across my naked nether regions and congratulated myself that things had gone reasonably well so far. Mum and Di were okay - the boys hadn't encountered anything serious to be dealt with and Roo hadn't turned into an axe-wielding maniac, running amok amongst the passengers. However, the large amount of body lotion I was using told me that there was definitely one small problem that needed to be addressed.

It was painfully obvious that I'd put on a pound, or two.

Something had to be done and I had to take positive action before the problem was really out of control. I could go into denial, convincing myself that all my clothes had shrunk and buy new (bigger) ones. I could lash myself to the railings on our deck for the remainder of the cruise, thus excluding me from temptation. I could ask Roo to advise the Maitre d' of each restaurant that I was harbouring Proximal Jejunitis, a disease usually found in horses and could not be allowed in the restaurants, or jump overboard, swim to a remote island and live on coconuts for a month.

None of the options were ideal, although in an emergency I would go with option one and the last option meant that I might never be seen again – fat, or otherwise, so I decided to remain on the seafood diet.

You know the one - see food and eat it.

I would resign myself to the fact that Roo would probably divorce me when we returned to England and I would have to become a Vicar.

On the other hand, think of the Vicarage Teas I could host…………

Just as I had creamy egg and cress sandwiches with the crusts daintily cut off in my minds' eye, Roo bounced into the bedroom and I dived for cover to conceal my flab.

He wanted to talk about 'Milk Thistle' supplement he'd started taking. He reckoned he hadn't had the liverish odour since he started the remedy and was cured! *"But surely"*, I said, *"It's much too soon for it to have made any sort of impact"* and with that, he left the room with his nose in the air and the kind of look on his face you'd expect if he'd been the one to discover Radium.

I spent the next twenty minutes trying to wipe off the body lotion I'd spilt on the duvet cover and whilst doing so thought about the 'Milk Thistle'. It couldn't have miraculously cured his liver so quickly, but if he thought it was doing him some good and had confidence in it, what the hell?

Having to pack was bad enough, but it was also another 'Formal' night, which meant I would have to squeeze into some sort of stunning outfit. I couldn't decide whether to wear my turquoise trousers and top, or my turquoise evening dress. Mmm… I hadn't realised how much I liked turquoise. I chose the trousers and top, deciding to save the dress for Tahiti, thinking we might be 'romantic' by then. This just made me look up to see if there were any pigs flying around. There weren't any.

I packed like mad, attempting to fit everything into two suitcases and thought I was doing really well, until I found a whole load of drawers (the wooden kind) full of clothes. With a dramatic sigh, I decided to stick my head in the sand and finish the packing tomorrow.

We'd been given the option of Roger packing our cases for us, but then we wouldn't have been able to (hand-on-heart) say at Auckland Airport check-in desk that we'd packed them ourselves. So, being the upright citizen that I was, I would fight with the task myself. With Roger in mind, I remembered that there was more laundry to come back in the morning, which meant even more stuff to go in the cases. Bugger.

In the ship's blurb, 'Princess Patter', it clearly stated that visits to the Bridge were not permitted. However, that morning we were delighted to receive an invitation to do just that. Twenty of us were met by a young Officer who led us up to Deck 14 and the driving seat of this enormous liner. It was huge – the whole width of the ship, with 'stations' in the middle and at each end and vast empty areas in between. (It would have been a fabulous venue for a party). There was no wheel with which to steer – just a tiny little knob! The view was exceptional, with an uninterrupted view of the ocean immediately below and pretty much everywhere else apart from the stern (where our suite was). But we discovered that we had not been alone after all. CCTV cameras are fixed in the places they can't see easily – ESPECIALLY at the stern. Pictures of our deck flashed up intermittently on several different screens while we were there, which made my toes curl up, because I'd been so sure no one could see us back there, I'd thought about going topless many times – thank God I didn't!

Back to the formal night ....

I persuaded Roo to wear the white dinner jacket. All men look handsome in a white DJ and Roo, with his tanned face and freshly-trimmed beard (not such a dead badger now) looked very dashing and I told him so. I swear he grew an inch in height, although he was visibly nervous at the thought of going out.

We'd purposely booked a table at 'Sabatini's' again, so at least the restaurant would be familiar. The Maitre d' was the same, chatty Romanian and Alex was the waiter who served us last time, so it wasn't long before Roo had settled down.

The first visit to this restaurant had taught us to be careful with what we ordered. It could so easily turn into a Gastronomic Marathon loaded with calories of the type that instantly attach themselves to my thighs in great big ridges – the technical term is 'cellulite' and also, (I had noticed only recently) – my upper arms. I suddenly pictured my grandmother playing the piano with great gusto and the fat under her Brachium flapping away merrily in time to the music. Anyway, this time we were careful to choose more simple dishes. But I was still stuffed after finishing the starter and felt we hadn't done the meal justice when we left some of the main course on our plates. Time for a breather. All we seemed to do was eat and you know I rarely have a dessert. If anything, I'll have cheese – which I adore, but with my shrunken clothes in the back of my mind, I was adamant that I wouldn't have any more to eat that evening. Roo usually has a pudding of some kind and of course, is able to absorb thousands of calories at a time without it making the slightest bit of difference to any part of his anatomy - not even his Brachium. So I wasn't surprised when he ordered an apple-something, or other. I WAS surprised though, when I saw Alex the waiter walking towards us with two plates and thought Roo must have ordered a small portion of two different puds. Setting a plate before us both, I looked up to tell Alex that I couldn't possibly eat another thing, but suddenly realised that it wasn't a pudding at all. It was the beautiful necklace I had admired in the 'Swarovski' shop sitting on the plate, surrounded by *"Thank You"* written in chocolate.

The expression on my face must have been hilarious. I just sat looking at the plate.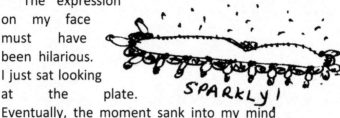

SPARKLY!

Eventually, the moment sank into my mind though and I carefully picked up the necklace, avoiding the chocolate letters. It was even more beautiful than I remembered it looking in the shop window and I couldn't wait to put it on. The Maitre d' and the waiters got on with their jobs, as if this was a regular occurrence, but a lady on the next table was visibly aghast and not wanting to appear like Elizabeth Taylor, we skipped coffee and left the restaurant post haste. Why he did it was a mystery. It was the most romantic thing he'd ever done and made me realise that perhaps he didn't see me just as his nurse, after all. Considering we were surely doomed six months ago, it was a miracle we were where we were now. So much had happened since Roo first became ill. I thought then, that he would simply fade away and die, or I'd be pushed to the limit and leave him. Then what would have happened? With all the other things going on while he was in the clinic I don't know why I was surprised to feel so despondent. The list of problems seemed endless. Mum had early Alzheimer's and was moving (reluctantly) out of her house into a sheltered apartment. Di was alone, desperately unhappy and even to this day is still trying to cope with the loss of her only child and had to move house again too. Harry was moving to Bristol – three hours away from us and Lukey was so obviously keen to keep his feelings secret, he hardly talked at all and I had no idea what he was thinking. My closest friends wanted to help and would have provided a shoulder to cry on, but they had their own problems and I had no intention of burdening them with more.

So, all I had left really was my faith and I wouldn't have survived without it. There are people who make fun of you, or think less of you when they discover that you believe in God – *any* god – but they're not only showing their ignorance by their lack of respect for the subject, I think they're also frightened to admit that there has to be more out there by choosing to deny the existence of something just because they can't see it.

For me, it was a bit of an accident that I was exposed to the church, when my mum, who had been looking for somewhere for me to go while she was at work in the early evenings, came across the Girl's Life Brigade, which was associated with the Baptist Church and their loving, genuine congregation who helped fill the gaps in my home life.

For eight years, I studied the Bible until I knew it backwards, took exams on the subject and was awarded so many GLB badges for everything from cooking to bicycle repairs, there was no room left to sew any more on the sleeves of my uniform. I had become 'Miss Wonderful, 1960' and there were great expectations for a rosy future, both as a nurse and a 'Crusader'. But those expectations flew out of the window when at the age of fifteen I discovered the existence of boys and totally went off the rails.

This isn't the time to tell you about that – that has to be very late bedtime reading! Another time, perhaps.

Throughout my nurse training and the riotous times that went with it, I pretty much lost every scrap of my faith. I knew I was a good nurse though and loved every moment of the work, but it wasn't until Harry was born that something happened to return my faith with a huge bump. (He was a very small bump actually).

DAY THIRTY-ONE: *"Tauranga, New Zealand"*

I opened my eyes and remembered the necklace, which I had left beside the bed. It should have gone in the safe last night and I told myself off for not putting it there. Of course, I had to put it on again and it looked fabulous with my pyjamas; but then it would look fabulous with a bin liner. I secretly wished I could remember how much it cost and hoped to be able to find a similar one in the sparkly shop so I could find out.

We had arrived in Tauranga, a Geo-thermal area where the Maoris had settled a zillion years ago and made use of the hot springs and bubbling mud pools; but I don't think for beauty treatments. This was what we were going to see today in a place called Rotorua. But first stop would be another farm. I was beginning to feel a bit 'farmed-out', but they're a big thing there, of course.

It was another well-run business, with the owner showing as much dedication to the well-being of his four-legged woolly things, as if they were his children. Declining the offer of the sheep-shearing exhibition (we could write articles on it by now) we headed for the Tea Room and sat taking in the sights and smells of yet more sheep. They're daft creatures, but quite sweet and the little ones are really cute.

Refreshed by the tea and obviously feeling confident, Roo was behaving in a crass and embarrassing sort of way, shouting "mint sauce" at them. Fortunately, he was ignored both by the sheep and our fellow tea-drinkers and when the others in the party had had their fill of clipping the poor old sheep, we moved on. We were driven through the town, where the pungent smell of sulphur was very strong and the sight of steaming geysers popping up from large cracks beside the road, in back gardens - and literally in front of us was a very weird sight.

The locals live with this phenomenon, caused by the earth's crust being very thin. It was like being on the set of 'Volcano' and I'm not sure if I'd like one in MY back garden.

We arrived at the very well-organised tourist centre, which was set up to feed several hundred people, buffet-style and entertain us at the same time. When we'd finished eating, the lights went down and six, or maybe seven Maoris appeared dressed in traditional costume and their skin covered in tattoos. They did the 'Haka' (you've seen the All Blacks do it), which we discovered wasn't always used as a War Dance – it could be a welcome too! That was great fun. The chaps finished their part of the show explaining their legends, culture and history by dancing to a moving backdrop of

'LADY KNOX'

light and sound, which was extremely effective. Next, it was the Maori women's turn to perform with their 'Poi' – ceremonial balls on string, which sounds really dull and boring, but I couldn't do it, if I tried!! They danced about with their Poi and it was all quite clever, in a juggling sort of way.

With the show over, we moved on to the really interesting geo-thermal area at Waiotapu. The air was thick with sulphur here and for safety's sake you had to keep to the slippery and tricky paths to avoid disappearing headfirst into the bubbling pools of mud. The mud is used in the on-site Spa as a skin treatment, but I'm sure they must cool it down first. The biggest geyser is known as the 'Lady Knox Geyser', which spouts to a height of 20metres, erupting at 10.15am on the dot most days, but can be a bit temperamental. It was discovered in 1901 by inmates of the first prison built in New Zealand and named after the governor's wife (lucky her). The geyser had been spouting furiously since the morning and could be seen way in the distance performing in full 'geyse'. Although we were warned that the walk to get close to it was long and arduous, I didn't want to miss it. However, I was on the point of collapse when we eventually reached the huge gushing water spout and sat on a shelf of hot rock opposite, until my bottom could take no more. (If only the heat could have melted some of the fat on it). It was a magnificent sight (the geyser, not my rear), with smaller geyser spouts erupting suddenly and surprisingly from the surrounding rock. With a glowing behind (probably), Roo and I continued on to see the bubbling mud, where the smell of sulphur (rotten eggs) was even stronger. The pools of "glooping" mud looked a bit dodgy to me and there were warnings about leaning over too far to get a better view of the boiling mud. The thought of falling in made you shiver – even in the searing heat; although you'd probably have very smooth skin when they'd yanked you out. Then we saw our first and only Kiwi. They're funny-looking things and nocturnal so aren't often seen, but the nesting house it lived in with a few others is kept in semi-darkness during the day, so fooling the Kiwis into thinking that it was dusk and time to get up for their breakfast allowing visitors get a look at them. They couldn't see us peering at them through the darkened glass and looking happy and healthy, didn't seem to mind their lives being turned upside down. The next stop in the Park was the inevitable shop, cleverly placed at the exit. We bought a Maori club – a dense piece of wood, ornately carved into something like the shape of a small ukulele. It really was used (a long time ago) in battle, to bash another Maori over the head, thus rendering them incapable with a severe headache, or worse. It would go very nicely with the Didgeridoo. (There will come a time, when the boys are clearing out our house, filling an enormous skip and I hear Lukey saying to Harry *"And why did they buy this?"*)

Leaving the Park, we chatted to Kay and Steven, the couple sitting behind us on the bus who were originally from Tottenham, north London. They had gone to live on the Gold Coast twenty-one years before and had been very happy since emigrating; not once doubting their decision.

Discovering that out of the 2,700 passengers on the ship, their cabin was right next door to ours' and with Kay busting to see our suite, we invited them for a drink on our deck when we left port for Auckland.

I was way behind with the packing. We were supposed to leave our suitcases in the corridor outside for collection before 8pm and hadn't even had dinner yet. Kay and Steven dashed off to finish theirs' when we realised it was already 7.30. It's amazing what you can get done when you're in a panic and I had it all finished with two minutes to spare. Roo was more exhausted than me and was quite "up the pole" in the brain department (I blamed all that sulphur). Knowing that even at his best, he wouldn't have been ready to go out until at least 9 o`clock - and as we had to be up really early to leave the ship, we decided not to go out for dinner. So, on our last night on the Sapphire Princess, we sat on our lovely deck just one more time – wearing our pyjamas and eating a yummy dinner from the room service menu instead.

DAY THIRTY-TWO:

"Auckland"

Our last port of call and a pleasant sunny day. We were sad to be leaving the ship and had thoroughly enjoyed ourselves. We'd seen a lot of Australia and most of the New Zealand coast. My favourite place had been the Fjords. But just to put a damper on things, Roo was terribly worried and jittery the moment he got out of bed. He was getting hot and panicky and headed off to the loo for the third time. We needed to hang it out in the suite for as long as possible. Appearing from the loo, he looked awful – in spite of his tan I could see we were in real trouble. *"I know what this is"*, I said, *"It's because we're leaving the ship."* He slid onto the sofa, closing his eyes and nodded. I could see he was scared, because he was visibly shaking. The last twelve days had been so good I'd almost forgotten what this was like. He lay on the sofa with all the windows and doors open around him. His colour began to improve slowly and he opened his eyes. *"Sorry"*, he whispered. I didn't reply, because there was nothing I could say that would help, but I did wonder if he'd be able to eat something and if that might buck him up a bit. He hadn't said he felt sick and I wasn't about to remind him by asking. I would mention food when I thought the time was right. We stayed put for another twenty minutes, with him on the sofa and me sitting at the dining table twiddling my thumbs. Time was marching on and there had to be a plan for getting him off the ship.

I peered outside the door. It was clear and strangely quiet. What do we do? Make a dash for it? For goodness sake, we're not bank robbers, I thought. Right. That's enough. Take charge. *"Come on"*, I said in my nurse's voice, *"We're going for something to eat"*. He looked at me, horrified. *"Oh, no .... I couldn't. I can't do that. You go. Just leave me here."* But it was too late. I was on my feet and pulling him to his. *"No, you're coming to the buffet – you're not dying, I won't let you,"* I barked. We walked slowly to the restaurant, which thankfully was almost empty. He flopped down in a seat at a table near the window as I went to the buffet to collect a small bowl of cereal and a glass of fresh orange juice for him and then went back to find something for myself. When I returned, he was looking at the bowl of cereal as if it had been poisoned. Sitting opposite him I didn't say a word, ignoring his patheticism and began to eat my fruit and yoghurt.

Stabbing at the cornflakes with his spoon, he swallowed a few and then dumping the spoon in the bowl, lifted his eyes up to mine holding my gaze as if I were the poisoner. I finished my breakfast without feeling the need to profess my innocence. I knew I wasn't Rasputin and so did he, really. It was so disappointing. I told myself off for expecting too much and assuming that just because we'd had some good days it would continue, but feeling more deflated than a burst balloon it was difficult to conceal my mood. I knew I was in desperate need of a light at the end of our long, dark tunnel and also knew that we couldn't go on like this much longer.

With most of the other passengers leaving the ship like a pack of rats ('A Mischief of Rats' is the correct expression, but that would sound daft), we planned to stay on board long enough to allow the majority of people to disembark, so returned to our suite one last time. Roo was still shaky and hot and I left him to his own devices while I sat pretending to read but was secretly worried and nervous about getting him off the ship.

Staying there for another twenty minutes or so, we could hang it out no longer. It was important to say goodbye and thank you to Roger and I rang his bleep. He was with us in a flash and seemed genuinely sorry to see us go. We hadn't been difficult to look after and had treated him with the respect he deserved. He would find the envelope I'd left for him later and hoped he would be pleased with the contents.

Leaving the ship was easy, but when we stepped ashore the queue to go through Customs was enormous. Roo's shoulders sunk and I looked up to heaven for divine inspiration, but with none immediately forthcoming, there was no alternative but to join the queue. A myriad of authority figures in smart New Zealand Customs uniforms wandered amongst the patiently-waiting people and with them, a very healthy-looking Beagle attached by lead to a female officer. The Beagle was a 'sniffer-dog' – but not the usual type seeking out drugs, this

PATAGONIAN TOOTHFISH

one was looking for fruit! In this part of the world, they're not bothered about you having illicit substances, but they are paranoid about an apple being taken ashore. This was to prevent the importation of pests and unwanted organisms. Looking sideways at some of the people in the queue, I felt there were many that fell into this category. In my bored state, I stood on one leg and then the other reading the poster telling us what you could and couldn't take into the country and knowing that I definitely did not have a 'Patagonian Tooth Fish', or an anti-personnel mine in my luggage, felt pretty safe. But as I continued to read the incredibly long list of very odd 'no-no's', the lovely Beagle on a lead sniffed my handbag and promptly sat down beside me. He might as well have pointed a paw directly at me shouting, *"Criminal!!"* The queue parted like Moses and the Red Sea and as we were suddenly isolated by a large ring of space a hush fell on those close enough to see what had happened. We were quite shocked, but this was the handbag that once tested positive for TNT at San Francisco Airport. That was a real shock and it wasn't until we discovered that the test then had shown traces of fertilizer (one of the elements in TNT), that we twigged the reason for their alarm. My bag had been sitting beside an open window at home and it must have been there when the fields around us were sprayed. Just shows you how even the most innocent of things can turn into an international incident. Anyway, back to New Zealand. The handler was joined immediately by another Officer, who told us to stay where we were and slowly put the bag on the floor. Then the interrogation began. *'Where had we been?'* (We both looked up at the huge ship sitting in the dock beside us).

'*Were we trying to smuggle fruit ashore?*' (Why would we want to do that?)

"*Thais dug ees specially trined to detect frate*" the New Zealand Officer said. My handbag was sitting all alone now and I felt quite aggrieved for it.

I expected the handler to shout, "*Stand back!*" and activate a controlled explosion, but instead she pounced on the thing, turning it upside down and smacked it, inevitably emptying the contents on the floor.

"*Hev yew git en eppel?*" She asked in her heavy accent. I had to think hard about what she was asking me and screwing up my eyes as I thought, tried to process her words as quickly as I could.

Of course! It suddenly dawned on me that she was talking about an 'apple' and didn't have a serious speech impediment after all. Assuring her that I wouldn't dream of flouting their laws and that I was an upstanding British citizen and 'No' – I didn't have an 'eppel', she remained unimpressed and with her head rocking from side to side in a patronising way, she asked if I had EVER had an 'eppel' in my bag at ANY time. I was beginning to feel as though I'd just arrived after six weeks at sea on a convict ship rather than a luxury liner and thought hard again. Tranquilizers = '*check*', tissues = '*check*', foot deodorant = '*check*', even a whistle in case the ship sunk, but no 'eppel'. Wait a minute though, weren't we given a snack bar on the train up to the Alps? Did it have 'eppel' in it? Perhaps it did and whatever it was, it had been in my bag all that day, because I'm not into snack bars. I was quite relieved to be able to confirm the vague presence of 'eppel'. *"But that was three days ago"*, I told the Fruit Police Officer. *"Aah! These digs have virry sensatuvv nazes"*, she replied, stuffing my property, drugs and all back into my bag and thrusting it into my arms before calmly moving away without another word – dog in tow. Phew!! I was saved from a cell in the Fruit Prison, but was quite annoyed at the way I'd been treated. I counted to one hundred and thirty-six and realising that I wasn't a threat to 'eppel' security, the queue of people – all thankful that they had not been the ones interrogated, closed in around us sympathising with the way the situation had been handled.

Sometimes you have to let things go and this time rather than be held up any longer and freak-out Roo, I wasn't about to cause us further delay by making a complaint. They were just doing their job after all, although it would have been worth all the hassle if I HAD been trying to smuggle in a 'Patagonian Tooth Fish'.

Fighting our way out of Customs (almost literally), next came the scramble for a taxi. It was bit like I imagined the fall of Saigon to be – except with cars, not helicopters. Was it that these ex-passengers already had post-cruise withdrawal symptoms and needed to eat? Roo spotted an empty cab that had just pulled up and with my jumble sale elbows in 'attack' mode we made a successful dash for it. The Asian driver chatted away in a very mixed-up accent – a cross between Peter Sellers-Indian-Gentleman-meets native New Zealander-meets Peckham. He said he'd left London because he thought there were too many foreigners being allowed in.

At the car hire place, we were greeted with, *"Shart if cares, made"*, which roughly translated meant that they were short of cars (Mate) and was the reason we were allocated a vehicle no bigger than a wheelbarrow. Roo had a devil of a job getting the luggage in it, but with an amazing amount of perseverance and a lot of swearing, we headed off to Hamilton, eighty miles south of Auckland loaded to the gunnels with stuff crammed onto the back seat and our extremities hanging out of the windows. We were so glad we'd had the presence of mind to ship the didgeridoo home by boat, otherwise that would have been trailing from the exhaust.

We had arranged to meet Martin, the son of our old friends living in Spain. Martin was now married to Lara – a native New Zealander and lived in a sprawling hilltop home with their two children, Piper, who was 2 and Mason, 4. It was strange to see Martin all grown up with a family and we stayed longer than we should, but after reiterating the story of the 'eppel' and eating barbequed Marlin under the shade of a Coolabah Tree (honestly!), we needed to say our goodbyes and get on the road north to the Bay of Islands before dark. It was going to be quite a trek by the look of the map, but at least we would be driving on the 'right' side of the road.

Up, down, through gorges, over bridges passing miles of hillocks, a mirror-image of 'Hobbiton' created for "Lord of the Rings" and filmed only a few miles away - it was all very green and tranquil. On the other side of the road though, the traffic was one long stream for at least half an hour. City dwellers, many with boats in tow headed back to Auckland after the weekend in Bay of Islands. I hoped this mass Exodus meant that it would be quiet and deserted when we arrived.

Eventually, we reached Opua, a tiny harbourside village, where Angie, who owned 'The Boathouse', greeted us. The building consisted of two apartments and had been built right over the water. We had opted for the ground floor, with an enormous lounge/diner/kitchen leading out to the deck, two bedrooms and a cool, serene bathroom. It was probably the best-equipped place we'd ever rented and must have cost a fortune to furnish. It even had big fluffy towels that covered ALL of my bottom for a change. Angie lived in a bungalow high up on a hill on the other side of the bay, but within 'binocular shot', so we'd better behave and not host any mad parties. The apartment was literally on the ferry ramp and beside this was a small restaurant and a very handy grocery store. We were hungry now, so popped into the restaurant where we enjoyed a good meal served by a chap from Lyons, France. He was amused with our French conversation and laughed when we told him we were *"rassasier"*, which is a very posh way of saying that you're stuffed, in French.

To hear the water lapping beneath the apartment when we were in bed was quite beautiful and there was no competition with listening to that, rather than Vesuvius erupting in the next room. Soon I was asleep.

DAY THIRTY-THREE:

"Yawn......"

I woke several times during the night thinking I was back on the ship. It must have been the water surrounding us, but in spite of feeling tired, the sight of the bay was so delightful I almost jumped out of bed. Roo had slept well, but his snoring had given him a muzzy head and I immediately thought, *"Here we go."* However, I was pleasantly surprised when he said he felt very at home already and that he too, was raring to go. He even volunteered to go to the shop returning with breakfast, which we ate out on the deck while we talked about just how much we could cram into the few days we would be in the Bay of Islands. Roo thought he'd like to swim with Dolphins (better than being away with the fairies) and rang a boat company offering the trip. He booked it for the following afternoon when hopefully, there would be a bit more energy in us. The rest of the day we spent sitting on the deck watching the ferry come and go and all the sailing activity of the boatty people. It was being lazy in the laziest and lovely of ways and we felt rejuvenated by the water and the beauty of the area.

A whole day passed and Roo had been great. He was so good that I felt a wave of optimism flow through me. It would be wonderful to return to life without the constant threat of him bursting into tears for no reason, or seeing him terrified of the unknown.

I really wanted to convince myself that this would happen one day, but every time I felt like this something happened to bring me heavily back down to earth again.

Continuing in 'lazy git' mode, I announced that I would not be cooking dinner that evening, but having spent the whole day lounging around knew we should do a bit of walking; or at least make an effort to get out. I can get ready in ten minutes flat but Roo takes an age, so I suggested he use the bathroom first. He almost skipped off to the shower and when I could hear him whistling too, I was quite looking forward to going out with him for once.

Anyone would think we were food connoisseurs the way we walked around looking at the different restaurants, perusing their menus and eyeing up the interiors, finally agreeing on one with tables outside in a pretty garden and both ate Snapper. I had smothered myself in 'Boots' own insect repellent, (being the decoy in the family, I usually get eaten alive). It would be interesting to see if it worked. If not, I'd be covered in red, itchy blobs by morning.

Lying in bed with the sound of the water beneath us, I went over the lovely day we'd had together. We'd hardly done a thing, but this part had been one of the best. Anyone meeting Roo for the first time would never have believed that he was so ill it could make him behave in the crazy way it does. If only every day could be the same.

DAY THIRTY-FOUR: *"Niagara in New Zealand"*

I found only one itchy, red blob on my ankle (the left one), so the repellent must have worked 99%. Good old 'Boots'.

The plan for today was to drive around exploring the area before we went for the Dolphin experience, but when we locked up and went outside to the car found the road was being tarmac'd, meaning we weren't going anywhere on four wheels! We sought out the person in charge to ask nicely if we could quickly move the car, only to discover that the Foreman was actually a Forelady – a tall, slim young Maori who was most unhelpful. She was clearly used to people being irate and more, or less told us that it was hard luck. We went back inside to telephone the Dolphin people and having explained the predicament, postponed our trip until the following afternoon. We caught the ferry to Russell as foot passengers instead. The small town of Russell across the water could be seen clearly from our apartment, but to drive there would take an age as it meant going inland and sort of doubling back somehow and it was only ten minutes on the pleasant ferry, so we were there in a flash. It was all very twee and unspoilt, with weatherboard houses and cosy eating places and after wandering about a bit, we sat on the grass leading down to the beach where Roo searched for pebbles to skim on the flat water. He was very good at it and the circles he made were quite mesmerising. When I had a go, they simply landed in the water with an almighty splash. But then Roo can't make an omelette the way I can. An hour, or so later, tearing ourselves away from the peace and tranquillity of Russell, we did the reverse trip on the ferry and found that the tarmac people and their scary boss had finished outside the apartment so we could get the car out. We had no idea where we were going and got all niggly with each other. It was probably because we were both geared up to go on the dolphin trip and were a bit disappointed. We'd also had the unpleasantness with Maori Forelady, which was a bit unnecessary. Thankfully, we saw a sign for 'Huvura Falls', which sounded interesting and headed off to find them, or it.

What we found was a miniature Niagara, complete with mini rainbow hovering above. It was cool here and we sat on the riverbank for a while watching the rushing water.

It was a fantastic sight and I wondered how we could be so niggly when things as beautiful as this were here for us to see.

It wasn't long though, before a young family arrived complete with screaming-baby-in pushchair and demanding two year old in wellies. With the peaceful moment wrecked, we left Huvura Falls to them and continued on our foray. Driving towards the coast, we came across Waitangi, another beautiful spot, where the British had signed a Treaty with the Maoris on February 6th, 1840, making New Zealand part of the British Empire.

On the beach where the signing took place, I pictured the scene one hundred and sixty-eight years earlier, when the Royal Navy frigate HMS Herald - sails billowing, appeared in the bay to drop anchor and the Maori's, wearing their brightly-coloured plumes and feathers standing on the same beach. They wouldn't have had any idea of how much the place they called Aotearoa, meaning 'long, white cloud' would change, or what they would really think of Pakeha – the white man in a few years' time.

In 1940, an amazing war canoe, with an equally amazing name – 'Ngatokimatawhaorua' was built here to commemorate the Treaty's first centenary. The canoe - dug out of a single huge tree and carved by Maori hand, takes to sea on the anniversary every February 6th, paddled by seventy-six people, which gives you an idea of how big it is. On the way back to Opua, we passed a small ceramics studio and stopped to have a look at what they were making. We bought an

"HMS HERALD"

unusual curved tray with two large cups and a teapot and arranged to have them shipped back to England. I hoped they would survive the journey. Fed up with fancy food, we thought we'd have a Pizza takeaway for dinner and while at the studio, asked if they could recommend anywhere. The owner raved about the local Pizzeria and gave us their number.

Unfortunately, we were unable to share the chap's enthusiasm about the Pizzeria, because around three hours after consumption, Roo saw his again ... and again ... and again. Whether the reason we didn't spend the evening in synchronised vomiting was because our toppings were different, I don't know. It could have been that, or because I have the constitution of an ox and Roo's more delicate digestive system can't handle anything remotely dodgy, but in one respect he's lucky because he's able to get rid of anything wrong instantaneously. I slept with one ear open, in case it developed into something nastier, but he went through the night without incident of any kind. Even better, I didn't have to play 'nurse' again; or worse, play the part of Janitor!

DAY THIRTY-FIVE: *"Dealing with the Blues again"*

By morning, the problem had settled down and he had improved physically. It was a pity his mind hadn't.

By 10am he was in woeful mood and I found him sitting huddled on the floor of the bathroom wrapped up in a towel 'being safe'. My heart sank. At times like this, whatever I say makes no difference and there's no point in telling him to pull his self together. I've done all the sitting beside him/cuddling/rocking/crying with him and it doesn't help.

It was cruel, but I left him to it and went out on the deck. Eventually an hour, or so later, he came out of the bathroom with tears streaming down his face and lay on the sofa. It looked like we'd be spending our last day trapped in the apartment, so I cancelled the Dolphin trip. The man there was as nice as pie about it fortunately and after my heart-rending description of Roo's physiological symptoms, he even offered to refund the money. (I should have taken that place I was offered at RADA).

There were worse places to be confined to. It was so pleasant simply watching the boats bobbing around and the ferry trundling backwards and forwards was entertainment enough. We were so lucky with the weather too.

Attempting to cajole Roo into a more positive mindset, I reminded him that he had simply eaten pizza with a suspicious ingredient (probably something to do with the mushrooms on it) and he didn't have Lassa fever or Beri-Beri. But you know how men are – they sneeze and they've got Pneumonia. (How would they cope with really bad PMS and have to channel a tiny tampon into their compartments? And don't even think about a dilating cervix and having a baby fight its' way through it!)

He tries so hard to act normally when he's like this, but resembles a frightened rabbit caught in headlights. Picks things up … puts them down, fumbles with nothing really, until he gradually comes out of it. I can only watch surreptitiously and be there – acting as mother, sister, friend, as well as remembering I'm actually his wife.

We sat on our "dock of the bay" and the day progressed, but Roo didn't. His mood was morbid and he was sad and weepy. Then he announced that despite all attempts at rehydration he still had a headache and lay like a corpse on a lounger in the shade. I tried to ignore the dramatics and wasn't particularly worried about this, but I was worried about checking in with Air Pacific for our flight the next day. This airline operates on routes encountering particularly bad weather, with the knock-on effect of frequent delays and cancellations and we'd just heard on the news that a cyclone was gathering strength in the region around Fiji. And where were we going tomorrow? Fiji. Well, we'd go with the flow (ha-ha) and deal with things if they happened, but it didn't stop me worrying. It didn't help either when Roo made another announcement, saying that he thought today was the worst one of the trip. He tried to explain his mood, using words like 'desolate', 'intense terror' and 'overwhelming sadness'. What with that and the thought of flying in a washing machine the next day, I really felt cheerful and sighed again. Lately, that was something I did a lot.

Perhaps we should cancel the trip to Fiji. Maybe ask Angie if we could stay at the apartment for a bit longer, but just as I was about to pick up the telephone, I had a brainwave. Get him to do something constructive. Make him think about something, other than himself. It's worked in the past to flush out these dark thoughts. Somehow, I persuaded him to go to the dolphin trip office and deal with the refund they'd promised. *"Have a shower"*, I suggested, *"See how you feel then"*, I said. So he did. He reluctantly had a shower, but there was no whistling this time and he dressed so slowly, I thought he was having trouble buttoning up his shirt or something. However, by the time he finally emerged, he looked much better. He went out without looking back, which was a good sign, but the next forty minutes were a bit nerve-wracking and I spent the time making him a check list for tomorrow. I've done this before and it's helped him to focus and feel as though he's in control by crossing things off the list. Honestly, I feel I could write a book about all this. "The Depressed Husband:

A Wife's Guide" I know I shouldn't joke, but there must be thousands of wives (and husbands) in a similar position – all trying to cope, not knowing if they're doing the right things and thinking no one understands what they're going through. There isn't a right, or wrong way to handle this illness. You just have to work through it with them and try not to end up mad yourself. Or do the other thing.

He rang from the office. *"Just checking in"*, he said, in a shaky voice. As soon as he walked through the apartment door, he wanted to lie down. I didn't let him. He was still very anxious and asked for a tranquiliser. I said he couldn't have one. Instead, I marched him outside and we wandered about a bit in the sunshine. Checking in on line with Air Pacific at the grocery store we discovered that the weather further north had improved and our flight was going to happen. We both wanted to go to Fiji (who wouldn't?) and saw this as a good omen.

Our last evening at the Boathouse was spent dealing with the logistical nightmare of my favourite pastime - packing. I juggled our clothes and souvenirs between three suitcases, one of which, we would store in Auckland.

I was sure that Fiji was an unsophisticated place and we wouldn't need our poshest evening wear and after carefully adding these to the storage suitcase, sat on it to make it close. This of course, made a mockery of my careful folding and could easily have damaged the souvenirs as well. Hey-ho.

I finally hit the sack at 11.30pm picturing in my mind the amount of souvenirs we had already. It was a change from counting sheep.

DAY THIRTY-SIX: "Fiji" (+12hrsGMT)

I'd had a lousy night (blame the Menopause), but my self-discipline got me out of bed. I sprang into action mentally, more than physically crossing things off 'the list' and appeared to be very in control, which helped Roo, but I really wanted to go back to bed and hide under the duvet while he did all the organising and sorting out. The digestive system seemed to be behaving itself, but Roo was still in a woeful mood and feeling very sorry for himself, so I continued my 'in charge' approach and ignored him. I was concerned that I'd somehow store the wrong suitcase and end up having to wear an evening dress for breakfast the next day, but with great confidence zipped up all three of them and locked the one I hoped was heading for storage.

Leaving the delightful Bay of Islands behind us, I found I could relax enough to actually enjoy the scenery and an uneventful journey took us back to Auckland where we headed straight for the airport and the luggage store. It was an easy-peasy procedure and the helpful staff whisked away, what I hoped was the right suitcase from my worried gaze.

From there, we went straight to check in where we were told that we could use the Quantas First Class Lounge, as we would be travelling in 'Tabua' with Air Pacific. The lounge was good with excellent facilities including a buffet with fabulous blue cheese and I had to talk to myself very sternly so as not to have 'thirds'. Roo was doing well and seemed as relieved as me that the luggage store worked out as well as it did. He read the newspaper for a bit, but wasn't particularly interested in Kiwi goings-on and went instead to check our emails, but had only just logged on when our flight was called. Walking towards the aircraft I caught sight of what I thought was our luggage being loaded into the hold, leading me once again, to believe that I'd stored the wrong suitcase. Too late now, I thought. Those are the ones coming with us whatever. Roo and I were almost the last two to board the plane. We'd deliberately dragged our feet so we weren't sitting for a long time before take off, but with only eight passengers at the front and oodles of room we were, of course extremely comfortable. Trying, once again, not to feel guilty about the squashed passengers at the back, I settled down for the sixth flight of the trip. The cabin crew, wearing Fijian National Dress were older than usual (rather like Pan Am when it was around) and very efficient.

We were looked after admirably for the uneventful three hour trip to Nadi, in the Fijian Islands and landed in brilliant sunshine on the western side of Viti Levu, less than an hour from Tonga. With no signs of cyclones or even a cloud in sight, we had high hopes of good weather for the few days we'd be on the island discovered by the Dutch explorer, Tasman in 1643. (Cap'n Jim wasn't there until 1773 – makes a change for someone else to get there first).

Having literally been waved through passport control, we found the Customs Officers conducting the strangest of procedures, which meant removing our luggage from one conveyor belt and then loading it onto another where it was passed through X-Ray once again. Goodness knows what they were looking for. Patagonian Tooth Fish, perhaps.

Having retrieved our cases – deemed free of contaminants, we were met by an official-looking lady with a clipboard, who after confirming our names ushered us outside to a taxi. She told us in no uncertain terms in front of the driver that he *WOULD* drive us straight to our hotel, *WITH* our luggage and *WOULD* only charge a certain amount. Roo and I looked at each other with sickly grins and instantly, I pictured a large Fijian lady wearing my new pyjamas stirring me into a big cauldron of soup over a fire. I couldn't see Roo in the picture at all and assumed she'd already eaten him.

The temperature outside matched that of a sauna and not expecting air conditioning, I wasn't looking forward to the trip to the hotel. The driver delicately picked up our cases, while Roo and I slid into the back of the beaten-up, but clean and polished yellow taxi to the sound of loud Indian music from the radio. Then we felt the full weight of the cases as the driver *indelicately* threw them into the boot. There was an aroma of curry, but thankfully it was surprisingly cool, despite the thick cream-coloured plastic very-sensibly covering the maroon PVC seats. At least the seats underneath would stay clean.

Off we sped –'seatbeltless' – something I absolutely hate. Why do we allow ourselves to be driven without wearing a seatbelt just because we're in a foreign country? Surely a small, dusty road is potentially more dangerous than driving on the M25? We clung to the 'hanging-on straps', which of course, would be totally inadequate to stop us being propelled through the windscreen during an emergency stop, but to give us some sense of security, we did it anyway.

Vatu, our driver was very chatty and keen to show us photographs of his enormous family, but it was difficult to grab the photos while we slid around on the plastic covering the seats and I started to giggle uncontrollably. He jabbered away in perfect 'Peter Sellers English', looking at us over his shoulder and leaning back across the front seat to point out 'Little Johnny' with the hand that should have been steering. I tried to glimpse an image of the hoards of children before sliding off with the motion of the car, but this made me giggle even more until I gave up and just kept saying, "*Lovely. Lovely*". Roo was hanging on to the strap with both hands now, looking straight ahead at the dirt road with saucer-sized eyes.

It soon became apparent just how poor this island was. The area had recently been hit by the cyclone and the roads were full of deep holes and tree branches, which the driver skated around like a rollerblader. It was the type of place you see on the news, where a car is suddenly surrounded by shouting soldiers brandishing guns and mortars land in the background with a thud, exploding in a hail of concrete covering the car in mud.

Our journey continued at speed despite the craters and detritus.

Skinny dogs directed their barks towards us and chickens dashing in front of the car narrowly missed being squashed. Some hadn't been missed though and it was difficult not to notice the remnants – a fresh meal for a four-legged animal later – or possibly something with only two. Between the bedraggled ferns and palms,

shanty, shack-like homes, some still with their tin roofs intact, lined the road surrounded by other peoples' roofs, rubbish and piles of bald tyres. Strangely, it was all cheered up by brightly coloured plants in earthenware pots, clothes flapping on long washing lines and children playing without toys. These desperately poor people were obviously used to picking themselves up and starting again and all seemed happy to be doing so. It was certainly organised chaos and very Third World, but such HAPPY organised chaos!

With the photographs back in the glove box, I was able to hang on to the hand strap above the door and watch my knuckles turning white. Roo and I hadn't said a word to each other, but must have been thinking the same thing. *What the hell were we doing in this awful place?* This was supposed to be paradise. We hadn't passed one road sign since we left the airport, but I reassured myself that surely cannibalism had gone out of fashion by now.

Whether there should have been road signs, or if they'd been blown away, I didn't know, but it was just then that we crossed a bridge and with the terrain altering with every foot we travelled, a different world appeared.

Once again, it was as though we'd passed into another dimension, leaving the real world behind us. Lush, manicured lawns and gardens – a perfect golf course and not a pothole in sight. Had the cyclone missed this part of the island? Clean, white, low-rise buildings lit by gas flares despite the late afternoon sun nestled amongst dense banks of huge flowers and foliage, with only hordes of noisy red and green parrots flying in and out breaking the peace and quiet.

A few tourists wandered along the white pavements and it was obviously the male staff wearing the full-length Sulus (sarongs) and tropical shirts. Very sensible in the heat. The taxi screeched to a halt, with the pair of us on our knees in front of the PVC seats, but thankfully not in the driver's lap and my giggling started all over again. Roo gave me a sideways look as we prised our fingers from the holding-on straps, but I looked away quickly before he could say what he was thinking.

Our driver shot out to open the door before the Sulu-clad employee could do it – as if it were some sort of competition and Roo and I literally slid out from the back seat. I was sure we had unwittingly polished the plastic even more. So much so, that the next fare would probably be on the floor the minute Vatu hit the gas. After paying him the exact price the official lady had quoted, he was back in the taxi in a flash and disappeared in a cloud of exhaust and blaring Indian music, back to the poverty-stricken place across the bridge no doubt.

The hotel reception area was of open plan design, allowing a view straight through to the white sandy beach and ocean behind it. There was paradise here after all. An enormous Fijian chap sat behind a Lali – a drum, hollowed out of a log, which he beat with a big stick to welcome us to the hotel. I didn't know if we were supposed to acknowledge this greeting in any sort of way, but just smiled at the drummer. You can't go wrong if you smile sweetly in most situations – sticky, or otherwise.

Staff flocked round us and it was all a bit confusing, until a pretty young woman in a long floral dress spoke sternly to them while clapping her hands and they stood to attention in silence. So did we. She turned to us and somehow knew who we were, explaining that we would be shown to our villa after we'd registered and that a refreshing drink was waiting for us. It was here that something really daft flashed through my mind. Knowing that the sarongs the men wore were called 'Sulus' reminded me of the early 'Star Trek' series and Mr Sulu – one of the crew. Remember him? The Oriental chappie? Anyway, do you recall the episode where Captain Kirk and the others in mustard-coloured tops were greeted on a strange planet with a 'refreshing drink'? Soon after they drank it, they went all peculiar and fell in love with the first person they saw – a bit like in 'A Midsummer Nights Dream'. Yes, I can hear you. You're quite right. I'm a nutcase. But I won't be wearing my red top here. The ones in the red tops always copped it in 'Star Trek'.

Checked in with mum. Nothing to report. Villa – clean and lovely. Enormous pond outside. Many insects. Lots of frogs. Haven't fallen in love with any yet.

DAY THIRTY-SEVEN: *"Bula"*

Eaten alive!! In spite of 80% DEET. Covered in big, red, itchy blobs. I had slept well, for a change and in that bliss had obviously given the insects a night to remember. Couldn't find the 'SOOV', so rather than frighten the locals into thinking I had Plague of some kind, Roo kindly went to the hotel shop to buy some more for me. I was glad I found some writing in English on the box before I used it, as he'd bought Haemarrhoid Cream. I tried not to be too cross with him. It might be useful later.

Weather cloudy, humid and quite oppressive after the cyclone. The small islands just offshore resembled the inevitable picture postcard and one view conjured up in my mind an old British Rail poster I'd seen once. Thanks to the cyclone, the Southern Pacific Ocean looked all churned-up and in spite of the obvious mad rush to clear it away before the tourists saw it, flotsam and jetsam still littered the beach. We would spend a lazy day today. Tomorrow would be a long one with an early start, as we were off on a boat to sail round the Mamanuca Islands, including Monuriki (or Mondriki), which was used as Tom Hanks island in the film, 'Castaway'. Roo = 8 out of 10, so far.

It wasn't long before the cloud lifted and the day improved, so we walked a short way up the beach away from the hotel and sat on the sand watching the surf and the birds. Some of them, like Orange and Golden Doves and the Shining Parrot aren't seen anywhere else. The ocean had calmed down a lot by now and had a more turquoise tinge to it. The tranquillity was further enhanced when we heard the slight hint of Fijian music drifting from the hotel. Having had a reasonable breakfast, we skipped lunch and went out for an early dinner. The resort area of the island operates a 'Bula Bus', a free service between the hotels using forty year old trucks with the sides cut out and replaced with railings. Passengers sit side by side on benches (no seatbelts) holding on to the railings if you're sober - not caring if you weren't. It always looked hilarious when it passed, like something between the works outing and St. Trinian's, with those aboard shouting "BULA" ("Hello") when it came to each stop. The atmosphere on these buses was a scream. It would never pass 'Health and Safety' in England, with people hanging onto the sides if there were no empty seats – a bit like those trains you see in India. The Fijians are always smiling and are so laid back, they're almost horizontal. I wondered if they suffer from depression here.

I did some homework about Fiji and found that in 1643 a Dutch chappie called Abel Tasman landed in the islands (hence Tasmania/Tasman Sea, etc), then of course dear old Cap'n Cook turned up in 1774 and in 1789, Captain Bligh passed through after the mutiny on the 'Bounty, but it wasn't until around the mid-1850's that Christianity was accepted and cannibalism stopped. From the late 1870's Indians (from India – not the Red kind) came to work on the sugar plantations and now they make up 44% of the population.

Somehow, we ended up in the 'Hard Rock Café', Fiji, which was a bit of a novelty and very un-Fijian. I would say that all in all, Roo had a good 8 out of 10 sort of day.

DAY THIRTY-EIGHT:

"Castaway Island"

U p early for the 'Seaspray'.

A bit too early actually, because Roo set the alarm wrongly and we were up at six instead of seven. Then he opened the fridge door and a bottle of wine fell out smashing on the floor and the third thing he did, was to pull the towel rail off the wall. All in the space of twenty minutes. A good start to the day. But I really can't talk, because I'd done some washing the night before and my pure white, lovely trousers were now an unusual shade of pink.

We were collected from the front of the hotel and delivered to the harbour, which was I imagine reminiscent of the D Day Landings with all sorts of craft – big and small taking on supplies and loading passengers with such pandemonium, that I expected to be strafed by a Stuka any moment. Now you know Roo doesn't do pandemonium. This was my penance for a calm day yesterday. Everyone else seemed to know where they were going and had formed orderly queues, but I couldn't find the right orderly queue to join. Presenting our tickets at the end of two of them, only resulted in being ushered to another, until I came to the end of my tether and 'got big' (as the boys used to call it, when they were little). There's no point in going into detail about this, because it's usually quite unpleasant, but needless to say, we were soon sitting inside the air conditioned part of a large catamaran and for a change, I was trying to calm ME down.

Funny thing, Roo kept really quiet and didn't moan once. But then he doesn't like it when I 'get big' either.

The catamaran left the jetty without being strafed and the atmosphere calmed down, as the craft headed out to deep water.

Our first stop was 'South Sea Island', which has a small resort on it and a dozen passengers left the cat for their stay there. It was a similar situation at the next two islands we stopped at – 'Bounty' and 'Treasure', although the accommodation seemed to get smaller and smaller and even more idyllic the further out to sea we went. This part of the world is definitely for young people and romantic fools and I am neither.

There are more than 300 islands. Most are covered in lush forests of palm trees, but some are simply sand dunes sticking out of the water. It's easy to see how the dunes turn into islands – all it takes is one coconut to land up on the sand and take root and a few years later – Bingo! Another bit of paradise – how clever! Until a cyclone comes along that is.

We arrived at Mana Island, to transfer to the 83' schooner and could see it anchored out a bit from the landing area. *"Oh, Goodee"*, I thought, *"I'll have to do my impersonation of a pole-vaulter once more"*. Sure enough, the tender pulled up alongside and once again, it was automatically assumed that none of the passengers had any qualms about transferring onto it. So with a hop and a leap and a great deal of faith, I managed to keep dry while maintaining my dignity at the same time.

The steps leading up to the good ship, 'Seaspray' were easier to manoeuvre, although the vessel was moving up and down with the swell, but I'd lost count of the number of bruises there were on my legs and a few more wouldn't matter. So many times on this trip, I've asked myself why I was doing this and so many times I've come to the same conclusion – I haven't a clue.

After the usual safety stuff, we set sail for Monuriki. The weather was beautiful and the wind bellowed around in the sails, while we passed smaller islands and dozens of floating coconuts. Monuriki is surrounded by reefs making it a perfect place to snorkel, but doesn't have the shelf causing the huge waves you see in the film – that was thingied-in (or whatever it's called), so it's a safe place to anchor.

The island itself is just the same – quiet and uninhabited apart from goats, which weren't in the film either. We anchored just off shore but first we were going to visit Yanuya, the island just opposite where we would attend a Kava Ceremony and formed an orderly queue to disembark onto a smaller boat.

Before leaving the schooner though, the Captain reminded us that the ceremony we would witness and participate in was the equivalent of a religious service and we should behave with the utmost respect. With this in mind, the boat transfer was conducted in a dignified way, in spite of my usual fear of rope ladders.

Yanuya and its village was quite an eye opener. The inhabitants – who depend on visits like ours' to survive - live very simply in small mud huts and bigger shacks made of corrugated iron, all with thatched roofs. The village was built on the sand only a few yards away from the ocean, which must have been used for every purpose since there was no electricity, or plumbing.

The ceremony would be held in the largest Bure (hut) and as shoes of any kind were not allowed inside, we flung our sandals off just as the heavens opened and everyone dashed barefoot inside. The Chief and the Elders sat on the floor and our group quietly sat opposite them. When I'd planned the day on the schooner, we were advised of the Kava Ceremony included in the trip. I was intrigued to know why we had been so 'advised' and did a bit of research into its origins. Kava is an age-old herbal drink, which is actually a mild narcotic made from the root of a pepper plant and has been used in sacred ceremonies to honour visitors for hundreds of years. Originally, Kava was chewed by the elders and mixed with saliva – *yummy* – but now (hopefully) they pound it with a mortar and pestle and mix it with water.

The Chief spoke in broken English, but we were able to get the gist of what he was saying as he poured Kava into half a coconut shell and passed it around the group – a bit like Communion back home. It was a grey and frothy solution and I thought it resembled the contents of the many spittoons I had disposed of as a young nurse.

Roo and I gingerly drank some. It had a woody taste and was really unpleasant. I would love to have washed it down with a slug of water, but that might have been rude I thought. It was supposed to make you feel soporific, but I couldn't stop thinking about the saliva that might have been in it and was concerned that it wouldn't mix well with Roo's Clomipramine.

I had forgotten to worry about Roo today, because in spite of the earlier incidents, he'd been fine. He chatted away to anyone who would listen and really seemed to be enjoying himself. He loved being out on the boat and had managed to feel comfortable amongst the other forty-eight passengers and crew. Yet again, to other people his illness wasn't obvious and had I mentioned it to anyone they wouldn't have believed me, or would have thought I was exaggerating Not a good thing for my ego.

The ceremony was to last about fifteen minutes, but after only five of them I was having trouble sitting cross-legged on the floor. I really hoped that the burning pain seeping into my knee wouldn't make me curse aloud, or I'd probably be boiled alive.

After the ceremony, the group wandered around the village and looked at items the villagers had made and of course, wanted you to buy. I found a pretty necklace made from coconut shells and a painted cloth in native design, which I thought would look good framed. (It's now on an upstairs wall at home and does look good). The souvenirs would always remind me of saliva though. Torrential rain kept us hanging around the Bure, but as it didn't look like it would stop we ventured outside to find our sandals. There was so much water we expected to see them floating down the path, but they were where we'd left them. We made a dash for the shore and once again, after I was fitted into the small boat we headed back to the 'Seaspray'. As we left, several village children ran into the water and waved us off. It was delightful and made us feel really special.

Back on the 'Seaspray', the crew had started the barbeque and the aroma as we climbed aboard was sensational. Chicken, burgers, massive prawns, salads and bread was washed down with pretty much anything alcoholic you liked. Some people seemed to like the booze a bit too much, which really wasn't the thing before snorkelling and I could see why we'd attended the Kava Ceremony before lunch.

The entertainment continued with soulful singing and music from the crew. Their voices were terrific and when two guys with a guitar and a ukulele joined in, the mood became very party-like.

My left knee had grown to the size of a grapefruit – probably due to sitting crossed legged for so long and I could still taste that ghastly, frothy stuff. I had to bite my lips to stop me from gagging at the thought that it might really have had saliva floating in it and the only reason I guzzled a glass of wine, was to sanitize my mouth.

While Roo and I sat in the shade eating, I told him that I wouldn't be going in the water because my knee was so bad. This was true to a certain extent, but the thought of stripping off in front of all those people also filled me with dread. Of course, none of them would have cared that I looked like two-ton Tessie, but *I* did.

Being full of food and booze didn't stop the majority of passengers diving overboard all at once. They looked like a load of Lemmings. I wouldn't have been surprised if some of them had sunk to the bottom and never surfaced, but every one did, flippering away from the boat to terrify some little sea creature, no doubt. The only

people left on board were the crew who were busy clearing away the barbeque food, me with my knee and a Canadian gentleman who was 'uncomfortable amongst fish'. We chatted away about his trip and our trip, until we noticed several snorkellers, including Roo, swimming towards the beach used in the film. I knew exactly what they were going to do. Sure enough, it wasn't long before they were all dancing around some sticks on the sand, telling the world that they had "made fire". Honestly! They did look daft. It was hilarious though and I laughed so much I had to cross my legs in spite of me knee. We stayed anchored for a couple more hours, until all the snorkellers had returned (a little more sobre than they had been) but with the sun blotted out by a sudden shower, we left Monuriki in exactlythe same misty way Tom Hanks did in the film. The rain closed in and the island disappeared, as if it had never been there at all.

With the rain coming down in torrents, it was quite cosy when tea and muffins were served. However, those with obviously tough livers started to drink all over again and by the time we reached Mana Island to meet the catamaran, they were probably sozzled once more.

Leaving the 'Seaspray' via the small boat was unavoidable unless I dived in the water and swam ashore, so steeling myself for the umpteenth time, I went for it. The knee appeared to be in danger of exploding by the time the small craft chugged its way up to the beach and having to step into the warm water up to my thighs was soothing, but my calf-length trousers had absorbed half of the Pacific and I didn't relish the thought of sitting with wet clothes.

Once on the beach, there was still a half mile walk to the jetty where the catamaran waited and I struggled to walk on the sand, sinking with every step. But you know how determined I can be in a challenging situation and I marched along as if in the Foreign Legion ignoring the pain. Roo, bless his heart, would have carried me had I been a size twelve, but said encouraging things while we trudged instead. I made it with a bit of speed-praying and now that the rain had stopped, went for a seat on the open-air deck with the idea that I'd dry off in the wind. As ever, the Japs on board dozed off and passing island, after island, so did we.

Arriving back at the villa, I was so glad to get into the shower – especially one without a myriad of knobs and levers and while I stood under the flurry of water from one sensible rose spray, thought about the day. It had been terrific and so had Roo. The only downside had been the Kava, which reminded me to brush my teeth.

I thought we'd be too tired to go out for dinner, but it's amazing how a shower can revitalise you and we were soon sitting at a table beside the moonlit pool where a local dance troupe had just begun a performance.

The light of the moon and the gas flares, the chanting, the haunting type of songs they were singing and the faint sound of the waves crashing onto the beach could have made a very romantic evening …. *had Roo been that way inclined.*

The menu was a very fishy one and I was spoilt for choice but couldn't resist ordering the lobster. When it was served, it was like no other lobster I'd ever seen before. It was an amazing purple colour, with green swirls and white stripes and would have made a fantastic ornament. We were intrigued and asked a bemused waitress to show us one uncooked. She returned with one, waving it in the air at us and plonked it on the table. It was bright green and could have been painted by Picasso. I felt very guilty eating the cooked one, but Roo had no guilt as he tucked into his lamb – even with the memory of those we'd recently seen up close still fresh in his mind.

We were nice and relaxed by the time we'd finished eating and felt ourselves glowing a bit from the day out on the schooner. The dance troupe had finished now, but music had started up in the area behind us, so we swapped the restaurant table for one where this group were playing. Two Maitai's and several foot-tapping 70's tunes later, I was ready to crash out for the night, but before closing my eyes I thought about Fiji. Bearing in mind that up to now, should I ever be captured with sensitive and important information, all you'd have to do to extract it from me, would be to tiggle me - *since the Kava episode*, all you'd have to do now, was threaten me with a mouthful of the stuff.

But if you're looking for one of the most romantic and gob-smackingly-beautiful places on earth - look no further than Fiji. Clothes — let alone posh frocks are really unnecessary, the people are lovely and won't eat you and the lobster is amazing in both taste and tattoo.

DAY THIRTY-NINE: "Towards Tahiti & French Polynesia"

We hadn't bothered to set the alarm clock and when I opened my eyes, I was surprised to see that it was already 9am but there was plenty of time to pack, so I began the process slowly and without panic. Roo was up already and came out of the bathroom looking perturbed. *"Here we go again"*, I thought.

"Do you want to start folding a few things?" I enquired. He nodded, but instead of heading towards the wardrobe where of course the clothes were, he sat down heavily on the edge of the bed immediately standing up again as though he'd been stung by something. Then he noticed his camera on the sideboard. He picked it up, clutched it close to his chest and began to pace around the room nursing it, only to replace it where he found it the next second. Wandering into the kitchen now, he opened the fridge and examined the empty space inside, closed the door with a thud then moved to the window where he stood looking out with a fixed gaze.

I wasn't sure how to handle this one. It was pretty obvious that he was confused and unable to perform the simple task I had set him, but I didn't want to raise the alarm by pointing it out. Very casually, I said, *"Oh, on second thoughts, would you go to the Business Office instead?"* (I needed to email the next hotel for an appointment with a hairdresser, as I had begun to look like a tortoiseshell cat and needed urgent chemical assistance). *"Yes, I could do that, couldn't I?"* He asked. *"Yes, of course you could"*, I assured him.

I was agitated when he left the villa. A whole ten minutes passed until I could stand it no longer and rang the Business Office to see if he'd arrived. He was certainly there, but discovered that he was just about to ring ME, because he couldn't remember what in the world he'd gone there for. I knew I should have written the details down and was annoyed with myself that I hadn't, but tried not to sound too discouraged and told him all over again. On his return, he was less anxious and pleased with himself, but looking at the suitcases sitting ready and waiting in the hall, asked if he could help me to pack!

Was it me?

It was true that occasionally, I questioned my own sanity and wanted to run around the villa screaming, but this time I just gritted my teeth and said, *"No, all done"*..

The hotel had called for a more salubrious version of a Taxi. This one had palpable cloth seats and no plastic. It was quite novel when the driver, Errol introduced himself in a very professional way and asked us to buckle up before he started the engine. Errol was not at all chatty. With photographs certainly not on the agenda, we sat in the back strapped in like stiff boards. Despite the ride from the airport being perilous, it was so hilarious I think I preferred it. Errol took the same route across the bridge and into the town. The homes we passed were a little more organised now and although the roads were in the same state, the drive was accomplished in such a way that our bottoms were in exactly the same places they had begun when we arrived at the airport. Cool, calm and collected, we walked into the noisy terminal feeling a bit deflated.

Miracle of miracles, the flight was on time and after checking in we headed for the Tabua Lounge, where we ate all their sandwiches. On board the aircraft we shared the Tabua Class cabin with only three others and had a smiling, attractive and burly Polynesian Steward to look after us. Very content and trying not to think about poor Roo's earlier behaviour I sat in anticipation of a nice flight.

The Purser – another big Polynesian chap, announced that he was about to close the door and we would soon be on our way to back to Auckland, where we had arranged a brief lay-over until our flight to Tahiti. We were strapped in and raring to go. All Ship-Shape and Bristol-Fashion then I assured myself. Lovely.

But in life, we never know what might be round the corner and the events of the next few seconds were certainly unusual, when a young man suddenly emerged from the rear of the plane and made a dash for the door shouting loudly that he had to get off!!

For once, it was worse being up the front, as we could see and hear everything that was going on and an unexpected surge of adrenaline made me feel light-headed. Having just closed the door the Purser was still standing and reeling around, placed his hands on the man's shoulders to keep him at arm's length. Our Steward, sitting beside the door ready for departure, threw off his seatbelt and was out of his seat in a flash to assist his colleague.

There was a deathly hush, as the five of us looked on in amazement. The white New Zealander, shouting loudly in a high state of emotion would not be pacified, stating that the only explanation for his hasty exit was that he needed to get off for personal reasons. When I heard this, I was sure something serious was going to happen and grabbed Roo's hand, not knowing if I was trying to comfort him, or wanting him to comfort me.

While the Purser held on to the now ashen-faced man, our Steward summoned help from Airport Security and fortunately, with the plane still attached to the loading bridge (you know the tunnel you walk down to board?) it wasn't long before a horde of officers were waiting outside the door.

When he left the plane there was quite a commotion as passengers, including Roo and I started to talk again until we were interrupted by an announcement from the Pilot. He sounded as astonished as us when he came over the PA., but there was no point in trying to hide what had just happened, so simply said, *"Well, the gentleman has left the aircraft now and as soon as we've offloaded all his belongings, we'll be on our way"*.

The cabin crew made a thorough search of the man's seat and the area around it, but finding nothing detrimental, calmly chatted to the passengers in a kind and comforting way. Then there were bangs and thuds outside, which made some of us jump, but it was only the noise of the baggage handlers furiously rummaging around in the hold to find his luggage so it could be removed.

Roo and I have flown millions of miles together and have friends, who have flown millions of miles, but we'd never ever heard of anything like that happening before. Perhaps there was nothing in it. Perhaps he adored Fiji so much, he couldn't leave. We'll never know. I would love to have read the Airport Security file on him, though.

Once the shock of it all had gone and my adrenaline levels returned to normal, I turned my attention to Roo. Not knowing how he would handle what had just happened, I was surprised to find him in such a jocular mood. *"If you've gotta go, you've gotta go"*, he said, which made me and our fellow passengers smile.

Eventually, we took to the air - minus the gentleman and his luggage, but it was obvious that the flight was going to be a subdued and thoughtful one.

Only forty five minutes into the flight we began to experience the most awful turbulence, with big bangs and drops in height that made your tummy somersault. The Captain warned us that due to amazing cloud formations and fork lightning, we were on a very slow 'rippled ascent' (whatever that was) and that consequently all cabin services would be suspended. After an hour though, the turbulence stopped and with the abrupt stomach-turning drops in height coming to an end, the cabin crew resumed their excellent service.

In spite of the unusual circumstances and impending arrival into Auckland, we accepted their offer of dinner, with just enough time for me to consume a very good vegetable curry and Roo a chicken dish.

The flight landed smoothly and was only forty-five minutes late, in spite of bizarre behaviour from both passengers and weather, but by the time we'd collected our luggage – including the extra suitcase from storage and had hailed a taxi, it was already 11pm. The journey to the Sebel Suites didn't take long though and we were soon leaning over the balcony of the fourth floor suite overlooking row upon row of beautiful yachts in every shape and size moored in the Marina below.

With just enough light from the pier to see in the darkness, Roo's eyes were the size of saucers again at the sight of so many lovely boats. The water caressing them gently and their hypnotic sway made us wish we were staying longer than twelve hours. I could have watched them sway all night, but as soon as I'd rearranged the luggage into four more manageable portions we both reluctantly hit the sack. I had no idea what Roo was thinking as we lay in bed but reflecting on the strange day it had been, I played it all over again in my mind.

Having to cope with Roo's unpredictable behaviour has taught me to expect the unexpected and I'm under no illusion that some humans need very little to trigger off some deep-seated emotion with the ability to unleash devastation on the rest of us. We were just lucky that a situation with the potential for disaster had been handled so well by the crew.

Roo made no answer when I said goodnight and must have slept as soon as the light went out. The events of the day hadn't bothered him at all. I thought they HAD bothered me actually and was thankful that we hadn't ended up as an item on Sky News,

DAY FORTY:

"Next stop Tahiti"

Lukey had sent a text to say he wasn't feeling too good, so I rang him. He told me that he was worried about his Level 2 ski exam and hadn't been sleeping properly. On top of that, he had a really bad stomach ache, his head hurt and he was convinced he had a high temperature as well. Although it didn't sound as though his life was in danger and vomiting wasn't mentioned, everything that could possibly be wrong with him went through my mind and I wasn't happy until I'd been able to rule out Appendicitis, Meningitis and an obstructed bowel. (Not that I EVER thought worse case scenario).

He promised to text later with a progress (or not) report and sounded happier to have had a chat and a bit of reassurance. It was good to hear his voice and I made a mental note to remind myself that his exam was only two days away. I didn't mention the fun and games on the plane yesterday.

Wandering into the sunshine, we scoured the pier for somewhere to have breakfast close enough to the yachts so we could continue to admire them and if we were seen dribbling, we could blame the food. It was St. Patrick's Day and the pub covered in green balloons and Shamrocks just had to be Irish. Although it was early morning, it was already full of people wearing Leprechaun hats and drinking Guinness. I preferred the Eggs Benedict so early in the morning though and Roo a fry-up, which we were very content to eat at a table outside, not only with a huge parasol, but also with a wonderful view of the biggest yacht in the Marina.

Leaving the Irish to their Guinness and the fabulous yacht to its lucky owner, I went back to the suite to finish fiddling with the luggage. Roo was happy to walk a few blocks into town to the All Blacks shop to retrieve the 'other' sock. (Remember the one we were given ONE in Dunedin?) He returned to the suite waving the sock above his head triumphantly and acted out a ceremonious 'joining of the sock' with the other one to make a pair. Daft idiot. But it was funny and I had to laugh. This was like the 'old' Roo I once knew.

It was time to leave and I was determined to be specific about booking the same suite again should we ever return. (Someone remind that it was number 417, if I have forgotten). With the sun shining in a cloudless sky, we chatted to the taxi driver, a true Kiwi in his 60's, who was sure New Zealand was heading for its share of immigration problems. We swapped notes on the subject, assuring him that New Zealand - with only four million people in a country the same size as England where there are seventy million *that we knew about*– they had a long way to go to catch us up. He was noticeably horrified and changed the subject.

In spite of the move to yet another part of world, Roo was showing no signs of panic and didn't even have the shakes. He jabbered away merrily, cooled by the breeze from the open window obviously enjoying the ride and the scenery. I was wearing my Optimistic Head once more and felt relaxed and content - until we reached the Airport that was.

It was much busier than the day we arrived and my Optimistic Head was instantly replaced by my Apprehensive Head. We went straight to the Air Tahiti desk to check in - glad to be relieved of our ever-expanding suitcases and headed for their Lounge.

Security was a bit odd and although this time I wasn't accused of smuggling 'eppels', I was asked if I had family living in New Zealand. I really couldn't be bothered to point out that I was, in fact, LEAVING the country and just said, "No". Perhaps the Officer usually worked in Arrivals and had forgotten he was in Departures.

Still with no signs of panic, Roo helped himself to a snack in the lounge and scanned the local newspaper. I pretended to study my book while he failed to notice that I was staring at the same sentence and not turning the pages. It was almost a week since his last bad day and I was beginning to think that the Milk Thistle really was doing him some good, in spite of the need for a daily 10mg dose of Clomiprimine.

The flight to Tahiti left Auckland on time, taking to the air without anyone charging around wanting to get off and with only one three other couples up front, we were spoiled by the attention of the two gorgeous French-speaking female attendants wearing National Dress and leis made from fresh flowers. When we levelled out, they removed the leis, replacing them with a single bloom behind the left ear and in their thick jet black hair. This was a local custom: left ear if you were taken/right ear if you were available. It was odd listening to them speak English with a French accent and when we reverted to their native language, they seemed to appreciate it.

We had just passed Tonga over to the left somewhere, when the Captain told us that we were about to cross the International Dateline, meaning that we had to subtract 24 hours and have Sunday all over again. I wondered what this would do to you if you made a habit of crossing it. Would it be good for your wrinkles, or bad for them? I felt a bit like a time-traveller, but apart from that, nothing else happened to me and Roo's behaviour was always bizarre, so I doubted that it was anything to do with the Dateline.

It was dark outside now. Roo and the other passengers were snoozing and all the windows had their blinds down. I'd been watching a Sci-Fi film, which had finished abruptly in typical sci-fi astonishment - with a totally blank and dazzling white screen. The brightness of the film gone, my eyes were diverted to the window beside me and the flash of light on the other side. Slowly lifting the blind, what I saw gave me a sharp intake of breath.

The streak of lightning intent on penetrating the Acrylic seemed to bounce off the window with shock and in its light, great soap sud-shaped clouds revealed themselves. I closed the blind quickly, but just as I did, the cabin lights came on and the lovely girls appeared in a flurry of fuss. I wasn't surprised to hear the announcement that we were approaching a storm.

We'd flown around it as much as we could apparently, but for the last few hundred miles, there was no alternative – we'd have to fly IN it. "*Oh, Goody*", I said to a sleepy Roo (as Tom Hanks in 'Castaway' swept into my mind) "*A Pacific storm*".

It was violent. There was no other word for it. It was as though Mrs. Nature didn't want us in her air and was showing her anger by trying to shake us to bits. The journey didn't improve until we were below the soap suds, which now had a strange pink glow about them. Then came the rain. The sound of water attacking the plane was like a wall being pebble-dashed and I wondered if there'd be any paint left on the fuselage.

With each flash of lightning, the plane was low enough for us to see the ocean and a million 'white horses'. Ploughing through them as best it could, the illuminated shape of a cruise ship came into focus.

But now we were making our final approach. The Captain had obviously done it all before and despite one final roller-coaster ride, landed the huge steel tube safely in Papeete, Tahiti, French Polynesia.

I felt exhausted. Goodness knows how the crew on the Flight Deck felt. But the lovely girls hadn't batted an eyelid and wearing their leis again, we left them behind with a thousand 'Thank You's' and made our way to Immigration.

Having been warned to expect interrogation of Gestapo proportions, I had made sure that all our paperwork was in excellent order, showing that although we had one-way tickets, we would be leaving Tahiti in thirteen days' time. Honestly!

We were given a questionnaire to complete and one of the questions asked if we were looking for work. I smiled at the thought of any Tahitian company wanting to employ an old bird with a gammy leg and a bloke who couldn't organise a social occasion in a beer-making factory – even if they did speak French. We dutifully filled in our answers and handed them back to the official, who scoured them and gave us another piece of paper saying that we'd completed it successfully. The French love paperwork.

Leaving the airport clutching our bits of paper, we searched for a Taxi, but none seemed immediately available. The only type of transportation we could see parked in the taxi rank looked like very old VW Campers. They were called 'Le Truck' and were actually vehicles with wooden cabins bolted onto the back.

'Health and Safety' – or the lack of it -sprang to mind once again.

Well, with no alternative, we secured a ride in one of these to take us to the Sheraton. My initial attempt at climbing up into the cabin was unsuccessful, but I mastered the technique the second time – although without any ladylike refinements. Roo and I sat side-by-side on the wooden bench and with a long sigh said together *"FIJI!"* And this time, without the hanging-on straps.

We must have been mad, but off we sped clinging to each other for dear life. There were no lights along the roads, so it was difficult to see much in the dark. It didn't look as poor as Fiji – but almost. The Sheraton looked like a safe haven though and it was a relief when we screeched to a halt in the covered, but open-air Lobby.

I was sure I'd pulled a muscle trying to stay upright and looking very dishevelled, we both tumbled out of Le Truck.

The softly-spoken beauty behind the Reception Desk got on with the paperwork quickly, while welcoming us to Tahiti at the same time. I hoped I wasn't becoming complacent with all this jet-setting and time travel and reminded myself that we were lucky enough to be standing in the foyer of a beautiful hotel built on one of the French Polynesian Society Islands in the middle of the South Pacific Ocean.

Our adjacent rooms on the first floor of the low rise building were large, nicely furnished and with splendid bathrooms. Full width windows with a sliding door led to a balcony and a lagoon view. We'd have to wait till morning to see the lagoon view though.

As usual, we were both desperate for a shower and headed for this refreshment before doing anything else. As I sat in a towel, drying my hair, there was a knock at the door. I hoped it was only Roo and not a waiter. Luckily it was a waitress, delivering a large selection of fruit, pastries and wine. Another knock at the door and this time it was Roo. He'd been marvellous all day, but I was ready and waiting for a nosedive, so it was no surprise when he began to complain about his room. The air conditioning didn't work and neither did the 'phone and why was it we didn't have an interconnecting door? I reminded him that when we'd checked in we were told that they'd all been taken by a wedding party and he was literally in the next room for goodness sake.

He stood at the door sulking and I just knew he was going to say that he'd have to stay in my room for the night. With the thought of trying to sleep beside a jet engine for eight hours, I picked up the 'phone to tell Reception about the faults. An Engineer arrived within a few minutes and Roo went off with him next door. My telephone rang shortly after. His 'phone had been fixed (obviously) and the air conditioning was fine, so I said goodnight and reluctantly, Roo stayed where he was.

The sliding door was open and I went to close it, but before I did, stepped out onto the balcony. Although it wasn't visible, the lagoon was out there somewhere and there was a smell of something fishy in the air. It was very windy, but so warm and comforting I could probably have slept outside. Instead, I closed the door, did a quick sweep of the room for mozzies and plopped into bed. I couldn't have been sleeping long, before a flash of light woke me up. For a minute I couldn't think where I was and stood up until I got my bearings. Bugger. I really had been out cold and knew I'd be lucky to get back into such a deep sleep again. Another flash of light made me jump and I pulled the curtain back from the window to see what was going on. There was nothing except blackness, but as I went to turn away, someone in the distance must have turned on a gigantic neon light, because suddenly the lagoon appeared as if night had become day.

It was the eeriest of sights, lasting a few seconds each time. This I must see, I thought and madly went out onto the balcony.

The air was still now and without noise, except for the faint rustle of palm leaves. Another flash gave me a black and white luminescent view of the lagoon and the distinct curve of the ocean on the horizon beyond. It scared the life out of me and I flew back to bed.

DAY FORTY-ONE: "Pirates and Brigands" (-10hrs GMT)

I still had a sheet over my head when I woke up and for a minute thought I was dead. But realising I was breathing, 'tutted' and told myself off. The room was bright for more than a few seconds, so it had to be daytime and looking at the clock on the television, it was – *just*.

Daring to emerge from under the sheet, I gingerly left the bed and peeped through the curtains to see that dawn had turned the raging sky into a dark blue – in fact exactly the same colour as the flower called 'Blue Dawn', or 'Morning Glory', which is more of a purple. Well, whatever colour you wanted to call it, it was beautiful.

The pyjamas I was wearing were my new best ones (the spotty turquoise ones I'd bought in Cairns) so I felt confident that they were good enough to be seen in, should any other mad person be up at this hour and nobly went out onto the balcony again. It was peculiar, because outside looked nothing like the view when we arrived.

Now I could see that the hotel stood right on the shore of the lagoon and of course, had the enviable manicured gardens we'd come to expect. A row of palm trees ran between the beach and the gardens and dotted in between, straw huts sat looking at the cyan-blue lagoon. It was all very Tahitian and in many ways, similar to Fiji.

Roo said he'd been banging on my door for ages, but honestly, I hadn't heard him. He was cross when I eventually opened the door, saying that he'd been woken up by a text from Lukey and I had to speak to him urgently. I don't like 'urgently'. It can go with words like 'serious' and 'dangerous'. The poor chap sounded dreadful when I got through to him and mentally, I was on the next plane to Canada. My worse case scenario came right down the scale though, when he explained that some bright spark had suggested taking a large dose of senna to cure his stomach ache.

Establishing the exact amount he'd taken, I was confident that he'd survive the overdose and cancelled the mental flight to the Rockies. With the advice that sometimes it was good to 'clear the system' and that taking a purgative is rarely fatal, I convinced him that he was not about to die, but that it would probably be a good idea to stay indoors for the rest of the day. I wasn't sure about his level 2 ski exam tomorrow though; we'd have to cross that bridge later on and didn't mention it.

As the morning progressed, the weather went downhill and it felt stormy again, so we chose not to do very much and sat around the pool even though it wasn't sunny. I wanted to go to the pearl market the next day and needed to rest my leg if I was to wander around for several hours, so I lazed on a lounger, trying not to look like a beached whale, while Roo went off for a swim. I'd been able to see him floating back and forth and thought he was fine, so I was taken by surprise when he stood over me dripping with water, both from his shorts and his eyes. He wasn't in control of himself again and I had to tell him to sit down before he fell down. When he did, he was inconsolable. What a disappointment. I really thought we were over these feelings of complete and utter uselessness.

We left the pool and went back to my room for a cup of PG and I put my Counselling hat on for the 93rd time. I said the same old things, because there really wasn't anything new to say and an hour and a half later, having come out the other side it was time for the distraction of dinner.

The main restaurant had been built over the lagoon, in a similar way that the apartment in the Bay of Islands had been and served very tasty, but expensive food. We had to agree that it was a good thing we weren't staying at the hotel for very long. The ocean was only a few feet below our table and to entertain us was a huge shoal of fish feeding around the rocks that held up the restaurant. They were obviously used to receiving titbits from diners and swam right up to us to nibble the morsels of bread we threw out of the window. Being away from the main hotel and most of the light pollution, my eyes couldn't help drifting above the fish to the vast ocean beyond giving me that shiver I get every time I see something big. I knew what was out there after the illuminations of the night before and had to force my gaze back to the fish.

It's amazing how much you can say about cold-blooded aquatic vertebrates and I rambled on about them the whole time we were eating. It was just the sort of inane chatter needed to stop me looking at the big expanse of water and saved Roo from having to talk at all, as he was still very down.

From the restaurant we headed for the open-air lounge. With a vast patio, comfy cane furniture and entertainment from Polynesian dancers cavorting around on a small stage, we sipped cocktails; alcoholic for me and the more boring kind for Roo.

On the way back to our rooms we strolled through a very French-looking courtyard with wrought iron tables and chairs, hanging lanterns lit with candles and old barrels placed amongst the palms. I wouldn't have been surprised if Black Beard himself had swung in on a rope shouting, *"Avast Me Hearties!"* Geckos croaking like frogs scurried around hunting for mosquitoes and instead of yesterdays' fishy smell, the fragrant aroma of jasmine and ginger wafted through the air.

That divine breeze was with us again and a bit of a moon so we could see white fluffy clouds speeding past a million twinkling stars. We sat down at one of the tables to look up at it all without getting giddy and I had to wonder why the vastness of the ocean had made me feel the way it did, but the sky didn't affect me in the same way.

As Freud said, '*the mind is like an iceberg, it floats with one seventh of its bulk above water*'. Not that his quote makes it any better of course, but it does make me sound very intelligent.

"AARGH JOHNNY!"

Roo had to drag me away from the lovely courtyard and I went up to bed feeling all romantic, but unless Johnny Depp appeared by grappling hook on my balcony in a puff of gunsmoke, romance was still off the menu. Hey-ho.

DAY FORTY-TWO: *"The Black Pearl"*

Tahiti had a calm night in spite of all the warning signs and by daybreak, it was clear, sunny and warm outside. Lukey sent a text to say that he was still suffering the after-effects of his self-medication and that the Level 2 exam was off. Probably a good thing. I rang the hotel hairdresser and in my best French, asked if she would be able to remove the tortoiseshell cat from my head. Well I said, *"Ecaille et blanc"* and she didn't reply with, *"Quoi?"* She just assured me that I had an appointment the next day and I hoped not to return with a 'crewCAT'. (Ha-ha).

After breakfast and a reasonable-looking Roo, we took a cab from the hotel lobby and went into Papeete (pronounced: par-pea-ate-ee) the capital. With the awful experience in Hong Kong's Stanley Market embossed in my mind, the last thing I wanted to do was drag Roo around the shops aimlessly, so I had asked the beauty in Reception exactly where to head for.

The town looks very run down and worn out – probably with all those pirates coming and going, but retains a French atmosphere of sorts and is full of character and odd smells. How it must have looked a hundred years ago, with French soldiers and traders milling around I don't know. Anyone with an ounce of imagination couldn't fail to see the legacy that robbery and criminal violence had left behind because of course the real facts are less romantic and swashbuckling.

History shows that things have been going on here in trading terms since the 16th century, with all sorts of explorers and spice merchants sailing to and fro from all over the world. From the mid 18th century, English and then French Missionaries had a huge influence on the islands and almost obliterated native culture, but has been French territory since 1842.

The artist Paul Gaugin painted here and the locals are very proud of the fact. Nuclear testing took place about 1,000 miles away – which isn't far in nuclear terms when you think about it and continued until the 1990's when rioting broke out during anti-nuke protests. Quite right too. How could you possibly think it was right to destroy such beauty? God must have been furious.

Roo and I walked the rough streets leading to the pearl market and eventually came across rows and rows of stalls selling the famous black pearls. We weren't so sure about buying anything from a stall, knowing we wouldn't be able to recognise a good one and coming across a store that looked a little more professional, decided to go in. We found the door locked and were puzzled, as it was nowhere near lunchtime. After looking us up and down through the window, a security chappee opened the door and asked what we wanted. *"A pearl, please"*, I said (as if there was anything else there to buy!) We were shown upstairs and came to another locked door. I have no idea what would happen if there was a fire, but at least the pearls would be safe from thieves. The pearls on display in this room were magnificent and most of them had magnificent prices to match, but the sales people in the shop were past masters at detecting what was in your wallet and one of them brought out a tray of pearls within the price range we had in mind. I chose a large, perfectly round and shiny dark grey pearl, which would always remind me of Tahiti.

Returning to the hotel we sat by the pool for a while, but it wasn't long before we heard PG Tips calling to us and off we went for a cuppa until it was time to get dressed for dinner. We ate massive prawns at the same restaurant, watched the same fish darting in and out of the rocks and yet another massive storm way out at sea. Roo was a bit niggly, but promised he was training himself to handle his dark moods and in spite of his bad company, I couldn't resist another cocktail at the same cocktail place. This time, we were served by a gorgeous softly-spoken 'lady-man', with immaculate hair and make-up. I know how awful it is to be trapped inside the wrong body – I'm a size 12 in my dreams.

Before we went to bed I reorganised the luggage for tomorrow. The ship would be in port when we woke up.

Just a bit of history about the ***Mutiny on 'The Bounty'*** In December, 1787, HMS Bounty set sail for Tahiti, to collect 'breadfruits' and transport them to the West Indies, where it was hoped they would be grown as cheap food for slaves. But five months later, following alleged cruelty by Captain William Bligh, Master's Mate Fletcher Christian led a mutiny and with seventeen others set Captain Bligh and most of those loyal to him afloat in a small boat. After scouring the South Pacific Ocean for a safe haven and abducting several Tahitian women in the process, Fletcher Christian and other mutineers settled on Pitcairn Island, where they set light to the ship to conceal their whereabouts. Miraculously, following an epic and eventful journey and probably due to his unusual navigational skills, Captain Bligh returned to England to report the mutiny. It was seen as an outrage and in 1790, the First Lord of the Admiralty despatched HMS Pandora to capture the mutineers and return them for trial. Many of the mutineers were caught and locked in a box on the Pandora, inevitably gaining the name 'Pandora's Box', from Greek Mythology, where they were kept in appalling conditions. Although Fletcher Christian was never caught, he was known to have died violently at the hands of Tahitian men in 1793, but it was not until 1808 that the mutineer's hiding place was discovered with John Adams still alive. Of the 134 men who set sail for Tahiti in the 'Pandora' to capture the mutineers, only 78 returned and only threee of the mutineers were executed.

DAY FORTY-THREE: "Tahitian Princess"

A pleasant sort of day greeted us. Not too hot with a bit of a breeze. Roo arrived at my door washed dressed and although without a smile, had no hint of panic or other brain anomalies – even though we were soon to leave the safety of the hotel. I felt confident enough to leave him alone in my room while I went to the hairdressers, but explained the exact whereabouts of the salon just in case he panicked. On arrival, I discovered that not one of the delightful staff spoke a word of English. It was to be a good test of my French vocabulary, but they could see from the look of me what needed doing. The only time I ran into trouble conversation-wise, was when they were talking amongst themselves and I didn't know what *'nuage orageuex'* meant, until in a very roundabout sort of way with much arm-waving in the air, I realised it was *'storm cloud'*. The next time I'm at our place in France, I'll impress the locals with that one. Sitting in front of a mirror wearing the tint, I wasn't surprised to see Roo's reflection too. He was "*just checking that I was alright*".

He didn't hang around when he saw that he was the only male in the salon and went back upstairs to wait for me. With the tortoiseshell cat removed from my locks for a second time, I collected Roo and our luggage and we departed by taxi with a lady driver, for the 'Tahitian Princess'. Her English was as good as our French and we nattered on in both languages, which now I think about it, was quite clever of the three of us.

The ship was a quarter of the size of the 'Sapphire', but with the same standard of cleanliness, hygiene and service. Another Fillipino called Rodeo was to be our Steward who was just as sweet as Rogellio. Eager to help in any way he could, he left us carrying loads of our laundry and still had a smile on his face all the way out of the door.

The ship was smaller and so was our suite, but equally as comfortable, with two loos – one in a powder room, the other in a large bathroom with an <u>ordinary</u> shower, a lounge-diner, separate bedroom and spacious deck.

Before unpacking, we went on a tour of the ship which didn't take long and as we'd skipped breakfast and thought we must be hungry, ate a delicious lunch. So far - so good.

No matter how often a woman receives flowers, it always makes them feel good, so when we returned from our exploration and found that flowers and Champagne had been delivered, I was delighted. It was a shame that the moment was spoiled by Roo pacing around the room – a sign of impending doom. Thinking quickly to avert whatever it was trying to be, I suggested we go out onto our deck and get some fresh air. We sat outside in the warm breeze until there was call to say that we would need to have dinner at six o'clock, because only a third of the passengers had arrived on board due to the bad weather and inevitable flight delays. I thought of those poor people flying around in the turbulence and was glad that we'd already had out turn.

The thought of having to make small-talk with our fellow passengers when Roo often felt anti-social filled me with dread and I knew we would both find it embarrassing, but with the ship being so small, we were allocated a nicely positioned table for two beside a huge picture window tucked away quite privately from other diners, thankfully.

The quality of the food was as good as the Sapphire and after eating five of the six courses offered, we somehow managed to stand up and move to the bar. Studying our companions surreptitiously, it would appear that most were honeymooners, or at least romantics.

Well we wouldn't see much of them then. This would be a very quiet cruise.

The film, 'The Queen' was showing on the big screen in the forward lounge and we decided to go and watch it, although we'd seen it at home already. It was difficult not to giggle listening to the mainly American audience and their comments about the story and the genuine sadness they felt for the subject.

Unwittingly, the seats we'd taken for the film, gave us a ring-side view of what was to follow - a noisy and very entertaining show from local Tahitian dancers. Beautiful girls in native dress and hunky chaps – *in not very much really*, impressed us with their native dancing. Boy, those drums were fantastic, or was it the hunky chaps that had made my blood pressure rise?

DAY FORTY-FOUR: "Off on the water again"

Roo was in a bad way despite having had a good nights' sleep aboard an anchored vessel and didn't seem to notice the beautiful morning. Breakfast was delivered on time, of course. Boiled eggs for him/scrambled for me. We ate and went back to bed, which sounds very decadent, but I just couldn't face spending time counselling him again and hoped the answer would be for him to sleep off the blues. He dozed off quickly and I lay there too, listening to his breathing with the echoes of the ship being made ready to leave port in the background.

Lunchtime came and went, with Roo slipping fitfully in and out of consciousness. What was going on in his mind? Why couldn't we stop his irrational behaviour? If only we could remove his brain and soak it in Ariel overnight ... I didn't know why I was making jokes, because it wasn't funny – the situation was quite dire; but I'd made myself smile, which had to be a good thing.

There was a tap on the door. I went to open it, although I was still in my PJ's and managed not to wake Sleeping Beauty. It was our Steward who was, I was quite sure, used to seeing passengers wearing very little. He told us that the evacuation procedure would be practised shortly and to be ready for the alarm, so I had no alternative but to wake Roo and tell him to get up. He was terribly anxious with this news and said he couldn't possibly go outside to stand with several hundred people. *"Well if you don't"*, I said, *"We won't be leaving Papeete, because it's a legal requirement that we all have to know what to do in an emergency"*. *"Perhaps it would be better if I went down with the ship"*, he replied in morose and dramatic tones. Looking up to heaven, I grabbed his arm and pulled him out of bed. *"Just get dressed quickly, will you?"* was my only answer.

The alarm would sound in less than forty minutes and I was thankful that Roo spent only half an hour showering and dressing, which was a record. I was sitting at the table ready to go clutching our lifejackets when he announced, *"I can't go, I can't. I'm just not …"*. But before he could finish the sentence, I had removed a tranquilizer from the blister pack, poured water into a glass and stood in front of him with them both. The alarm sounded as soon as he'd swallowed the pill. Good timing I thought and thrusting his lifejacket into his left hand, held the other tightly and led him along the corridor, up the stairs and into the Bar, which was our Muster Station. (Very handy for Brandy if we needed it during an evacuation). Every single passenger listened intently to the Evacuation Officer including Roo, although I knew that the empty look on his face wasn't exactly one of concentration. With instructions of what to do, should the ship strike an iceberg or similar firmly in our minds (well mine, anyway) we felt the ship move. Passengers and crew dispersed in every direction and Roo and I returned to our suite, where I suggested we sit on deck to watch the departure.

The deck was only two-thirds of the size of the last one, but would have been more than adequate for twelve people, let alone two and bent around the side of the ship, giving a marvellous, uninterrupted view of where we had been as we left it. We leant on the rail, waving to no one in particular and when the people were too small to see, sat in the mahogany loungers watching the sun set in a blue sky behind fluffy white clouds.

A few miles out, the island of Moorea soon came into sight, but we would be making a visit there on our return to Papeete nine days later, so sped past its towering peaks without stopping. A little further on, both islands came into view together, silhouetted by a massive sky.

Roo was much happier now and had been reading his book all this time, but I had to interrupt him to tell him to look at what was going on above us. Pink, cumulus clouds were congregating atop dense, blue-tinged, fluffier ones and it was beautiful enough to make me feel quite choked-up.

Then the moon appeared, rising up just to the left of Moorea in the still-bright sky. A huge, perfect silver orb smiling down happily on all it perceived, as if it recognised and approved of the beauty of it all. Disinterested in what he called, "another one of those skies", Roo went inside, but I couldn't get enough of "those skies" and stayed until the very last minute, waiting for the first star of the evening to appear. The blue sky gradually changed to a darker hue and the light from the moon grew in intensity, until it cast a long glistening white line in the water. There was very little time before dinner, but just as I went to turn away, a star winked at me right on cue.

Roo was much better and hungry. He enjoyed prime rib of roast beef and my dense, tasty tuna went down very nicely too, as we sat at our very private table. Dinner finished, we made a brief stop at the evening's entertainment, a Welsh chap with a voice similar to Barry Manilow, but for some reason I was really tired and went to bed listening ... not to the romantic sound of water splashing against the hull, but to the sound of my gizzards trying hard to devour that tuna – which wasn't romantic at all.

DAY FORTY-FIVE: "Good Friday on Huahine"

Good Friday didn't start in a very good way and I can never understand why we call it 'Good' Friday anyway. It is of course, when we're supposed to celebrate the day that Jesus was crucified – breaking the barrier of sin and making it a 'good' day, but perhaps it should be called "Not Such a Good Day for Jesus", or "Bad for Sin Day", which seems much more appropriate to me.

So as I said, not such a good day for Roo either when we arrived at Huahine (pronounced 'who-a-heenee') where it was very windy and a bit cloudy. The ship swayed in the breeze as the anchor was dropped and breakfast arrived. Roo was panicky, frightened and anxious again. He left most of his breakfast and as I was still having trouble digesting that tuna, left mine too. Roo dived for the security of the duvet and not knowing what else to do, I joined him there.

The ship was really swinging wildly in the strong wind, as if trying to escape its shackles giving us ever-changing glimpses of Huahine through the big picture window. Moving about so much we were enjoying 180 degree sweeps of the island without actually going anywhere. It looked intriguing. So much so, that after a few more sweeps, Roo said he felt well enough to go ashore.

The ship used the lifeboats to ferry passengers ashore. No row boats, these were tough, covered boats with powerful engines and big enough to hold one hundred-and-fifty people. It took less than a minute to reach the tiny jetty on the island and once on terra firma, we walked on a bit inheriting a chubby local dog. However, seeing an abundance of local chubby dogs around, we realised this might not be such a good idea to encourage them. We didn't want a pack following us – chubby, or otherwise – even if they were friendly, so turned circle and made our way back to the jetty depositing 'chubby' on the way.

Walking on the sandy path beside the lagoon, we were puzzled by the dozens of very large holes, about the size of a dinner plate at intervals along the shoreline and wondered, with a certain amount of trepidation, what might be living in them. With the dinner plate size in mind, I wasn't too desperate to establish who, or what lived down them, but Roo was. Close examination gave us no clues although outside some, deep scratches were visible. Could the occupants have claws? There was no sign of an animal this size around – something nocturnal perhaps? Roo was tempted to push a stick into one of the holes, but with visions of him impaling something vicious on the end and having to run for our lives being chased by a clawed monster, I managed to deter him.

Coming across hole, after hole, eventually we reached a little row of shacks. I would like to have said that they were simply huts for fisherman, but of course, they were homes for some of the local people. 'Home' in the loosest sense of the word. The inhabitants, however, were yet more of those happy souls we kept seeing who were content to live their lives in the simplest of ways and appeared to be healthy and stress-free with it. We discovered the holes were crab holes - for **very large** crabs - the staple diet for the populous, along with fish and pork. Every night, they were collected in the dark — simply picked up and taken home, where the crabs were caged and fed on coconut (which the crabs love). The coconut not only cleaned them up, but it also gave a wonderful flavour when they were cooked and eaten a week, or so later. Ingenious. No hunting, no trauma and everyone is happy — apart for the crabs at the very end (fed on so much coconut, they're probably sozzled and don't care anyway).

Hoping to see as much of the island as possible, we caught the local bus to the town centre. A rusty charabanc, it was held together with brown paper and string and was loaded to the gunnels with smiling Huahines and cheering children hanging

ALL ABOARD THE 'BULA' BUS

off the windows. The Health and Safety Executive in England would have had kittens if they'd seen it. Most of the trading places (it would be difficult to use the word 'shops') were closed, but at least there were no crab holes. The few people exhibiting the local craft were closing early for Easter, but we had a quick look round anyway and then joined the queue of Princess passengers to return to the ship.

When the next charabanc arrived, I was reminded once more of a St. Trinian's film, with the children shouting the equivalent of Hooray' leaning out of the windows this time. The driver even looked like Terry Thomas, complete with moustache and gap between his teeth.

Huahine is really worth a visit, should you ever be in that neck of the woods. It's two islands actually – Huahine-Nui and Huahine-Iti (Big and Little Islands) connected by a bridge and with its steep mountains covered with lush green tropical plants, blue lagoons and white, sandy beaches, they (who know about these things) say it's the most relaxing of all the Polynesian Islands, because there isn't anything else there – and never will be. Let's hope they never run out of coconuts for those crabs.

Back on board, a Good Friday Service (of sorts) was to be held, but Roo wasn't sure that he could handle it and I didn't want to go alone, so we decided not to attend. Sailing through the turquoise waters of the lagoon and away from Huahine, a mist was rising above the high volcanic peaks untouched by anyone able to do them harm. Huahine is another island totally unsuitable for development. It's amazing how many like this there are. We're constantly told about the bad things going on in the world, but don't realise how much good stuff there is out there.

Sitting on our lovely deck, we sailed away and Roo dozed off. I was trying hard to think what my fashion options were for the evening and without my lovely white trousers (washed pink in Fiji) an important part of my remaining outfits was out of the equation. Tomorrow was the last formal night. As on the last cruise, Roo should have had both a black and a white DJ, but this time, the white one hadn't materialised. Fortunately, the black one was a very nice double-breasted affair and although he looks good in white, I thought he would look really debonair in this one. I hoped to squeeze into my black evening top, but having resembled a large barrage balloon the last time I looked in a full length mirror, that might be out of the equation too. Looking back towards Huahine, a rainbow appeared on one end of the island hitting the water at the other. It marked the exact spot we had been, as if it were saying, "You were here". More pink clouds followed the ship and I thought they looked beautiful – until I remembered my trousers.

There was a French theme at dinner, but avoiding the snails and frog legs, Roo chose Orange Roughy – a fish a bit like Plaice and I revelled in Lobster Tagliatelle. It was all lovely and Roo was being lovely too. Perhaps Huahine was the place to be.

Jump ship … set up a crab sanctuary …

Not ready for bed immediately after dinner, we sat in the Internet Café and emailed Harry with last minute notes before he left home for San Francisco in two days' time and also checked that we hadn't won the lottery, which was unlikely; because the only thing I had ever won in my entire life was the Prize for Bandaging when I was training to be a nurse. Then after a quick spin on the breezy deck to check out the stars, it was back to the ranch for bed.

245

DAY FORTY-SIX:

"Cook's Islands"

Rang mum first thing, who said she was fine. Di said she wasn't.

I had a hairdressers' appointment for later on to get a 'do' for the formal evening and nagging in the back of my mind was the thought of what to wear other than the shantung blouse. If there was no alternative, I'd have to put the *'small breath procedure'* in place. It seemed to work before.

The book I'd been reading, *"Do I look Fat in This?"* was not the most enlightening of novels, but I'd persevered and finished it. Whether the information gleaned from its pages would stop me hating my body and help me to start loving myself was doubtful and when I looked at the next book I'd chosen, *"How to be a Better Person"*, knew I must be suffering from some sort of mental affliction.

Perhaps I should apply the **Diatheses-Stress Model** to determine exactly which mental affliction as soon as possible. (I'm sure you're very impressed with the subtle mention of this psychological theory. The truth is that it's actually the sum-total of my Psychiatric knowledge – although I could write a book about living with a Depressive).

The hairdresser was a delightful Aussie who did a good job, but made me look like a cross between Diana

Dors and Doris Day – one of whom is dead and the other is eighty-something. On my way back to the suite, I felt a spring in my step and thought my hair looked quite nice, even if I did resemble an old or dead film star. However, my jaunty air disappeared in a puff of hairspray when instead of greeting me with *"Oh that looks nice. You remind me of someone."* Roo was in floods of tears. It didn't look as though I needed to worry about what to wear, because the formal evening for us was probably off.

He was bad enough for a tranquilizer, which I gave him straight away and tucked him up on the sofa.

Instantly resigned to a night in, we spent the afternoon snuggled up watching (of all things) the film, *'Casablanca'* on TV.

The formal evening should have started with a cocktail party, but there was no way Roo could handle that and Room Service was a mere 'phone call away – so we wouldn't starve. (Anyway, the way I looked after more than six weeks away and two cruises on, I could have gone on a 'Maxi-Lent Fast' - without food for forty weeks, let alone forty days and forty nights).

'Casablanca' was great – no matter how many times you see it, it's always great and it wasn't long before Roo was asleep – *again*. Despite the amazing amount of sleep he gets, he needs a positive mind for quality rest and I don't think he gets this.

His negative thoughts lead to negative activity (that's a mouthful). He shuts down, because he wants to be alone with his depressed mind and doesn't want to take part in anything that will stimulate him. The fatigue and physical symptoms such as stomach ache, muscle pain and headaches just add to the overall feelings of despair and on top of this, his liver is screaming at him. I know it must be hell for him, because it's hell for me just watching it all happen.

Leaving the sofa to Sleeping Beauty, I looked in the mirror at my hair. It was all lopsided, where I'd been laying and apart from the money I'd spent on having it done, I supposed it was fortunate that we were staying in. I poked it around a bit, but it didn't make much difference, but just then the 'Cracken' awoke and jumped to its feet. *"Look at the time"*, it said. *"We'd better hurry."*

"Where are we hurrying to?" I replied quizzically, with one finger still in my hair as if pointing to my ear.

"Well, the Formal Evening. Don't you want to go?"

Had I stood there much longer with my mouth open in disbelief, I might have caught an insect, so I closed it and bolted for the loo where I sat with the door locked.

Stupid, stupid woman. Yes, I am a stupid woman and I know I shouldn't let it get to me, but I still howled my eyes out and had to stay there until I'd calmed down.

When I finally came out, Roo knew nothing of my frustration, but did say, *"Your hair looks nice, but it's more puffed-up on one side."* It was times like these that I wished I was the type to come out with something clever, but it always comes too late for me to make an impact. 'Impact' was a good word though. *"I could impact you with the window right now."* I said under my breath.

Revitalised and raring to go, Roo sped through the preparation stage and was ready in a flash. He looked very posh in his black DJ – the style really suited him and he sat on the sofa with his legs crossed, revealing his shiny black shoes and his hands resting beside him on the sofa, as if he might suddenly get up and do a tap dance. Meanwhile, I attempted to work some sort of miracle on my hair with one hand and frantically go through the wardrobe with the other.

It had to be the black shantung blouse after all, but in spite of wearing my 'serious' knickers, with the elasticated midriff, it fitted like a second skin. It looked good once your eyes had reached my cleavage though. That was usually my saving grace – the décolletage – as the French say sounding much more romantic than 'cleavage', which could be what a lumberjack shouts when he's felling a tree.

With my black chiffon palazzo pants (BIG trousers), 'THE' necklace to dazzle them and my décolletage to admire, perhaps our fellow diners wouldn't notice the shantung straining at the seams and if I kept my head tilted on one side, my hair appeared almost normal. The dark pink-rimmed eyes would just have to look pink, but then there were no children aboard to frighten. My little howling escapade in the loo had delayed us long enough to have to forgo the cocktail party. I was relieved actually. What with my lopsided hair and eyes that were now turning blood red people might have thought I was a vampire and I had no wish to make small talk when I felt so drained, so we just went to dinner.

The lovely waiters were Romanian, so Roo would be able to practice his fourth language (after English, French and American) and the Maitre 'D being Italian was easy to talk to as well. All that was required was to add an 'O' on the end of every word and he understood everything I said.

With another sumptuous meal delivered and despatched, we staggered back to our suite just in time for me to get out of the shantung and take a deep breath before contracting double pneumonia. The 'serious' underwear came off and as I slid into my heavenly, freshly-laundered new pyjamas, ruffled my hair with both hands.

Bliss.

DAY FORTY-SEVEN:

"Easter Day"

Felt sick all night long. Not surprising with the amount of food I put away last night and the emotional bit hadn't helped either. (Not sure if I'd ever be able to wear the shantung blouse again).

We'd sailed away from Huahine during the night and now we were moored off Raratonga in the Cook Islands. It was Easter Day and the first time for years that I'd missed the service in our tiny village church. I could picture all the flower arrangements cleverly contrived by the local ladies and the lovely one which will be sitting above the altar. I knew it would be lovely, because someone else would have done it instead of me. I was useless at flowers.

We swallowed just enough solid food for Roo to take his med's and me my vit's then went down to the bottom of the ship to catch the boat over to Raratonga. We didn't intend to stay all day, as there was a multi-faith service planned for 4pm and I couldn't miss that. The boat headed for the 'port', which was really a glorified landing stage, but tying up to allow us to disembark was difficult for the crew as the swell of the ocean (they said) was around 8'. An indication of things to come, perhaps. Apparently, the last time the ship was moored in Raratonga, it broke an anchor, which shows you just how strong the currents are here.

Interesting things about Raratonga .... 31kms of island coast can be driven all the way round in forty-five minutes. The root vegetable Taro is grown for its edible corm. The name came from Rara ('down') and Tonga ('south') – perhaps from a sailor being heard to say that he was "going down south". Coconut palms and jungle-clad peaks are surrounded by a lagoon and skinny wild chickens are seen scooting around everywhere. People might have arrived on Raratonga 5,000 years ago, but nothing seems to have been written about it until the 16th century, when its beauty and what it had to offer was raved about. The most interesting piece of history was made when the 'Cumberland' stopped there in 1814 looking for sandalwood. There was no sandalwood, but there was a lot of trouble between the sailors and the Raratongan's – so much so, that the Captain's girlfriend was killed and eaten by the islanders! That's a real claim to fame!! For church services on Sundays, the men turn out in their best clothes and the ladies wear stiff 'rito' hats made from coconut fibres. When France attempted to take over Tahiti and the Society Islands in 1843, the Rartongans asked Britain to protect them. I'm not sure how they would have done this when there was no telephone, or email, but they got the message somehow and came to their aide.

Roo and I had a quick look around the 'port' and then wandered along the shoreline. God obviously grew Raratonga for couples hopelessly in love with the need to be terribly romantic, because we saw so many of these incurables laying on the beach sifting white sand between their fingers as they gazed into each others' eyes. With a backdrop so beautiful, heaven itself would be jealous. Of course, Roo and I weren't IN love now. We love each other, but that's different and doesn't require sand-sifting anymore.

In spite of the 8' swell, we were in good time for the service, which was to be held in the Panoramic Lounge on the top deck at the stern, giving an enchanting view of the island as the ship swung slowly around.

The Priest, a tanned, portly South American with white hair and scruffy beard to match, wore a full-length bleached white cassock with a rope belt slung round the portion of his body where his waist had once been. He was to conduct the service in both English and Spanish, hoping to cater for as many nationalities as possible, but the Russians, who spoke neither English nor Spanish would have to make do with just being there. I don't think the Priest was expecting many passengers to attend, but I counted 63 and then gave up, which meant that at least 15% of the whole ship wanted to celebrate Easter. That was pleasing.

As more people piled into the Panoramic Lounge, Roo became increasingly shaky and was heading for a panic attack, so moving to one side away from the majority of the group I made small talk about the incredible view, hoping to keep him there for as long as possible. Once the service started and his attention was captured he was less likely to disappear.

The Priest kicked off and although it was the oddest service I've ever attended, it was also quaint and somehow endearing in a funny sort of way. With so many people to minister to, the Priest soon ran out of wafers, which was a shame and I nearly offered to dash off to the kitchen for some substitute bread, but those who didn't receive a wafer, or drop of wine weren't upset and when we all sang 'Amazing Grace' in Spanish, English, Russian and goodness-knows-what, it was especially moving.

I could easily have written his sermon for him. It was on 'Depression', which the Priest understood first-hand, since he was also recovering from his own battle with the dreaded illness. Isn't it amazing how many people are affected by it and the assortment of people it targets?

I persuaded Roo to have a talk with him afterwards and while they were nattering, I started a conversation with two ladies from Arizona. We had a laugh about them taking our old London Bridge and the fact that they thought they were getting Tower Bridge. They said everyone was really puzzled when it arrived.

The Arizonians headed off to the bar to celebrate Easter in their own way and I found Roo sitting on a window seat alone looking out to sea in a forlorn sort of way. The Priest, as lovely as he was, hadn't been able to conjure up any divine intervention, but it had been good to swap notes with a fellow sufferer.

We returned to our suite with Roo in ponderous mood and not looking forward to the evening. The early-evening singer was the one who sounded like Barry Manilow and had a 7pm slot, so if we wanted to catch his performance, we'd need to get our skates on. But like a naughty schoolgirl with a dark secret, I wondered if it might do Roo some good to do something without me for a change and I hatched a cunning plan. At 6.50pm. – ten minutes before we should leave to get a decent seat, he found me in a conveniently dishevelled state and in a terrible quandary because none of my clothes fitted me.

I stomped around the bedroom, throwing everything onto the bed saying, *"Well, that's no good – and neither is this"* and by the time I'd emptied out the wardrobe, he'd had enough of hearing me moan.

Then very casually I said, *"Oh, you might as well go on ahead of me – just save me a seat"*, I could see that he was actually thinking about it and almost held my breath. He didn't look too horrified, but it was transparently obvious that he wasn't mad keen on the idea and it took a few more minutes of stomping to persuade him to go.

When he actually walked out of the door, I felt quite elated and saw this as some sort of achievement. Triumphantly, I joined him for the tail-end of the singing and was only a little disappointed when he said he'd never, ever go anywhere alone again and wished he hadn't done it, because he was terrified and thought he was going to be sick.

But done it, he had!

We wandered along to the foyer of the restaurant, to find that the catering staff had been more than busy creating an 'Easter Tableau'. A massive array of Easter-orientated ice sculptures, surrounded by bunnies and chickens carved from vegetables and melons, chocolate fountains and sorbet waterfalls. I'd honestly never seen anything like it before. These were very clever and artistic people – perhaps a little eccentric, but obviously ingenious and they can cook too. I can do a lot of things, which includes cooking, but carving a lesser-spotted Woodpecker from a courgette was not – *and never would be* - part of my repertoire.

Surprise, surprise, another gorgeous meal. A dozen Alaskan crab legs swept past my lips and Roo said his steak was magnificent, even though *I had* made him feel sick earlier and he wasn't allowed the liqueur sauce. He learnt more Romanian and was becoming quite popular with the Eastern Block staff, but this was one more occasion when I felt irritated that I had to cope with his madness in private with no witnesses.

Having to deal with what was really going on alone, I wasn't sure if I could contain all this in MY mind, without it sending ME round the twist. All quiet on the brain front tonight, though. Or was it that I was taking less tonic with my Gin and wasn't noticing as much?

Returning to base camp, we thought we'd listen to the radio for a change. Once we were in bed, Roo found a station playing something nice and I turned off the light to relax us even more. But the relaxed moment was short-lived, when we realised that we were listening to BBC Radio 2!

It was most peculiar to hear about the chaos on the M25 and the sorry Easter weather, when we were lying in bed floating around the South Pacific on the other side of the world.

DAY FORTY-EIGHT: "Bobbing Around"

That 8' swell had greatly increased throughout the night and the ship was rising up to meet the sky one second and returning abruptly to the sea the next, which made my tummy turn over in spite of the size of the ship. We'd been woken by flashes of lightning – even with the blackout blinds tightly closed and both felt we'd been to another all-night party we hadn't enjoyed. Polynesian Immigration Officers would be on board today and we had to report at 8.40am sharp, which we dutifully did, but it was after 9am by the time we reached the front of the queue. The Officer glanced at our passports and waved us on with a yawn. He must have been woken up too.

There was no land in sight and a few spots of rain were hitting the windows when we got back to the suite. Roo was down in the dumps again, worrying about the daftest of things – even about our Steward having a cold! Just to put the lid on the morning, I realised that I'd lost some of my vitamins, which must have fallen out of my bag in the New Zealand Customs Hall. *'Bugger'.* I said to myself. It would be the sniffer dog's fault if I started to shrivel up the way Urusla Andress did in that film *"**She**"*. I remember that scene terrified me when I was 12, but now with time marching on forty-something years later the thought of her wrinkled face terrifies me for a different reason.

I booked a table for dinner at the Steakhouse for a change to the main restaurant that had the formal eating time. Although there was a surcharge, it meant we could eat later putting less pressure on Roo to be somewhere 'on time'.

It was a 'Tropical night' tomorrow and passengers were encouraged to dress appropriately; whatever that meant. Roo had several suitable shirts to choose from including my favourite, which was Hawaiia'n and one I'd bought him on an earlier trip to Maui. Thinking it was cheap; I'd not noticed an additional '0' at the end of the numbers and nearly fainted when the figure was rung up on the till. At least he'd look good. But I wasn't sure what was expected of the ladies. No one in their right mind would want to see me in a grass skirt and I knew there were no coconut shells big enough on any continent to make me a suitable top for wearing in mixed company; but maybe I could find a garland of fresh flowers to plonk on my head at our next stop in Raitea.

Roo was asleep in the shade. It was a good job I was no longer the party animal I had been in my earlier years and knowing I shouldn't start thinking about that part of my life, turned my attention to the sea and sky. I had no idea what most of the birds were called, but it was easy to recognise an Albatross, what with them being so huge. Then I couldn't stop the Monty Python sketch popping into my head, where John Cleese has one for sale, instead of ice cream in the cinema and sat looking at the sky trying not to wake Roo with my chuckling.

I was slow at getting ready for dinner, because the sunset kept distracting me. It was more than beautiful and I couldn't think of the right word to fit the appearance of such splendour. Each time I peered out of the window, the colour had changed from deepest pink and then lilac, to the darkest red. It was a real 'enchanted evening', but instead of singing that song from 'South Pacific', hummed 'Bali Hai', which was where we would be going to meet the boys – well Kauai, anyway. The Hawaii'n island where the film was shot.

Off to the Steakhouse then. Roo was jittery to begin with, but slowly improved when he recognised the waiters from Sabatinis, which seemed to please both him and them and he was able to practice his Romanian again. Good food. (Thank God). Steak for Roo/Swordfish pour mois.

Arm-in-arm, like old-timers, Roo and I wandered around the ship without meeting a soul. (I told you we wouldn't see much of those Honeymooners). The clear, black sky shone with the usual million sparkly stars and the warm breeze brushed softly on our faces and the bare skin of our arms. For all we knew, or cared, everyone else could have been sucked off the ship and disappeared into thin air.

DAY FORTY-NINE:

"Gone Tropical"

Dawn.

Raiatea (pronounced 'rah-you-tay-uh').

This is the second largest island in the French Archipelago, lying midway between Tahiti (the biggest island) and Bora-Bora. It shares a lagoon with a smaller island called Tahaa, or Vanilla Island, where 80% of the vanilla in the region is grown. Raiatea means "faraway heaven" and "sky with soft light" and is the sacred religious centre of the area. Hardly anyone works, but the French-speaking people are able to live off the abundant sea life, so there's really no need for paid employment.

Roo was fine this morning, so we took advantage immediately, going ashore straight after breakfast and found that Raitea had a nice, clean port with some shops. After a wander, we found a bench to sit on where we watched yachts, catamarans and fishing boats coming and going and then miracle-of-miracles, on our way back to the ship, we came across a lady selling garlands of fresh flowers and one that fitted my head perfectly. I would look 'tropical' after all.

Back on board, Harry rang to tell us that he was going to have an increase in salary and Lukey also rang to say that he'd just skied down his last run in Whistler. All good news. Lukey admitted that the day before, he'd bungyjumped off a bridge into a 200' cavern and could tell me only now. He said he's screamed like a big girl and was only admitting it to us because it was all on camera. We'd look forward to seeing that soon, but I was just glad that he had survived. They were both excited about the imminent trip and seeing us again and we too, were **_longing_** – in the most longing-of-ways - for the meet-up in Hawaii.

The garland was comfortable and a perfect fit. The perfume of the orchids, plumeria and pikake was glorious and kept wafting around my head in waves of heavy scent. I'd decided to wear my turquoise trousers and matching top that had a white organza background, but I didn't look particularly 'tropical' until I donned the garland, which completely altered the whole effect. I felt like a Polynesian Princess, but with Roo wearing a floral Hawaiian shirt and cream trousers, we probably resembled a Columbian drug Baron and his floozy.

Even before reaching the restaurant, the air was filled with the intense smell of a thousand-thousand flowers and walking to our table, it looked as though everyone had made an effort to look 'tropical'. Some had gone a little bit over the top, but it was the spirit of the thing that was important. I did feel a bit sorry for the lady wearing the 'Carmen Miranda' fruit on her head though. She was having big trouble balancing the heavy conglomeration of real apples, bananas, oranges and you-name-it, while attempting to cut up her dinner. Someone should have done it for her.

The evening continued its' Tropical theme with entertainment from a marvellous troupe of Polynesian

261

dancers. The costumes were fantastic and the heavy drumming of the tribal music really got you going – enough for many of the passengers to join in. It was hilarious watching them attempt to match the lithe, 'pumped' dancers, but of course it's easy to laugh when you're not brave enough to participate yourself. An hour or so later, with the music finished and the dancers gone, it was all a bit of an anti-climax, when back in our suite we listened to Radio 2 again. We were instantly transported to England and in spite of our exotic location, the familiar chatter, travel news and weather reports made us feel a bit homesick.

Loathe to remove the lovely garland, which still looked beautiful and smelt divine, I wanted to leave it on my head for as long as possible. I took my makeup off around it, brushed my teeth standing bolt upright so it wouldn't slide off and carefully pulled on my pyjamas bottoms still wearing it. Roo laughed at me, because I didn't take it off until my head was an inch from the pillow.

But it wasn't often I felt like a Princess.

DAY FIFTY: "Bora Bora"

The ship had left Raiatea as the sun rose and sailed just twenty, or so miles to Bora Bora an island in the Leeward group of the Society Islands of French Polynesia famous for its unbelieveable beauty and romaticism. This was destined to be one of the highlights of our trip, for more ways than one.

Breakfast was delivered early to make us get out of bed so we wouldn't miss the arrival, but fresh fruit, crab quiche, smoked salmon, cream cheese, bagels and pastries was a bit much as 7.30am.

If he was feeling up to it, Roo was booked to scuba dive at 1.30pm., so he didn't eat much anyway, but not wanting to waste the quiche it was a good job I wasn't joining him, as I may never have surfaced again. Roo nibbled a bagel and I asked him if he thought it would be sensible to go scuba diving. *"Of course"*, he replied stuffing the remainder of the bagel into his mouth in one go.

The sun was really scorching by 8am, but the Pacific was as calm as mill pond as we slowly, slowly, drifted into the lagoon surrounding the island. In spite of our gentle approach, the ship still created a pressure wave at the bow and even though we were at the stern, it would have been difficult to miss the dozens of dolphins really enjoying themselves surfing the wave. But neither of us was prepared for what we were going to see next.

The first thing that hit us on the approach to Bora Bora was the twin peaks of Mount Otemanu and Mount Pahia, two extinct volcanoes sitting right in the middle of an unreal lagoon. What your eyes were seeing was so unbelievably beautiful, I could only liken it to one of those paintings in the Galleries you see illuminated by turquoise neon lights. But this wasn't manmade.

The truth is, the beauty of it all is so crazy it's hard to know where to look next and when the dolphins at the bow were joined by two giant Manta Rays literally flying through the clear water, it was such a joy to see that it made me almost tearful and I held out my hands to try to touch them.

KONG
BLONDE

(Interrupting the calm and bringing us back to the real world, Harry sent a text to say that he was on his way to the Marriott at Heathrow, which was a good start to his journey, until I remembered he should have been on his way to the Sheraton. I was sure the Marriott would redirect him, so returned my mind and eyes to the wonders of Bora Bora). Known as the centre of the Romantic Universe, it was originally called Pora Pora ("first born"), but when our friend Captain Cook arrived, he mistook the 'P' for a 'B', which was daft really, when the letter 'B' doesn't even exist in the Tahitian language. Then nothing much historically happened here, until the Japanese attacked Pearl Harbour in Hawaii in 1941 and the island became a military supply base. Fortunately, there was never any combat to destroy the beauty and majesty of it all. The servicemen posted here must have thought they'd died and gone to heaven.

With the sheer black rock of the volcanoes covered in a giant smoke-ring of cloud, I wouldn't have been surprised to see King Kong appear any minute, holding a blonde in one hand and shaking the other at us in a defiant fist. But instead, inching our way further and further into the lagoon, we passed a tall ship at anchor on one side where the crew struggled to take down the billowing sails and several locals in outrigger canoes ploughed through the water to meet us on the other. It was if we'd gone back in time and were coming in on 'The Bounty'. We felt honoured to be allowed to visit such a magical place just as we had in New Zealand. Sailing closer and closer to the edge of the lagoon, 'over-water' Bures, with their distinctive thatched roofs dotted around the many secluded coves began to appear. It was easy to see why this was a popular honeymoon destination. Pure solitude within paradise and the added bonus of having the ocean beneath your feet. I wouldn't be surprised if Bora Bora had been the original Garden of Eden.

We tore ourselves away from the dolphins to go ashore as soon as the ship dropped anchor. Even before reaching dry land, the smell of Copra, Ginger and oranges hit us and the heavy scent of Hibiscus was overwhelming. It was more than handy that the ship's tender had dropped us off right beside the jetty where the Scuba School met and when another couple joined Roo for his dive, I slipped away, before he had time to change his mind; although he looked at me alarmingly as I left.

The few shops were all full of wonderful things, but I found it difficult to concentrate. All I kept thinking about was Roo under the water and how he was handling the whole thing. I went back to the ship alone, having bought a couple of shot glasses, the usual amount of postcards with stamps and an engraved mother of pearl shell. I was pleased with myself, because I'd managed to purchase the whole lot without speaking a word of English on this French-speaking Island, but wasn't pleased with myself for agreeing that Roo should go diving. He wasn't a suitable candidate anyway, what with his panic-attacks and they had said so in the blurb before the part where you signed the disclaimer. While he signed it, I remember him asking me if I'd ever seen him have a panic attack under water and insisted that this didn't apply to him. You can imagine what my reply was.

I sat down in our suite to write the cards but still couldn't concentrate and looked at my watch every five minutes. Whose stupid idea was this scuba diving anyway? I should have either gone with him, or not let him go at all. It was bad enough that we were going 100` down in a submarine tomorrow.

Two hours went by with me in sheer agony and I was close to the wringing-hands stage when he popped through the door unscathed. He'd had a wonderful time and was proud of himself once again. I was so relieved I could have passed out on the floor.

He was totally exhausted though, looked awful and was unable to do anything for the rest of the day, but it didn't matter. We'd gone up another notch in the plan of things. We were heading in the right direction and at least we knew that he didn't experience panic attacks under water, which he assured me, would be very helpful in the future.

We spent that evening in a very gentle way. After dinner, we sat in the piano bar listening to the ivories being tinkled, until 9.30pm and then went to bed feeling very satisfied. The display of courage and determination Roo had shown on day fifty of our trip had made me realise that the old Roo was in there somewhere. We just had to get him out more often.

DAY FIFTY-ONE:

"An Underwater Experience"

Rang mum – weather in England still cold, wet and windy.

We had an invitation to visit the Bridge - just as we had on the Sapphire, which we accepted. The Bridge was tiny in comparison and more like you would imagine a Bridge to be, with a proper steering wheel and maps and everything. I really preferred it to the more up-to-date version, although there were still loads of flashy-lighty things and we spent nearly an hour on the Bridge chatting to the lovely 2nd Officer from Norwich, who looked about twelve.

Then it was time to go ashore for the submarine descent, which I have to admit I was more than apprehensive about. Roo was full of bravado after his epic dive yesterday and I couldn't show any sign of weakness with him doing so well, so without emotion made ready for the trip.

What DOES one wear in a submarine though?

Once ashore, with me in white three-quarter length pants and stripey tee shirt (very nautical, I thought), Roo and I were joined by two large Argentinians, who didn't speak a word of English and a slip-of-a-chap, who piled the four of us into a speedboat. I really hoped he wouldn't be driving the submarine too, as he looked so young, but then so had the lovely Officer on the 'Tahitian' and he was in charge of a liner!

The speedboat did just that – sped off between a gap in the reef, passing the turquoise ring of water and the thousands of clumps of oysters happily growing there in their shells blissfully unaware that one day, having given up their precious treasure, they would be sliding down an oesophagus to be digested by gastric juices, without even having been properly tasted. With that image conjured up in your mind, I will quickly return you to the magnificence of Bora Bora.

Bouncing into deeper water, we slowed down. In the distance, a yellow dot appeared and my tummy started to do somersaults. But by the time the dot had grown into the large round dome of the yellow submarine, my insides were doing acrobats good enough for the Olympics. *Why do I plan these things? It always looks so good on the Internet and I'm never scared when I hit the 'purchase' key.*

Once the young chap had tied the speedboat to this nautical vessel, the French pilot/driver, or whatever he was called greeted us as a group and then being French, offered his hand to me first to pull me across the water and onto the sub. Miraculously, I managed this in one very wide step hoping that the gap wouldn't widen as I stepped. So far … so good. But standing safely on the body of the sub he had to prise his fingers from my grip, which was rather embarrassing although perhaps not the first time he'd done it. (Surely I wasn't the only nervous passenger he'd encountered).

With the pilot helping the others aboard, it gave me a chance to look more closely at the thing we'd be encased in without any proper air for the next hour and a half. The sub didn't look very big close-up, but then, of course, most of it was under water and it was really only the tiny hatch at the top you could see. The hatch door lay open and there was a wooden ladder sticking out of it. 'hatch/door' – 'ladder'. 'hatch/door' – 'ladder. I repeated this over and over again in my mind. I had done boats and planes, but never had it been necessary to climb down such a small ladder, through such a small hole – I mean, 'hatch'. It just hadn't occurred to me. Why hadn't I thought about getting into the ruddy thing? Just as I was about to dive into the water and head for the hills, the pilot began to explain the entry procedure. The five of us stood together precariously perched at one end of the sub, as our Jacques Cousteau told us that there were sixteen rungs on the ladder for the completely vertical descent into the capsule. As he finished speaking, he realised that the Argies hadn't understood a word he said, so went into paroxysms of amusing explanations by hand, until the Argies nodded and seemed to be 'au fait' with what he was saying.

Hang on though. Capsule? What capsule? I thought we were going to be in a submarine lounging on sofas watching the ocean go by. You know – like in the series,

'*Voyage to the Bottom of the Sea*'. No one said anything about a 'Capsule' and as if that wasn't bad enough, the size of the door - I mean hatch dawned on me.

The hatch was round. Without a tape measure I couldn't be sure, but mentally I thought the size was comparable with my rump. This might be the challenge to end all challenges and the seaplane episodes entered my mind in glorious technicolour along with the headlines .... *"Brit Winched from Sub – Stuck Fast, said Pilot"* and *"Big Bottoms are Best"*, say Argies.

This could be my 'Waterloo', I thought.

Continuing in perfect gentlemanly-French of course, I was offered first go at the ladder. Hoping my shaking body was not visible to the naked eye I accepted the hand to assist my descent and slid through the hatch by the skin of my bottom, rather than the greatest of ease. I counted every rung and was so grateful when I reached number sixteen.

Being the first at the bottom of the ladder, I stood there for a minute and looked around realising that this was nothing like the 'Seaview'. Rather than a futuristic nuclear submarine, it was quite simply a 9" thick, 8`x 6` Perspex bubble.

It was very quiet, apart from bubbling noises similar to those you hear standing next to a fish tank and the sound of slopping water in a swimming pool and I was glad when Roo joined me to break the silence but he too, looked around and took a deep breath without saying a word. When the two Argentinians climbed down, they weren't able to stand upright and we huddled together in the middle of the bubble like four lemons, until Captain Nemo came down the ladder without using any of the rungs. *"What a show-off"*, I thought.

Six stools were positioned around three quarters of the bubble. The other quarter was taken up with a seat for Captain Nemo, surrounded by those flashy-lighty things I just love to hate, numerous oxygen cylinders and – *thank God* - a very obvious First Aid Kit. Just in case we'd need a plaster 100` under the water.

Had there been passengers on each of the stools, I would have found it rather claustrophobic, but with just four of us - even though the Argies were so big, it was comfortable.

I told myself that it was very reassuring when the pilot showed us which knobs to turn to effect a hasty ascent should he be incapacitated, but the only thing I could visualise during the talk was the shower on the Sapphire.

Then, with the sound of hydraulics and water under pressure, we began our descent. I clung to my stool to stop me from heading back up the ladder to the world above and its fresh air. But everyone else was behaving in such a relaxed manner, as if it was perfectly normal to be deprived of life on earth sinking to the bottom of the ocean in a Perspex bubble. I couldn't take my eyes off the hatch and the water flowing on top of it and the inevitable change in the colour, as we sank deeper and deeper away from the light of the sky, with only the glow of one low volt red bulb to comfort me.

100`doesn't sound like much when you say it quickly and I suppose that a few feet – even a few inches under water would be pretty much the same drowning-wise, so resigning myself to whatever fate had in store for me, I tried to relax like everyone else. Sinking deeper and deeper, I was startled when the pilot turned on the external lights and the reef came up to meet us, appearing in a blaze of glorious colour.

Drawn to the amazing sight outside the bubble, I stopped thinking about myself, fascinated by what I was seeing. Reaching the very bottom, the sub followed the reef and headed further out to sea. The pilot constantly pointed out different fish and gave the names of the coral living on the healthy ocean floor.

Eels – or what looked like eels, popped in and out of the reef and when a turtle appeared, we followed her graceful flight through the clear water. We saw a lot of sharks - obviously annoyed at the intrusion, they turned to have a look at us as we approached and I was glad the window was 9" thick, when a few of them actually bumped the sub with their noses. We must have looked really strange to them on the other side of the Perspex. Perhaps they thought we were the ones on show – and I suppose we were really. We were the trespassers in their world.

The sub isn't allowed to dive at night, but if it was you would be able to see the Octopusses and the bigger sharks who feed on them. I didn't want to see bigger ones – the ones outside were bigger than me as it was.

By the time the dive was over, I was so comfortable under water, I could have stayed down for much longer. Considering I was so scared at first and terrified that I'd be banging on the hatch to be let out, I would definitely go again. The four of us had loved it. The Argies had jabbered away in Argentinian, but amazement was the same in any language.

We bubbled our way to the surface and the light grew brighter through the hatch, until the water had disappeared above us completely. All that was left was to say goodbye to the deep and give the sharks some peace and quiet. We let the Argies climb the ladder first and Roo brought up the rear – well, my rear actually, since he had to give it a shove at the ninth rung for a bit of momentum.

The return journey to shore was in a skiff this time, which was even quicker than the speedboat. The Argies went their own way, but Roo and I needed some liquid refreshment after all the excitement. We'd heard that the place to go was 'Bloody Mary's'- a bar named after the matriarch who presided over the going's-on in the island of Bali Hai, in the original film 'South Pacific'.

There was a truck serving as a local bus and we caught this to the bar on the other side of the bay, passing an arc of beach with pure white sand. 'Bloody Mary's' was a huge bure of a hut. At the entrance

was a board with dozens of names of the famous and infamous people who had visited over the years, such as Raquel Welch, Rod Stewart, Sting, Ronald Reagan and some I'd never heard of – but someone must have thought they were famous. Built on sand, with no hard floors anywhere, the bar and restaurant was in WWII style, with wooden stools, round tables and heaps of nostalgia.

After a drink and a burger, we both used the loos. These were just as novel as the rest of the place with sand floors too. Bamboo screens were the only things dividing the ladies from the gents, but they still allowed discrete use of the facilities. The hand basin was really unusual. It was a black rock carved into the shape of one of the Easter Island Heads - without taps, but when you were ready for the water, pulling on a dangling handle allowed a trickle to run through the rock producing a freezing cold waterfall.

Reluctantly, it was time to leave Bora Bora and we caught the tender back to the ship, (a treat in itself). It was another formal night and after a shower to remove all the sand I'd brought back from 'Bloody Mary's', I laid out Roo's DJ., checked my long, sparkly dress that I bought on e-Bay for £32 and gave my tiny little tiara (that wasn't £32 on e-Bay) a rub over. We'd certainly look formal tonight. Ready to go, with Roo looking quite splendid and an extremely sparkly me, off we went to join the other diners who had made the effort to dress up. But reaching the restaurant, Roo's mood suddenly plummeted. He hardly said a word the whole evening and any attempt to start a conversation over dinner was futile.

After we'd eaten, I felt like going to the bar on my own, but I knew I'd never be able to get up on the ruddy stool, so we just went back to our suite together. It was a case of "all dressed up and nowhere to go" and I wanted to scream when Roo sat on the sofa and switched on the TV. There he sat in his DJ and shiny shoes and I stood behind him sparkling like a firework in more than appearance. It was times like this I wished I had something heavy in my hand. Just in the nick of time before I chucked him and the TV overboard, Harry rang to say that he'd arrived in San Francisco safely.

I was instantly cheered up and as if God thought I deserved yet another treat, Lukey rang straight after. He'd bungey-jumped twice without mishap and was on HIS way to San Francisco. The two of them would be together there for a day and a half and I tried not to worry about what they might get up to Downtown. At least our American friends Dean and Marje would be able to rescue them, if necessary – but I hoped it wouldn't be.

After their calls, I didn't mind getting out of my evening dress and started packing bits and pieces into our suitcases ignoring Roo's doldrums.

He was still watching TV when I went to bed.

DAY FIFTY-TWO:
"Cruising Complete"

I half expected to see Roo still sitting in front of the television this morning, but he had obviously gone to bed and was now awake. He was still miserable though and didn't know why. When breakfast was delivered I ate alone. He was still in bed, sighing and 'tutting' when I'd finished, so I went and sat beside him, attempting to be jolly. But I can always tell when this ploy isn't going to help and rather than continue with my usual counselling session, turned on some music to give us something else to hear other than his sighs and 'tuts'.

The ship slowly came to a stop and the usual banging around to secure a mooring could be heard outside and I went out on deck to see where we were. This was our last port of call and I was especially interested, because it was used as Bali Hai in the second 'South Pacific' film.

As I mentioned before, the real Bali Hai is on the Hawaiian Island of Kaua'i, but for some reason, this island was deemed more suitable to be the island holding enough mystical power for the film.

From our deck all I could see at first was ocean but once again, the ship was swinging around on its anchor and as it turned, Moorea came into view. It's like one of those places you visit in a dream. Dramatic, tall peaks surrounded by beaches of black sand on one side and white on the other, sit on this triangular island paradise surrounded by a teal green lagoon. A perfect finale to our cruising.

Roo was still miserable, but I dragged him ashore anyway, just so we could say we set foot on the awe-strikingly beautiful island of Moorea. We were back on the ship an hour later, with Roo on the sofa doing his impression of a Victorian lady overcome by 'the vapours'. *(Now I'm being horrible – but honestly, sometimes I can't help it)*. I was quite happy to sit out on our deck, perhaps for the last time and breathe in every last ounce the island had to offer. I stayed there until we left for the short sail back to Tahiti and Moorea was a mere blob in the distance. This meant that I would have to hurry the packing if I didn't want to do it after dinner. Roo was still prostrate on the sofa and when I mentioned the need to pack before our last meal on the ship, he said he didn't want to eat. *"That's okay"*, I replied jauntily and with enthusiasm. *"I'll go alone"*.

An hour later, Roo was ready to go. Would I have gone alone? No, of course not. I would have ordered Room Service, wouldn't I?

Our delightful waiters Catalin and Simona deserved a good tip and after the inevitable photographs, goodbyes and sly envelope handovers we left them and the restaurant, just as we slid into the dock at Papeete the end of the line for us and exactly where we had begun. I wanted to check in on line for our flight to Hawaii at half-past midnight, because it was important not to allow any hiccups with getting there and our subsequent meet up with the boys. We waited on our deck in the darkness watching busy Papeete until the time came.

Roo seemed a bit better, but my concern was more for the time we actually left the security of the ship. We'd be in limbo for twelve hours after disembarking, as our flight wasn't until much later. However, I'd booked a Day Room at the same Sheraton Hotel we'd stayed at on our arrival, so at least we'd be in a familiar place.

I had no idea I would be so sorry to say goodbye to cruising. I had enjoyed it so much and would do it again. With only a Mediterranean cruise to compare it to, I would say that these two ships couldn't go anywhere near a comparison. Of course, you get what you pay for, but even if we'd only been able to afford an inside cabin, it would still have been marvellous. The only difference was having the luxury of space allowing me to get away from Roo when I needed to, which was probably fortunate. At least I wasn't leaving the ship in handcuffs accused of murder.

Roo had been dozing, but just before 12.30am, I dragged him along to the business office and checked in with Hawaiian Airlines. It didn't take long and we were both tucked up in bed by 1am.

DAY FIFTY-THREE:

"The Sheraton again"

Early breakfast and off the ship.

Finding a cab amongst the melee of Papeete wasn't difficult, in spite of the traffic honking at our driver while he threw our cases unceremoniously into the boot. Roo looked very concerned and kept his gaze on the ship until it was completely out of sight. Feeling his apprehension, I was relieved the driver flew along the road at top speed, until we screeched to a halt at the hotel.

"Oh, yes. Here we are again." Roo said wearily. Repeating the same checking-in procedure as before, we were shown to a ground floor room only a few yards from the beach – not a bad place to relax for the next twelve hours. The flight to Honolulu and then on to Maui would be tiring, even with decent seats, so we could do with all the rest we could get. We sat quietly outside on the terrace watching the sun set behind Moorea igniting the peaks in a blaze of reds and orange. I asked Roo what he would remember most about cruising. *"It's all been lovely"*, he said softly, *"I just wish I hadn't felt so ill."* He was close to tears, but I wasn't going to let that happen now and dragged him from his chair. *"Have a nice long shower"*, I suggested.

While he was gone, I wondered what was coming next. I hoped he would improve once we had the boys in our grasp, otherwise they might wish they'd never come. That would be disastrous.

DAY FIFTY-FOUR:

"The Sandwich Islands"

(-10hrs GMT)

It was good to board the aircraft taking us to Hawaii, because the Terminal at Papeete lacks any sort of comfort, let alone a nice Lounge. The cabin lights were dimmed to suit the time of day and I was almost halfway there already listening to the sound of the ukulele playing in the background like lift music and watching the images of palms swaying in the breeze on the screen in front of me. It was a soporific moment and I could have drifted off, had I not been disturbed by Roo snoring loudly. Each time I elbowed him he stopped, only to start up again two minutes later. We played this game at regular intervals for what seemed like an eternity.

Witnessing the sunrise from an aeroplane is somehow always better than the picture you see from the ground. The stars had stopped twinkling and seemed to be replaced one-by-one by the light of a new day. Roo had slept around three hours, but I hadn't closed my eyes once and felt really tired. I perked up as soon as I spotted the first sign of land though; a feat in itself, when you remember that Hawaii is three thousand miles from the mainland. I was glad we didn't miss it and fly right past, but then I suppose modern aircraft use more than a compass these days.

The island of O'ahu is about the same size as Maui and to land at Honolulu Airport means passing Pearl Harbour. It's still a major US Naval Station, even with the remains of the Arizona – still leaking oil all these years later sitting just below the water where it was sunk by the Japanese on December 7th, 1941. This and the other submerged ships that were attacked on 'the day of infamy' are covered by shrines honouring the men killed and the land memorial that America built to commemorate the significant event is visited by millions each year - including the Japanese. Some throw flowers, or leis into the water, which is just what we did with the boys on our first trip. It's a very sad place.

Having visited Hawaii several times before, it's so familiar to us that we always feel very at home and despite muzzy heads, we both felt comfortable with our surroundings the moment we stepped off the plane and felt the warm breeze. Honolulu even in the early morning was already 72 degrees.

Immigration and Customs were no problem – I played the dumb blonde (they hate that) and we were through in a matter of minutes, which was a good thing, as the next flight to Kaua'i was leaving in less than an hour. A bit like getting on and off a bus, we hadn't time to get comfortable and our seats hadn't even warmed up before we were out of them, finding ourselves on the tarmac again twenty minutes later.

The State of Hawaii is actually a string of eight islands – *the Big Island* … *Maui* – the Valley Isle … *Kaho'olawe* – the Target Isle (used as a bombing range by the US Military, from WWII until 1990 and now only used for

Native Hawaiian culture and spiritual purposes) ... *Lana'i* – the Pineapple Isle (for obvious reasons) ... *Moloka'i* – the Friendly Isle ... *O'ahu* – the Gathering Isle ... *Kaua'i* – the Garden Isle and *Ni'ihau* – the Forbidden Isle (this is the smallest of the inhabited islands, privately-owned by the Robinson Family ((yes, really)) and off-limits for anyone unrelated giving it the name, although a small number of visits can be arranged if you know the right people. The islands became the 50th State in the US in 1959.

So I bet you can't guess who landed here in 1778. Now think hard. Yes, well done! It WAS our friend Captain Cook. He called them the Sandwich Islands after the first Lord of the Admiralty, an Earl of the family of the Sandwich's, John Montagu who invented the buttered toast, which has been called a sandwich to this very day. Of course, the Hawaiian Islands bear no resemblance to a sandwich, but in many nautical charts, they are still referred to as The Sandwich Islands.

You'll be pleased to hear that I won't be mentioning poor old Captain Cook again, because he finally met his end when the Hawaiians stabbed him to death, although I can't believe the story that they ate him afterwards; they're such nice people.

At the car hire office, we collected a Chevrolet and wound our way round the west coast of Kaua'i, passing the dreamiest of views. It's a Director's Paradise. Films made here include 'Jurassic Park', 'Raiders of the Lost Ark' and of course, good old 'South Pacific. You can see why. The dramatic terrain is able to provide the backdrop for all manner of eras and subjects. Taro fields resembling rice paddies stretch far into the distance and behind them, dense jungle with Cheese Plants growing up around trees as Ivy does in England. Red Jungle Fowl (a Tropical cousin of the Pheasant, but looks more like a cockerel) roam freely – on the roads, in the jungle, up the trees and even on the beach. Finding the resort housing the apartment was easy, as it was just off the main highway in an outrageously fantastic position right opposite Bali Hai with the curve of Hanalei Bay in between. I started singing *'the song'* again and actually made Roo laugh. He'd been 'okayish', and was hungry, so we literally dropped the suitcases and went back to the car to look for a restaurant.

We found a candlelit table on an open-air terrace surrounded by giant Cheese Plants curling round forty foot trees with gracefully twisted limbs and lush, fern-like leaves. It was a romantic setting with the usual ukulele and soft singing to accompany it drifting on the breeze. But instead of holding hands across the table and looking into each others' eyes dreamily, we messily ate the coconut shrimp with our fingers, which was very yummy.

Desperate for sleep, we dragged our PJ's and toothbrushes from the cases and sank into the gorgeous king size beds. The last thing I saw before closing my eyes was the blackness of the sky and the sparkly things I adored. But I was too tired to star-hop tonight.

DAY FIFTY-FIVE: "The Boys Arrive"

Roo woke several times during the night and inevitably woke me too. He was anxious about getting to the airport to collect the boys and the excitement I'd felt yesterday was melting into concern too. I could imagine them on the plane together coming in from San Francisco and looked at my watch to visualise what they would be doing at that moment.

They would be having their breakfast – enjoying everything the cabin crew offered them and then later, as they swept past Pearl, could see them pointing at the enormous US Air Force C5 Galaxy aircraft sitting on the ground in Honolulu.

I brought myself back from the daydream and cooked a few boiled eggs, which we ate on the balcony. The view was breathtaking and the sound of surf crashing on the sand made us want to be there, so after clearing breakfast away we drove to the Bali Hai beach where most of 'South Pacific' was filmed, although some of it was shot in Ibiza for some reason. Still as beautiful as it had been in the movie, I tried to lighten the mood a bit, by doing my impersonation of Mitzi Gaynor, skipping along the beach (albeit like Hop-along-Cassidy) 'washing that man out of her hair'. It didn't work. Roo couldn't even manage a smile, until I suggested we take a slow drive to the airport to collect the boys and he instantly came to attention.

The slow drive turned into a mad dash though, when we were caught up behind a tractor on the single lane carriageway and my vision of waiting for them to come through the door at Arrivals like you see on the telly disappeared as the minutes flew past. By the time we pulled up outside the Terminal they were already there, which was disappointing, but there they stood in the sunshine wearing the flower leis around their necks that they'd been given in Honolulu. They both looked terrific, in spite of such a long day. Lukey had lost some weight, but had grown a couple of inches at least and Harry had put on a few pounds (which I didn't mention). I had trouble flinging my arms around them both at the same time, but managed to kiss them a million times anyway, much to the amusement of the other people waiting to be collected. Roo tried hard to be the big macho-father figure, but kissed them too and they didn't seem to mind. On the way back to the apartment we talked and talked and while we laughed at the funny stories they were telling, I sent a huge thank you up to heaven for bringing them safely to us. They hardly noticed the views and vistas we were passing, but thought the apartment was 'awesome' and stayed out on the balcony for some time marvelling at the location and close proximity to the 'Bali Hai' I'd so often mentioned at home. I left them on the balcony with Roo while I cooked dinner, humming to myself in contentment and with a permanent smile on my face.

They weren't really hungry, but still ate as though they were and then thought they'd have a lie down. Ten minutes later they were both sound asleep flat on their faces. I dreaded to think what was going on in their digestive systems with stomachs full of chicken and mashed potato, but thought it probably wouldn't hurt for once and left them where they were.

Roo and I were drained too. He'd had a moody day, but without serious trauma and the satisfaction of having the boys with us was enough to make me happily go off to bed looking forward to tomorrow. My prayers were not only full of gratitude. I also asked for the strength to cope with Roo successfully without the boys detecting it. Whether I would be granted this was one thing. Whether it would last for the remaining twenty-one days if it was, was another.

DAY FIFTY-SIX: "Sharks"

Torrential rain during the night had created a 300´ waterfall dropping from the dormant volcano opposite. The amount of falling water was tremendous and a marvellous sight.

It was wonderful to be together again. I cooked us all a huge breakfast and served it on the balcony finding it difficult not to fuss over the boys. I would have spoon-fed them if they'd have let me, but quickly told myself off for thinking something so stupid. With them sitting opposite, it gave me a chance to study these lovely people. Lukey had changed somehow, but Harry was his usual self – jabbering away nineteen-to-the-dozen. Yes, I know I'm biased, but they really are super blokes.

After we'd devoured the fry-up, I rang mum and passed the 'phone around so everyone could speak to her. She was delighted to hear our voices and thankful that we had the boys with us at last. I could see Roo was trying to think hard and concentrate so he would behave like a normal human being, but to see the struggle on his face was pitiful. It was a relief when I heard Harry suggest the three of them went snorkelling. Roo could hardly contain his excitement, obviously elated at the thought of being included in their activities. I had a difficult job to make them wait a bit longer after eating and they wandered about clock-watching in their swim shorts and slapping on sunscreen.

After tidying up, I put some washing on. It would be a doddle to write a book called 'Washing Machines of the World' having used so many different types in various parts of the globe over the years, but I wasn't sure who would find it useful. Then I constructed an enormous chicken baguette and cut it into an unequal three – the biggest portion destined for Lukey. I would be content with some fruit. Roo called the concierge for a buggy to drive me down to the beach as it was a very steep and awkward path to get there and I waited alone as the three of them flew off to the surf.

The buggy driver was a gorgeous young tanned guy, who helped me into the seat and strapped me in, as if I were his Granny. I smiled sweetly, until I realised that I WAS old enough to be his Granny! It was a good thing I was strapped in, because the path was almost vertical in places, but the driver had done it all a million times before and avoided the big bumps as he came across them, delivering me to the sand in one piece and with the baguettes intact. I thanked him and said I'd 'catch him later' (for a tip) and he replied, *"Sure thing, Ma'am."*

The beach wasn't busy. Just a few couples and a family, or two had spread themselves around and I could easily see where the boys had left their towels, so taking my sandals off wandered across to the spot. Shielding my eyes from the sun and looking out to sea, I could see that the men in my life were already in the water. It was difficult to distinguish who was who, but I imagined that the one splashing furiously and going round in circles was Roo. The other two, side-by-side swimming in an orderly, splashless-fashion had to be Harry and Lukey.

Lowering myself onto the sand as gracefully as I could, I sat watching for sharks (six had been seen on Sunday). I wasn't sure what I would do if I saw one and panicked a bit when I realised that my three were the only ones in the water. Did the others know something? But looking around, if the couples weren't kissing, they were either feeding toddlers, or sleeping, so perhaps it was alright after all. However, I continued on 'shark watch' until I counted three pairs of legs wading through the water and walking up the beach with all the right number of limbs to where I was sitting.

While they dried-off, a local chappee wandered up and asked if the boys would like to sail in their boat 'for a good price'. Little did I know at the time, that the chap and his companion lived in a shack somewhere up the mountain and needed money to pay their rent. Being the adventurers the boys are, they were keen to go and I let Roo do the bargaining, so it wasn't until they'd left the shore and I could actually see the craft that I became alarmed. The 'boat' was hardly a boat at all, but a traditional Hawaiian skiff with a flat bottom. It looked as though it was made out of an advertising board or something similar, with an 'arm' hewn from a tree branch on one side to keep it upright in the water, a net strung from one side to the other for seating and one flimsy sail.

I scrambled up from the sand to get a better look as

'BOAT?'

my baby boys waved their arms at me in long slow sweeps and I watched them head out towards a gap in the reef where the shimmering blue sea turned into big white water. The boat suddenly disappeared from view amongst the surf and all I could see was the top of the sail where it had dipped in between the waves. It reappeared seconds later and repeated this process until they were over the reef and then turning right, the wind caught the poor excuse for a sail and they were out of sight. Just then Roo returned. *"How could you let them go out on that thing?"* I said loudly. *"Oh, it's alright, they know what they're doing."* He replied sarcastically. *"And the Shark Reports?"* I asked. It was only a second, or two later that Roo stood beside me shielding his eyes from the sun, scouring the ocean for our offspring.

The two chaps sailing the thing obviously knew what they were doing, but it was one of the longest hours of my life and boy, was I happy watching them crunch their way through the chicken baguettes back on the beach. They were full of the short trip out on the ocean in nothing much more than a flimsy raft and couldn't understand my terror. They'd seen lots of flying fish, but no sharks!

We left the beach in the late afternoon and after showering, waited on the balcony wearing nothing more than towels to see the sun set behind Bali Hai. It had been an eventful day, which thankfully had ended without mishap and one where Roo had things to think about other than himself.

It was dark by the time we left the apartment and I suggested we take the boys to the restaurant with the good coconut shrimp. We had to wait a bit for a table outside on the terrace, but it was worth the wait. The breeze was still warm and a brief shower while we were eating gave the air a sweet-smelling aroma.

There was much heated discussion on the next table and we discovered that Aloha Airlines had gone into liquidation. We were lucky, as we always flew with Hawaiian Airlines, but it didn't stop us feeling sorry for everyone involved.

We'd spent a wonderful day together and I think I was still sending 'Thank You's' up to heaven when I lost consciousness.

DAY FIFTY-SEVEN: "Last Day In Kaua'i"

I'd spent ages trying to get through to Hawaiian Airlines on the telephone to check in for our flight the next day because the line was constantly engaged; obviously taken up by all those poor souls with Aloha tickets making frantic attempts to change their plans. We would have to keep our fingers crossed that all was well with ours'.

Roo rang his dad and the boys had a few words with him too and then someone suggested kayaking up the Hanalei River to the wildlife Sanctuary.

Now we all know that kayaks are not built for the likes of me, so it was pretty obvious that I was not included in the scheme of things, but I didn't mind at all and they left me in the apartment to catch up with the packing and writing even more postcards after I'd loaded them up with sunscreen and insect repellent.

They were gone such a long time, I was able to make sure my diary was up to date too until they walked through the door in very good spirits, including Roo. One of them had to have fallen in and it was Harry, whose Kayak had been pushed over into the water by his dear brother. Bless him. So then all I could think about was Leptospirosis – also known as Weil's Disease, which is spread by water rats and supposing there were rats even in Hawaii, marched Harry off to the shower to remove all traces of the river.

Scrubbed, de-loused and smelling a lot sweeter, Harry and Lukey went off for their usual foray. I supposed they were woman-hunting. It's what they're supposed to do, I supposed. I knew I shouldn't worry, but you don't know where these girls have been. I was sure Lukey had picked up Glandular Fever from one he kissed on a beach here the last time. Until now, I had never understood my mother's angst when I came home resembling something the cat didn't even want to drag in, or worse – not come home at all. There was more to worry about here though. There were no sharks of the watery-kind in the East End.

Roo was whacked-out from all that paddling and happily sat on the balcony with his book, while I conjured up the energy to start the packing. The boys' bedroom looked like it had been burgled, but I knew I mustn't touch anything because they'd moan and say that THEY knew where everything was, so I concentrated on the clothes I could safely launder without being accused of anything. When they returned, they had everything packed in a flash. 'Packed' being the operative word. I would call it 'Stuffed', but there you are. It was all ready-to-go in one bag, or another and that's all that mattered.

After another glorious setting sun fizzed into the ocean, we walked to the resort restaurant called 'The Happy Talk Lounge', where a guitarist entertained the diners while they ate. In between his songs, we listened to the bullfrogs croaking just outside and as usual, those big stars twinkled at us in the black sky. I was more than content with the day and after dinner had no trouble falling asleep in that wonderful King size bed.

DAY FIFTY-EIGHT: *"The Magic of Maui" (as 'they' say)*

Up at 7am.

A mist covered Bali Hai but the mountain was still visible and looked even more magical in the morning light.

The boys loaded up the buggy with our luggage, which had grown into a veritable land mass of its own and then transferred it all to our car. Oh to be young again! And after one last look at Bali Hai we left the resort. As we drove along the highway, those crazy chickens darted in and out of the undergrowth, attempting Hari Kari without the need to fall on a sword. Thankfully, we missed them all.

When we reached the airport, it was incredibly busy with a lot of stranded Aloha passengers milling around on 'standby' waiting for empty seats with any airline that could fly them home. Roo was desperate to behave in an 'okay' fashion in front of the boys but the look of alarm on his face told me we couldn't hang around the terminal for very long. Once we'd cleared all the necessary channels, it was a relief to be entitled to use the Hawaiian Airlines lounge and we waited there in the peace and quiet until it was time to board for the short flight to Honolulu. Roo calmed down completely; although he spent most of the time there in the loo.

Viewing Kaua'i from the air, it looked really green and friendly. With absolutely nothing in the centre of the island apart from plant-covered mountain and with strict construction rules, it should never be spoilt. Let's hope it stays that way.

Twenty minutes later, our 'bus' ride came to an end when we landed in Oahu. Pearl Harbour and the Visitor's Centre could be seen bathed in sunshine out to the left of the airport and dozens of menacing-looking C5's sat baking in the heat beside the runway as if waiting for some terrible emergency. Harry said the sum total of those planes was the annual budget for the RAF and we agreed that it was a good thing that USAF was on our side.

Fortunately, we didn't have to leave the aircraft for the next leg of our journey to Maui, so we remained in our seats while everyone but a few left the plane. The Aloha downfall was good economically for Hawaiian Airlines and a few dozen flight attendants and four pilots joined us. Some were going on to Portland and others to Seattle to fly in extra aircraft to help move passengers stranded in the islands. The reorganisation for them at such short notice must have been quite something, but they were all very jolly and made jokes about so many of them looking after us and which one of them would take over if there was an emergency.

"Ho-ho. Very funny. I don't think!"

On to Maui then. Lukey always says it's like coming home and I suppose he should feel that way, having made seven trips here since he was six years old. The familiar sight of the first bit of volcano on the west side when it came into view had been altered in 2008 by the installation of a wind farm consisting of twenty turbines. The farm is owned and operated by a company called 'First Wind' and provides 70% of Maui's energy. Somehow, the turbines don't look ugly, or out of place in an area of natural beauty and spin constantly due to the amount of wind enveloping the island. Wind energy has been used in Hawaii forever and the ancient Hawaiians relied on it to sail their canoes as far away as Polynesia (where we'd just been) and of course they still use a sail to go fishing. All the winds have names, but the only one I know is the name of the prevailing trade wind from the northeast, which is called Moa'e. I remember the name, because Roo's Mum had the nickname 'Moey'. We were robbed of a lovely person when she died.

Sweeping over the sugar cane factory as you do on the approach to Kahului Airport, I half expected the landmark to be gone this time, because it's been threatened with closure for years. But there it was, with its chimney belching out the black smoke that's supposed to be harmless – something to do with the cane, *'they'* say.

So we landed in our most favourite of places. We'd seen a bit of Hong Kong, Australia, New Zealand, Fiji, Polynesia and Tahiti, but for us, there's nowhere quite as perfect as Maui. After we'd collected yet another car, we drove off in a familiar way as if we'd done it a hundred times before taking the short cut we knew off the highway to the south of the island.

The two bedroom ground floor apartment was beautiful and one I'd admired during past holidays in Makena. Spacious and airy, it was only 100` from the ocean, with a safe sandy beach a hop, skip and a jump in between. While the men were bringing in the luggage, I went out onto the lanai (terrace) to see if there were any whales about. I scoured the waves, but couldn't see any tell-tale 'V'-shaped white splashes caused when a whale reaches the surface of the water and blows out warm air. Unsurprisingly this part of the whales 'nose' is called a 'blowhole'. It was quite late in the season and most of the whales would have left with their calves for Alaska by now, but this part of the Pacific is so safe for them, there were bound to be some latecomers loath to leave.

By the end of April they really are all gone and don't return until November to start the process all over again.

The chaps had joined me by this time and we all stood gazing out to sea. Harry and Lukey went inside to unpack, but Roo stayed where he was staring hard at the water without blinking. I asked him how he was feeling and he admitted that he'd had some sad thoughts, but none of impending doom since the boys had arrived, which was pretty good going. *"Keep him occupied"*, I thought and with just a cursory glance at the unpacked suitcases said, *"Supermarket"*.

Passing the boys' bedroom, we couldn't help noticing that their 'unpacking' consisted of emptying the contents of their suitcases onto the beds and a rummage around to enable them to find their swim shorts and by the time we left to get supplies they were in the pool, which was right outside the front door.

On the way to the Safeway food store we always use (we even have a loyalty card), we noticed a few new houses and a discretely-placed, low-rise apartment block, but apart from that little had changed on the main road since our last visit two years before; although we knew that the two luxury apartment complexes in the other direction had been given the go-ahead and would be completed by now. We'd go and look at them later.

Our local supermarket is always clean, tidy and full of lovely helpful assistants. It's actually a joy to go there - and I'm someone who will usually shop on-line whenever she can! But that's in England. When I'm in Maui, I conveniently forget things so I have to go back to 'our' Safeway.

The fruit and veg there is arranged in 'Harvest Festival' fashion and every so often in this particular aisle you hear the sound of thunder, which is a warning to stand back. A few seconds later a 'rain shower' sprays all the perishable things keeping the food fresh and mouth-wateringly irresistible. The first time we shopped there I had no idea about this and just thought there was a storm coming. The water I was sprayed with that time was however, quite refreshing – although I did look a bit bedraggled with mascara streaming down my cheeks at the checkout. With just enough grub to satisfy Lukey, but adequately feed the rest of us, the girl on the checkout and the packer dealt with the contents of the trolley while we stood watching.

Back at the apartment, literally chucking neat tuna steaks and giant prawns onto the barbeque on our lanai and smothering massive chunks of crusty bread with butter, we ate while we waited for the sun to set. The sun sets quite quickly here. Geographically, the islands are more than a thousand miles from the Equator, so it's nothing to do with that. I think it's something to do with being close to the Tropic of Cancer and the tilt of the earth. But then I'm known as 'Medical Mumma' and 'Legal Lady', not 'Geology Girl'.

Hawaiian beach weddings are very popular and Makena Beach – literally opposite our lanai, with its palm trees, a rocky point, the islands of Molokini and Kahoolawe in the background and a glorious setting sun makes a stunning location for a wedding, or even an excuse to have one. Halfway through dinner, we heard the sound of a conch shell horn being blow, which could only mean that one was about to take place! Of course, I was thrilled and had no hesitation in sacrificing the rest of my dinner to have a closer look. The boys thought I was totally mad and carried on eating.

On the far left of the beach, I could see a ring a flowers on the sand where the Bride and Groom would stand for the ceremony, two of those tall bamboo torches – already flaming away in the breeze and a man sitting to one side with a lap steel guitar (this is the instrument that gives Hawaiian music its *"peeoingy"* sound).

As I watched, the guitarist began to play the 'Hawaiian Wedding Song', just as two Hula girls danced onto the beach followed by the Minister in a flowing white robe and the Groom - in white suit and green lei and about a dozen guests all dolled-up and wearing colourful leis. Everyone was barefoot, which somehow looked perfectly natural on the creamy gold sand.

The Minister stood between the two torches and the Groom inside the flower ring and when everyone turned round to face the opposite direction, I knew the Bride had made her approach. Sylphlike and looking gorgeous in a simple calf-length, strapless dress of pure white - *'floatty' enough to have been Organza* - a traditional head dress of fresh flowers and holding a bouquet of Plumeria, she made her way across the sand holding onto the arm of whoever was giving her away – maybe her Dad, maybe not, I'll never know. The ceremony didn't take more than ten minutes and then the conch shell horn was blown again and everyone clapped furiously - *including me.*

It was wonderful and certainly worth forgoing my dinner for. I watched the photographs being taken, while listening to the music from the lap steel guitarist and thoroughly enjoyed the whole thing as if I'd been an invited and important guest and when the sun finally turned itself off and everyone disappeared, I felt quite left out.

It was dark by the time I dragged myself away from the lanai and went back inside. The boys were watching TV, having made some sort of 'man-wise' dent in the clearing-up (it's always a job half-done with men, isn't it?) So I had to finish off the finer details of the evening's eating, which was a bit of an anti-climax after attending a wedding, but at least I didn't have to change out of my finery to do it. When I'd finished, I thought the sky looked so beautiful, that I braved the insects and went back outside to study the stars, but I wasn't out there very long before the peace and quiet was shattered by the sound of a low-flying helicopter.

At first, I thought it was just someone very rich doing a night-time look at Maui (Tom Hanks and Oprah Winfrey have homes here), but when it circled over the ocean for the third time, it was quite obvious that something was up and I called the boys to come and see. Harry thought it looked serious enough to be 'Search and Rescue', but we all hoped it wasn't because we knew what that would mean. When it was joined by a Hercules heading out to sea, it meant that Harry was right and someone was missing.

We could see the helicopter pinpointing its powerful searchlight on the surface of the water about half a mile from shore. It went back and forth, round and round for nearly two hours. The Hercules was further out to sea, but the glow of its light was clearly visible from where we sat. We had no idea who was missing but I could picture the family or friends of the person who was lost frantically praying for their safe return and I prayed too.

Although I was absolutely done-in, I did unpack. The boys stuff remained on the floor of their room, where they'd tipped it off their beds, but I gave them the benefit of the doubt and hoped they would deal with it in the morning.

We live in hope.

DAY FIFTY-NINE: "Aloha"

I woke up at first light, instantly knowing I was in Maui. The surf crashing on the shore, the birds tweeting madly and the sweet smell of Hibiscus told me so. Leaping out of bed (well, *'getting'* out of bed) and looking out of the window, I could see that it was really breezy and that the ocean was full of white caps. We were off whale-watching lunchtime and by the look of the weather – could expect a rough ride.

Purposely breakfasting late, I fussed about knowing I'd need to be accessible to Roo before embarking on the trip. Even though we'd done it four or five times before, he was already in panic-mode and I was grateful that the boys had gone for a swim and a wander until it was time to go. I didn't want them to catch Roo experiencing his early morning terrors. They were not for the faint-hearted.

Usually, the whale-watching boats leave from Lahaina – a thirty minute drive up the coast, but a small company had started this trip from the Maui Prince, which was the hotel we stayed at on our very first trip, just five minutes away from Makena Surf where we were now. It was very handy and we'd also be supporting a small company to literally stay afloat.

The boys returned after their foray and without even noticing Roo's spaced-out appearance, joined us for the short journey to the beach at the Maui Prince Hotel to board the whale-watching catamaran.

Dragging Roo along, I had mixed feelings about the trip. If he freaked-out once we'd left the shore, there would be nothing I could do about it. I would simply sit him down somewhere and finish the trip hanging on to him if necessary. It would be okay. We've been in worse situations. He wasn't in charge of anything, or operating anything, so all he had to do was be still. I would lay on him to stop him doing anything stupid, if necessary.

Reaching Maui Prince Beach, the large catamaran we could see moving up and down in the 8` swell twenty feet short of the shore just had to be the vessel we were waiting for. Of course it was. Not only was it wandering around the ocean like the 'Titanic' in the last throes of its life, it was also (wo)manned by the slimmest, most gorgeous things on earth. A double-whammy for me, but I saw the boys' eyes widening. Leaving our sandals in lockers at the entrance to the beach, we trooped towards the shore together.

Stopping so short of the beach as the catamaran had, meant a trawl through the surf to reach the boarding ladder. *"Ha-ha"*, I thought. *"I climbed up and down a ladder with sixteen rungs in the sub - and this only has about ten"*. However, those ten rungs were moving up and down with all the ferociousness of the Pacific behind them.

Waves … sand … catamaran intent on destruction … gorgeous creatures …loads of Maui Prince people sitting on the beach watching ……

Oh, where was me deckchair and a cup of tea?

In my head, I heard that music again. You know the piece they play when you're on your way to the gallows. *"I don't think I can do this"*, I thought. *"I'll just make an idiot of myself again and this time, I'll embarrass the boys"*.

What to do? What to do? But we were at the water's edge now and intent on getting a closer look at the girls, the boys were already wading through the waves like soldiers evacuating from the beach at Dunkirk. The cat looked much bigger close up and I was really worried about getting on it. I thought I needed the loo and felt dizzy too, but just then, Roo grabbed my arm and said, *"I'm a bit worried about this. All these people. I will be alright, won't I?"* Without answering him, I hitched up my calf-length trousers and waded out into the water with him hanging on to me!

I saw the huge wave coming towards us, but could do nothing about it as we were both enveloped in warm Pacific Ocean up to our waists. Knowing my trousers and 'undies' would be see-through now, I was humiliated further by the helpful ebony water nymphs in skimpy bikinis, who hauled me up reassuringly with *"You're okay Ma'am"* and *"We've got you. There you go"*.

Oh how I wanted the salt water to have dissolved me! Dripping with water, I headed away from the other passengers choosing a safe corner to sit well away from the nymphs, hoping they'd forget all about the decrepit fat woman they'd just heaved on board. The only good thing was that in my terror I didn't need the loo any more. (Fortunately, the Pacific is a vast ocean and this anti-social behaviour would probably go undetected). Roo sat on the deck beside me, hanging on to my ankle as if to stop me from jumping ship. It was nothing of the kind, of course, but a bit of physical contact did it for him – even if it WAS only my ankle.

After a brief and comical safety talk from the bronzed Captain, we motored off with engine power at first and leaving the shore at speed, were soon in deeper water where we had our first sighting of a Humpback Whale with her calf. Incidentally, the birth of a baby whale has never been filmed.

Humpbacks are not the largest whales in the world, but they can grow up to 50` long and weigh something like 80,000 pounds. If you like snorkelling, you might be lucky enough to hear one of the wonderful things Humpbacks do, which is sing. Their songs can last up to twenty minutes and can be repeated for hours. It's only the males who sing and only in their breeding grounds but every singing North Pacific male sings the same song, slowly changing it in small ways throughout the season. As they make these changes, they each sing the new and improved version. It's not known what the songs mean, but scientists think it might be something to do with sparring for a female; although they know it isn't the female, but another male who responds – maybe they swap notes on all the available girls.

In the summer months Humpbacks live in the cold waters off the coast of Alaska feeding on fish and krill and it's not until winter that they migrate south to the warm Maui waters to breed, but it's too warm for small fish and krill here, so the whales don't eat while they're in Maui. In the last few years, the whale population here has doubled and fierce battles have been witnessed between rival males. The fights lasting several hours above and below the water can be bloody, with a serious outcome and even when it's over, the female might not fancy the male anyway and as she's bigger - what she says goes! With the thought of carrying a calf during an eleven and a half month pregnancy, I should think so too.

Next to elephants (and now Koalas), whales are my favourite creatures. I don't know why, because they're certainly not pretty or fluffy and not even a nice colour. I think I admire their power. The mum we were watching breached (jumped out of the water) constantly and every time she did, the little one followed. It's amazing that something so big has the ability to leap up into the air and come crashing back down again in a plume of water without harming itself. There are several theories about breaching, but no one knows the reason for sure. Federal law in Maui is very strict about what you can and can't do near a whale. Boats are supposed to maintain a distance of at least 100 yards, but if the whale swims closer to you, it's difficult to keep that distance. At one time, mum and baby were fin-slapping and waving at us only about thirty feet from the boat, so everyone was able to take masses of close-up photographs.

Eventually bored with the sight of us, mum swam off with

her darling baby and we motored further out to sea passing the moon-shaped crater of Molokini, an extinct submerged volcano. It's always surrounded by divers and snorkellers the minute the sun comes up until it goes down, because of the amount of fish to be seen there.

Reaching the smallest island In Hawaii, Kaho'olawe, we dropped anchor for snacks and drinks and some people went for a swim. Roo had let go of my ankle by now, but still sat beside me. *"Swim?"* I asked. He shook his head slowly and instead of trying to change his mind, I turned my attention to Kaho'olawe.

Fifty years of bombing something – even if it was just a big rock, would alter most things and looking at the island now, it's hard to believe that this was once a wasteland of eroding soil and blowing red dust. Decades without decent topsoil meant that nothing would grow, so the starting point had to be a clean-up including the removal of unexploded bombs, scraps of jagged metal and military equipment that had been left all over the island. Regeneration is ongoing, but the planting programme must be difficult as there is no fresh water. It will probably be another fifty years before it's back to how it was, but it's already looking good and one day might even be another island to visit. At the moment though, unless you're an archeologist hoping to look for a bit of anciient culture or a native Hawaiian performing a religious ritual, it's a no-go area.

After half-an-hour or so, we motored off again. Roo was still looking miserable, but had eaten something and downed a pint of lemonade. The boys were still trying to chat up the female crew, but weren't having much luck and I was just happy to be out on the water watching Hawaii go by. A couple of the passengers were seasick. A combination of the swell of the ocean and drinking too much alcohol, no doubt.

Midway between Kaho'olawe and Lani'i we had several more sightings of whales to delight everyone and there seemed to be a bit of competition going on to see which of us could spot one first. There was one pod just off shore that was particularly wonderful. There must have been three or four of them and they were playing around like kids. I don't care what anyone says – they were. Behind them, the peaks of Lahaina framed their antics. It's a corny thing to say, but it was enchanting.

Three hours later and with the sun sinking lower and lower and the wind in our favour, the engine was turned off. The lovely things helped to hoist the sail and with the wind moving us quietly and effortlessly over the ocean, we made our way back to the Maui Prince beach.

We were all tired. The couples amongst us huddled together romantically, while others lounged silently on deck. Light poured through gaps in the clouds, making turquoise pools of water amid a deeper blue and to cap it all not one, but two rainbows sat glowing happily over the Iao Valley peaks. The only thing to spoil the moment was the news that the helicopter and Hercules we'd seen last night had been looking for a windsurfer. The futile search had been abandoned early in the morning.

The cat was closing in on the beach and it would soon be time to get off, so I needed to formulate a 'Disembarkation Plan' fast. But before I knew it, we were twenty feet from the shore. The lovely things dived into the water like the nymphs they were, without their forms causing a ripple and expertly swam to shore holding the ropes between their teeth to tie up. Once the vessel was secured, everyone except Roo and the boys either leapt into the water, or easily slid down the ladder. Then inevitably, came my turn. Hoping the Disembarkation Plan would materialise in my mind any second, I suggested the others leave first, but the three of them stood looking at me shaking their heads slowly in a dutiful way. I wasn't sure if I was pleased, or not.

Well, do you know the expression *'Gay Abandon'*?

No?

It's the same as *'Impulsive Madness'*.

Knowing it was too late for a 'Disembarkation Plan', sudden *'Gay Abandon'* came upon me. Without warning, I took a deep breath and with a running jump hurled myself off the side of the catamaran and into the water eight feet below. Spread-eagled on the surface, I sank fast but fortunately emerged just as quickly. I have no idea if the boys went down the ladder or jumped in after me, but the three of them seemed to be right there the minute I surfaced in waist-deep water. With a contorted look on my face, I ignored their looks of disbelief and shouts of horror and with salt water streaming from my nose, dripping hair stuck firmly to my head and opaque knickers for the second time I marched up the beach triumphantly like a successful cross-Channel swimmer.

How attractive I must have looked.

Showered and in dry clothes, we lounged around in the apartment recovering from the adventure. *"I wondered where you were going"*, Roo said. *"When?"* I asked casually, (knowing dam well what he was talking about). *"You know"*, he replied, biting both lips. *"When you suddenly launched yourself off the side of the boat"*. Lukey chimed in with,

"The amount of water you shifted was like a meteor landing, mum". *"Thank you darling."* I grimaced. Surreptitiously rubbing my red, stinging midriff, thankful that he could have compared me to Moses parting the Red Sea and hadn't. Harry just put his arm round me smiling, the way he does sometimes when he loves me more than usual.

For some reason, I really wanted to cry. Roo had only been about five out of ten all day and the boys hadn't scored with the nymphs, but it had been fabulous on the boat and we'd seen loads of whales, so I don't know why I felt so emotional. Maybe it was because I'd looked such an idiot again. How was it that I could be in charge of an anesthetised patient while they were being operated on, but was unable to get off a boat?

I went into the kitchen and made some tea for us all. Taking mine outside, I was just in time for two more weddings on the beach! What was this, 'Wedding Week'?

"You mad fools", I shouted. (I didn't really).

They were conducted at opposite ends of the beach this time and the music from each one interrupted the speaking part of one and then vice versa, but it was still lovely and helped to cheer me up a bit. Roo was sound asleep on the sofa by this time and the boys were subconsciously watching a film. We were all so tired doing nothing all day. It was the sea air, I thought. Lukey (being the Geographer in the family) would argue that 'air' couldn't possibly make you feel tired and although I didn't think it was an Old Wives' Tale, there didn't seem to be a real explanation for our lethargy. If it was an old tale, it was probably as true as the one that says a wish will come true if you make it while burning onions. That really makes sense, doesn't it?

I needed to get some shopping at Safeway (what a nuisance), but as we were all hungry we reversed the shopping procedure, deciding to eat in the steakhouse opposite the supermarket first and shop later. Once there, Lukey ordered a T Bone Steak and was told that if he could eat the whole thing, he was entitled to a second one. It was the biggest steak I'd ever seen and although he ate the lot, he would have turned green if he'd had another. The atmosphere as well as the food was great, although it had an Australian theme, which was a bit weird in Hawaii, but it helped to lighten Roo's mood a bit and at least he was trying to make conversation. When we'd finished, the last thing I wanted to do was go shopping, but as soon as I walked into Safeway, I changed my mind.

Back at the apartment, it didn't take long to put away the few bits I'd bought, but would have to go back again soon though. (Tut!)

I went straight to bed after, trying not to re-live my impetuous dive off that catamaran.

DAY SIXTY: "How time was Flying".

Nothing planned today. I made pancakes for breakfast (how American) and the boys scoffed them up as fast as I made them, until I ran out of batter.

There was no news about the windsurfer and without sights or sounds of the rescue craft this morning we supposed the news was not good.

I decided it was going to be a lazy day and meandered out onto the grass barefoot. The emerald green Seashore Paspalum – the thick grass grown on the seashore because it tolerates salt, felt good between my toes and I stood scrunching it while I fed the dickies. Here on Maui, some of the birds look like Starlings but with yellow beaks. There are good old 'sparras' too and very posh-looking birds we call red hats, which are in fact Cardinals. The males are bright red or green and the ladies are yellow, but they both have a Mohawk haircut. They're almost tame and bounce up to within a few feet of you if they think there's food going. For some reason we call them all 'red hats' and if a green Cardinal pops in to see us we say, *"Oh look a green red hat"*. (That was a useless piece of information, but I just thought I'd mention it).

Big butterflies and stealth bees flapped around the deep pink and mauve hibiscus hiding amongst the hedgerow separating us from the sandy beach and a gentle breeze moved the foliage sideways occasionally, straightening up each time the wind dropped. It was clear enough to be able to see the wind farm and the sails of the turbines flying around making safe power for us all and with hardly a soul on the beach and a clear blue sky - save for scanty, fluffy, white clouds hurtling along, it was all very beautiful. The peace and tranquillity was there to see, if only you could be bothered to take the time to look. I would have been happy to stand there all day being peaceful and tranquil, but instead there was food to cook and other domestic duties to perform.

Roo was behaving a bit weird today - spaced out and quiet uninterested in anything. He said he was fine, so I left him alone to get on with it. I should have gone indoors and cleared away the breakfast things, but I continued to busy myself with the dickies, in between scanning the waves for whales. It would be wonderful to spot that windsurfer alive and well, but I knew that was unlikely now.

I couldn't believe my ears when they told me another wedding was traipsing up the beach disturbing the peace and quiet. All the trimmings this time, with hula dancers, blazing flares, guitars, drums, white chairs and everyone in the most extravagant leis.

It took a while to position the chairs on the wetter sand safely enough for them to stay put and not sink, but after much fussing and laughter the ceremony began. It was heart-warming to see the happy couple with their well-wishers and I wished them well too as the Minister made the sign of the cross over their flower-strewn heads and a whole herd of white doves were released from a wicker basket.

"No …… oh please – how will that work?" I thought when two more processions turned up simultaneously. There could be a battle of the beach weddings at this rate.

I doubted there would be a battle, but I didn't think the new arrivals were very happy, when instead of the doves taking to the air they landed en masse amongst the new arrivals. Much flapping of arms and shouting to try to shoo them away altered the gracious scene somewhat, as one dove cheekily sat on the end of a guitar chewing at the strings and two more bounced up and down the Yamaha piano making an awful row. It was really comical, but they were soon chased away and the wedding guest who had released them sneaked off with the empty basket.

The later weddings began and finished pretty much at the same time and although they were too early for photo's with a setting sun, the photographers had enough of a backdrop with crashing surf and palm trees and everyone went away looking happy.

The rest of the day was much the same. The four of us lounged about then the boys swam and walked along the beach until it was time for dinner. I cooked 'Chicken a la Vivienne' for them and 'Prawn a la Me' for me (chucked anything and everything in a frying pan and it somehow always tastes great).

Roo hadn't improved much and as I loaded up the dishwasher, I tried not to notice that he was doing his impersonation of a Victorian lady on the sofa again. The boys had walked into the village together and hadn't asked him to go with them, so he was probably feeling left out. The slightest little thing seemed to set him off, sending him into a downward spiral. He simply can't cope unless all is going well and even when it is, he can find a situation difficult to manage. I wondered if he had some sort of deep-seated psychological problem from childhood. My sister and I had some dreadful stuff happen when we were little and I know it altered our lives. I was constantly trying to work it all out and one day, be able to say, "*Eureka*!" But all I seemed to do was go round in circles. Oh! Isn't the mind a minefield!

With a tidy kitchen and the low hum from the dishwasher, Roo's breathing told me he was in a deep sleep, so rather than disturb him I went outside again. I just love 'outside'. I'm sure I must have Viking ancestry. Blue eyes, turned-up nose … horns growing out of my head … No, I know I don't have horns growing out of my head - I was just trying to amuse myself. I don't know a lot about my heritage, but I do know that my Grandmothers' parents (my Great Grandparents, of course) had lived in Bethnal Green in the 1850's, which had given me some romantic notion that they had farmed 'the Green' there and lived an idyllic lifestyle. I could imagine Great Grand Papa at the till, with his Shire Horse and Great Grand Mama in her white pinny bringing him his lunch. The truth was that this area just outside London had become a dumping ground for the very poorest of families and the amount of buildings that went up caused disease and squalor. There was even an asylum there. So I have no idea why I like 'outside' so much but it could be nothing to do with ancestry.

In seventeen days' time, I would be back at my computer putting the May issue of the parish magazine together and madly trying to find something smart to squeeze into to wear in Court. But for now, I was very happy to watch the sun strike the water and wait for my stars to come out.

DAY SIXTY-ONE: *"More Maui"*

The sunset last night had been so perfect, that when I woke up this morning, I could still picture the green flash that sometimes goes with it. I know that this phenomenon (a big word for a Saturday) has something to do with light refraction, or a prism – isn't that the same thing? And it's only there for a second, or two. If you can catch it, as I did last night, it's an amazing sight.

The boys said they would divide their time between the beach – where the waves were enormous today, the pool and the Jacuzzi, in that order. Roo and I sat out on the lanai. It was a hot day and I suggested he get some rays and absorb a bit of Vitamin D, which would give his yellow skin a boost and do his liver some good too. I helped him slap on a thick layer of 'factor twenty' and he pulled a lounger out into the sunshine, but after only ten minutes he'd had enough and huffing and puffing like a steam train and moaning under his breath about the heat, he shot back into the shade.

Trying not to get annoyed, I stood up and looked out to sea. This time, my grass toe-scrunching was in irritation, rather than the caressing way I'd enjoyed yesterday. He was just so difficult to get on with and absolutely no fun whatsoever, but I reminded myself that it wasn't his fault and he had no control over his behaviour.

I felt as though I was being constantly tested to see how much I could take before I ran off with an Italian ice cream seller, which was the first person that came to mind for some reason. Right on cue, as if to save me from screaming like a banshee (whose wail is so loud it's supposed to be able to shatter glass), I spotted the boys in the surf and my full attention turned to what they were up to.

The waves on some parts of the island – especially a place called 'Jaws' (Pe'ahi in Hawaiian) can reach a height of 120 feet moving as fast as 30 mph., caused by water breaking on a deep reef. Surfers have to be towed out to the waves and must have nerves of steel to face something so enormous. 'Jaws' is famous for its ability to form waves into gigantic barrels of hollow water and the surfers tuck themselves right inside them for as long as the wave will carry them. Phew!!

Harry and Lukey were mucking about in waves of around four feet, which was a bit different to 'Jaws', but they were still being knocked off their feet with the weight of the water when it crashed onto the shore. They floundered amongst the bubbles together, tumbling onto the sand and laid there laughing, which made me smile. I waved at them, but they were too busy to see me. I wished I was down there with them, but I knew I shouldn't leave Roo alone when he was in such low spirits.

The boys left the beach and must have made their second watery stop at the pool. I started to get lunch. Salad, crusty bread and burgers. Brainwave! Get Roo to barbeque them – give him a job. But by the look on his face, you would have thought I'd asked him to climb a 250 foot Tualang tree to collect honey from the hive of the biggest bee in the world, not suggested he Barbie some burgers!

With a deep sigh, he stood up and pulled the cover off the barbeque. *"There's stuff in it"*, he groaned. *"Well get it out!"* I replied sarcastically. He washed it out with the hose on the lanai and left it in the sun to dry off a bit *"otherwise the burgers will stick"*, he said informatively. *"Oh really?"* I said under my breath.

Just then Harry and Lukey bounced in. Harry was bright pink and immediately, I started to moan at him about the dangers of getting burnt, but he interrupted my bewailing to say that it was heat from the Jacuzzi and not sunburn. *"That's alright then"* I conceded.

"Where's food?" Lukey asked and moving outside to the lanai picked up the barbeque tray. *"It's wet"*, he said and grabbing the kitchen roll he dried the rungs enough to make them shine, poured the coals in and proceeded to light them completely taking over the job and foiling my cunning plan. Roo sat back down again with a relieved look on his face. Lukey made such a good job of the burgers, he barbied a side of salmon as well. We'd have that for dinner.

Roo's doldrums continued. I suggested we go into Wailea, but as I was saying this, I knew it wasn't a good idea because he looked so exhausted. I didn't know what to do about his sleep pattern at night. He wasn't able to have tablets for it and being a bad sleeper myself, I did sympathise. But my sleeplessness was different. I'm sure most women who have had kids are light sleepers having one ear open in case you're needed. A Depressive has a very different sleep pattern. They can sleep instantly, but it takes much longer to get into a deep sleep and be at total rest, because their mind is in such a jumble. Rapid Eye Movement occurs earlier in the night and they wake up a lot and start worrying - not only about having insomnia, but also the fact that they're depressed.

It's a real vicious circle. We've tried all the usual things and read everything on websites dedicated to help you solve the problem, but nothing works for him.

So we stayed put. The boys went out again and seemed to be having a good time and if they'd noticed Roo was 'up the pole', they didn't mention it.

Only a few hours later it seemed, Lukey was asking for food again, so by five o'clock, I was serving up the salmon, complete with the smoky taste of the barbeque and the whole time we were eating, we watched a couple of whales jumping about just off shore. I let the boys clear away the plates and rang Mum. It was snowing again in England, which seemed peculiar when we were sitting in the warmth of seventy-five degrees with whales.

With the sun calming down and eventually disappearing, so did the whales. We'd see them again tomorrow.

Roo had improved a bit and feeling the need to entertain the boys we drove to Maalea to a mini golf range we knew. It sounds naff, but it's good fun with a swashbuckling theme and it's quite novel playing in the dark, with just the light from gas flares.

But we forgot it was Sunday! When we arrived, it was closed, which did wonders for Roo's mood. Although the boys and I were disappointed, we knew we'd go another night, but for Roo it was as if he'd had his head sewn to the carpet and he'd never get up again. He went on and on saying how sorry he was … and that he should have phoned them … and that he'd … *"Oh, for God's sake"*, I thought … I had to think fast for an alternative.

It's difficult enough to know what to do in England on a Sunday evening, but something to satisfy the four of us at eight o'clock at night in Maui, when the locals are all in bed by nine, was a tricky one. *"I know"*, I shouted. *"Let's find a place to have some dessert!"*

Fortunately, anything to do with food is okay with Lukey and anything to do with puddings is definitely okay with Harry, so we drove back the way we'd come and pulled into one of the shopping precinct car parks. A Bar called "The Sports Page" would be open late and they did a mean syrupy-bananas with ice cream. Roo obviously felt well enough to play a few rounds of pool with the boys and the combination passed the time nicely. A pat on the back for me!! It was a very 'American' thing to do – to go out for dessert. It's something they do often and even have dedicated 'Coffee and Dessert' cafes. But I can't see it catching on at home somehow. It can't possibly compare with afternoon tea and cucumber sandwiches with a tier of little cakes.

Roo and I went straight to bed afterwards, but the boys stayed up to watch a film. It was ages before they turned the TV off and I could hear them still jabbering away in the next room for ages after that.

They'd be tired in the morning.

DAY SIXTY-TWO:

"Old Lahaina"

Roo admitted that he was up the creek and totally without a paddle this morning. A pep talk helped, but believe it or not, he'd got himself in a tizzy again about what we'd find when we get home in two weeks' time. (Sigh). He still LOOKS well though. I'd need to buy him some more 'Milk Thistle' and honestly thought it had helped him liver-wise; although of course, I don't have X-Ray eyes and know it might be wishful-thinking.

After breakfast, we sat outside in the shade together with him insisting he was alright although we both knew he wasn't. He was doing his best to keep it from the boys – good! I didn't want it to ruin our time together.

He had cheered up a bit by lunchtime and actually sat in the sun for a whole seventeen minutes (I timed it) and ate most of a triple-decker sandwich, so he wasn't too bad.

While we were outside, the weather changed. The birds disappeared and there wasn't one tweet to be heard. A huge black (and I mean, BLACK) cloud had covered half the sky, while out at sea it was a beautiful blue as if it had been sliced down the middle with an enormous knife and there was a sort of stillness to the air. But then a rush of wind – the type that takes your breath away – suddenly hit us, instantly throwing anything that wasn't heavy, or tied down into the air. On the beach, a couple of boogy-boards had been left, waiting for their owners to return and these plus all the stuff beside them were hurled up into a twister about thirty feet in diameter. The whole lot – boards, towels, flip-flops and I think someone's lunch moved along the beach in a twisting torrent of sand like a scene from 'The Mummy'. Then, as fast as it had picked everything up, it dropped them. We both just stared at it, until like a hungry animal catching sight of more food, the spinning sand left the beach and turned towards us. By the time it reached our lanai, it must have lost power because it just dumped loads of sand over us until we were covered in the stuff.

Weird. We've never seen that before. It disappeared as quickly as it came and the birds started tweeting again the minute it stopped. Then that black cloud let go and the heavens opened, so we rushed indoors, meeting the boys as they rushed out of the torrential rain from the other direction. *"Whoa"*, said Harry, *"Did you see that?"* We both nodded. *"Well, we are in the middle of the Pacific Ocean, three thousand miles from the mainland"* Lukey added and walked away mumbling something geographical about high (or it might have been low) pressure, shaking his head as if he was amongst complete idiots. As far as the weather was concerned, he was and it's easy to forget that you're sitting in the middle of the most remote island chain in the world. We swept up sand days after.

The rain looked as though it was set to stay for quite a while, so it was an ideal time to drive to the old town of Lahaina, once the whaling capital of the world. There's a museum there to prove it, but we've never been brave enough to go in. Today, Lahaina is the most historic town on Maui, so close to the island of Lanai'i you could almost touch it with the dramatic fertile peaks and valleys of the western mountain range looming high above it.

In 1825 Hawaii's ghastly whaling history began, which was to last thirty-five years and I won't, or can't say too much about it because it's just too horrible for words; but you all know how dreadful it must have been. Apparently, there was a constant battle between the whalers and the missionaries revolving around the lax morals of the whalers! Around the time they stopped massacring the wonderful whales, exportation of sugar cane began and then in 1912, another source of income was found by growing pineapples with the first cannery being built here in 1892. It wasn't until the 1970's that Maui - and especially Lahaina became a lively tourist destination. Front Street is the main area, but instead of the disorderly taverns, Restaurants, Art Galleries and stores now line the street, which sits right beside the ocean.

We split up and the boys disappeared off somewhere, but Roo and I were content to wander around the stores in the warm evening breeze. Roo needed a new hat, so we made a beeline for the one we knew which was less touristy and he chose yet another 'Maui' baseball cap to join the others at home. I managed to stop myself going inside the most expensive shops, but couldn't resist a look at the Wyland Gallery.

I don't think anyone could love whales more than Wyland. This artists' work is collected by millions of Americans and the non-profit Foundation he built supports all sorts of conservation projects, including his monumental '**Whaling Wall**' mural project — a series of one hundred life size marine life murals, spanning twelve countries on four continents, viewed (it's estimated) by a billion people every year. The Foundation also teaches thousands of students about our oceans and does wonderful work towards whale conservation. Wyland is definitely MY kind of person. In the Gallery, we saw a photograph of him in a rowing boat actually kissing a migrant whale on its beak! How he managed that is a mystery to me.

Meeting up an hour, or so later, we ate at 'Cheeseburger in Paradise', where it's not only the waitresses who wear grass skirts, the waiters do too (over shorts). The food here is actually just burgers – nothing fancy to eat at all, but it's worth waiting in the queue (hungry and just before sunset) to get a table upstairs in the wooden open-air building. The bamboo walls and ceilings are covered with tiki-hut knick-knacks - parrots, strings of coloured lights, hula girl dolls, plumeria flowers, coconut cups, moai carvings, tin signs and everything 'surfboard'. It's difficult to concentrate on anything but the knick-knacks and as if this isn't entertainment enough, the live music just adds to the atmosphere and when the sun has gone, the mood intensifies – or it could be the strength of their 'MaiTais'. (my fave drink of all time).

We all had burgers (including me – you can't go here without eating a cheeseburger). With chips the size of firewood and three Mai Tais later we wandered back to the car, where we found we'd been presented with a parking ticket. For some reason, we didn't seem to care.

DAY SIXTY-THREE: "A Quiet Day"

Scrambled some eggs and cooked the American version of 'bacon'. Even after our lovely evening last night, Roo woke up like a bear with a sore head, so I was glad the boys went off to Big Beach a few miles away, but not glad that once again I had this problem to deal with. His red-rimmed eyes told me that he hadn't had a good night and he anxiously pottered about achieving absolutely nothing, saying he couldn't eat and wanted to go back to bed. I quickly nipped off and pulled the bed straight so it would deter him. We would be home in two weeks' time. Would he get worse the nearer we moved towards England?

The boys returned to find Roo lounging on the sofa but made no comment. Their tans were coming along nicely, in spite of high factor sunscreen and me religiously dotting their moles with total block. (Am I paranoid?) I made several triple-decker BLT sandwiches, without the 'T' for Lukey and left Roo's beside him. I really wasn't bothered if he ate it or not. It would go to the dickies if he hadn't swallowed it in ten minutes. The boys took Roo's demeanour with a pinch of salt and said that as there wasn't much going on at Big Beach (no girls, probably) they would have a look at Polo Beach. I suggested they didn't stay too long, as I knew they wanted to go to Long's – a really good and interesting

Pharmacy/Electrical/Everything store, which Roo and I enjoyed visiting too.

I noticed Roo's sarnee had been nibbled, so I didn't threaten him with the dickies and took mine - without the 'B' out onto the lanai. It was a beautiful day – too beautiful to be inside and far too beautiful to be miserable. Doing what I usually did outside, I shielded my eyes from the sun and looked out to sea. It was very misty from the beach onwards and difficult to make out the shape of Molokini crater, so it would be even more difficult to spot a whale.

My feathered friends turned up and I gave them most of my lunch. Bugger. I wished Roo hadn't eaten his – the dickies were really hungry. Something caught my eye in the hedge and I moved forward a little scattering them in all directions. Peering closely into the Oleander, two tiny eyes met mine and I jumped back in surprise. It was a mongoose. Keeping very still so I wouldn't alarm him or her it shot out from the hedge, grabbed a piece of bread and shot off again. I probably shouldn't have encouraged it, because I know they eat bird's eggs, but it was so cute and if he ate a bit of bread, perhaps it would save an egg, or two.

Roo staggered onto the Lanai, squinting in the brightness. He'd showered and dressed and I could see his plate was empty. *"I'm going for a walk"*, he announced. There was no *"Do you want to come with me?"* so, assuming he wanted to be alone, I nodded saying, *"Good idea",* but the addition of *"Don't drown yourself"*, was fortunately lost on the breeze.

Knowing I should keep busy while he was gone, I tidied up the lanai and swept away more of that sand from the tornado. A teeny-weeny green dickie the size of a Malteser standing on legs as thin as cocktail sticks kept me company and I could see that the mongoose was still scampering around amongst the Oleander. The beach was almost empty – it always was (apart from weddings). Lucky us - except if there was an emergency and we needed someone to run for help. (Having Roo in mind).

Shaking my head at the thought of Roo's illness, I took my plate into the kitchen. It took less than ten minutes to clear up inside and not wanting to miss a moment of the sunshine went back onto the lanai and sat on a lounger. It was impossible to see the beach from where I sat, so I moved to the table and plonked onto a chair. Then I sat on the edge of the chair. Then I stood up and walked to the other side of the lanai..... and inevitably moved to the hedge. I knew I was being ridiculous but the worry of where he was had got the better of me.

I must have looked like Peggy Mount in one of those black and white films. All I needed was a rolling pin. But you know it wasn't anger making me stand there. When he appeared, I pretended I was standing up to tan the backs of my legs, but I don't think he believed me. Although a bit tearful, he joked about falling off a rock on the next beach and finding a rope hanging from a tree. I tried hard to laugh, but my mouth was too dry. The boys interrupted the awkward moment returning just at the right time and the four of us quickly changed for our bit of retail therapy.

We could spend a whole day in Long's. Sounds crazy? It's like an Aladdin's cave. You'd love it too. One of us had to be strong though and it was Lukey who dragged us away. He was hungry of course and back at the apartment, he barbied for the full-time carnivores again and I had a salad of huge prawns.

It would be early to bed. Very early. We were going to drive up to the Haleakala crater 10,000 feet above sea level before dawn to see the sunrise and needed to leave at 3am. Now that was crazy.

DAY SIXTY-FOUR: 'Haleakala'

When the alarm went off at 2.45am I was already up, dressed and raring to go. The boys were very good, but Roo needed a little coaxing with, *"If you don't get up, I'll pour a jug of cold water over you"* and we left the apartment a fraction after 3am. There was a large storm in the distance, which probably wouldn't make for a good sunrise but off we went anyway. The first hour was fine.

We chatted – well I chatted - and watched the lightning and tried to name the star systems, but it wasn't looking good up there.

The temperature on the way up drops around three degrees F for every thousand feet you go, making the summit (10.023ft) something like thirty degrees cooler than the coast, with clouds and rain replacing sunshine in seconds. The high altitude can complicate health conditions and cause breathing difficulties in any but the fittest and it's important to remember to walk very slowly and drink plenty of water. It's the most inhospitable place we've ever visited, but also one of the most amazing. Some people, like us go to Haleakala ('House of the Sun') to see the sun rise over the crater, but the more robust go to hike and camp and the really mad ones go for the thrill of a bike ride straight down the long and winding thirty-seven mile road built on the side of the volcano.

Before reaching the actual summit the road passes the University of Hawaii Observatory, which has been there for forty years. This area isn't open to the public but the domes housing the telescopes are easy to spot. It's one of the most important observing sites in the world because it lies above something called the 'Tropical Inversion Layer' and consequently has superb seeing conditions with the clarity of the air. The other advantages are the lack of light pollution and the fact that the volcano sits above one-third of the Earth's atmosphere.

Eventually reaching the summit, we wriggled around in the car pulling on our warm clothes and I tried not to think about the journey down, or how high up we were. It was eighty-seven degrees F in Wailea and only forty-nine degrees up top. The howling wind rocked the car and extreme gusts shook it, as if it was trying to rid this sacred place of an intruder. The oldest part of my brain told me were mad, but like the others, I continued the struggle in the confines of the car. We noticed lots of people hadn't exactly prepared themselves for the experience, shivering in tee shirts, shorts and flip-flops. Twits! Some had beach towels wrapped around them and others seemed happy to freeze, but most like us wore woolly hats and ski gear.

It's thought that Haleakala became Haleakala about two million years ago. It isn't extinct, only dormant, with the last eruption (perhaps, probably, maybe, 'they' think) in the fifteenth century; but 'they' don't think it will go off again any time soon. It's a massive volcano – what you can see of it, because 97% of it below sea level – so when it DOES go bang again, it might be quite a LOUD bang!

My two baby boys were insufficiently dressed until I had pulled their woolly hats further down their foreheads – much to their disgust; but who needs to 'look cool'

10,000 feet up a volcano? I asked them. With more dexterity than their old Mum and Dad, they were ready before I had my trousers over my knees and opening their doors gingerly, Harry's was flung open by the wind causing a rush of cold air inside the car, instantly freezing my bare thighs. (This may sound a little erotic to anyone who doesn't know how big my thighs are). Closing the doors with difficulty, they ran up the observation area steps taking two at a time, ignoring my *'walk slowly'* talk. Roo and I both took a few deep breaths – like a couple of 'free divers' and looking at each as if we were about to tip headfirst off   the 'Titanic holding hands romantically, reluctantly went to join them - *walking slowly.*

The observation area gives a magnificent view of the crater, which is 3,000 feet deep, seven miles long, two miles wide and twenty-one miles in circumference. (I told you it was big!) It's similar to a Martian landscape apparently, but here on our own earth in the middle of the Pacific Ocean, we miraculously find an alien landscape in the middle of an island paradise. Believe it, or not there are a few plants growing around the crater.

It's only Maui and on top of the volcano on the Big Island of Hawaii and 4,900 feet above sea level, that the Silversword plant lives happily amongst the rocky lava flows, which is a feat in itself. It's not a marvellous-looking plant, but it is marvellous that it can grow at such a height and extremes of temperature. Even with our insulated clothes and huddling together we were chilly waiting for the sun. The sky gradually grew lighter, until a glimmer of red appeared through the clouds below us and although the weather had spoilt the experience to a certain extent a few people cheered and became quite emotional, as if it were a different sun up here to the one we usually see. We heard one person say that the cloudier it is, the better the colour of the sky, but the only real colour in evidence was a deep, deep red. It was a bit mesmerising and Roo and I stood watching in silence probably contemplating different things. Harry clicked away merrily with his camera and took photos of what I thought were very peculiar subjects; but then I've never been very photographic. When he shows the pictures later, I know we'll say, "Aah!............ Of course". He has this ability to see things in a different way.

The sun switched it's light full on exposing the sightseers. We all looked dishevelled and tired, but the ones in flip-flops had already gone to warm up in the Visitor Centre further down the volcano. Lukey, of course was starving so we thought we'd go straight to have some breakfast, rather than stop halfway. Roo had hardly said a word since yesterday. I was beginning to wonder what to expect next with him. He was probably getting worked up about leaving Maui and going on to the next location. I knew he found this difficult, but surely having the boys with us was a comfort.

Around 8,000 feet, the temperature began to rise and it was 'all-change' out of our warm clothes. Lukey complained of painful ears and I hoped it was just the difference in pressure and not an infection, which he's prone to. If he was still in pain when we reached the bottom, I thought maybe he should see the Doc. for some drops. We would be off to Vegas soon and there's nothing worse than ear pain when you're in a plane. (That was almost a poem. I could have said, 'Earplane'. Ha-Ha)

It was 8.30am when we finally completed our descent. Looking back at Haleakala, it was amazing to think we'd stood on top of it and had witnessed the dawning of a new day. The weather had improved and there were breaks in the clouds, but it must have rained here and there, because several rainbows shone over the sugar cane making it sparkle and we could see that the pineapples in the plantation we passed were soaking wet. Everything looked very well-nourished and healthy. What else would happen though in a climate of warm rain and nutrient-rich volcanic ash?

We'd used a lot of petrol going up and down so before doing anything else, thought we'd better fill the car up with 'gas'. Right besdide the gas station, a Huey helicopter was hovering with what looked like a massive air conditioning unit hanging from a net beneath it. The noise was deafening. We'd never have been allowed to get so close in the same situation in England – they'd have closed the whole road off; but they're so laid-back in Hawaii. It was quite exciting for us and our fellow motorists to watch the pilot plonk it in the right place with the help of a chap hanging out of the door in the side, release the net and fly off.

The ears were still hurting, so rather than wait for them to get worse, we stopped at the Medical Centre, which has a small 'walking wounded' bit. The investigation determined the problem – sand on his drums! He was given drops and tablets for the pain and was annoyed that he wouldn't be able to go in the sea for a few days, although he insisted he could swim with his head above water. I was just grateful that there was time to get them clear before our next flight.

We were all tired and the rain had caught us up when we came out of the Medical Centre. A few hours kip wouldn't go amiss and it would give the storm time to pass, so when we reached the apartment I made us all tea and toast and went straight to bed, sleeping soundly until I was woken up by a huge thunderclap. It was one o`clock. Good. We'd had at least three hours' sleep. That would do until nightime. More food was required. All I seemed to do was make triple-decker sandwiches. Roo, of course declined the offer and wanted to stay in bed. For a moment, I thought I'd leave him there, but the vision of him pacing around the apartment in the early hours of the next morning made me decide to drag the curtains open flooding the room with light. He protested and I relented a little by telling him I'd get him a cup of tea to drink in bed.

There was a crackly storm raging outside. Heavy rain, bright lightning and booming thunder. A good time to put the washing machine on and start the sorting out for Vegas. The boys were still jaded and were happily lolling around. Harry was reading and Lukey poked at his computer. It seemed as long as they were warm, fed and watered, they were fine. They were still my babies. Roo on the other hand was a giant problem. His illness continued to be hard work and it was painful for us both.

The torrential rain continued, but the thunder and lightning had stopped. We'd perked up a bit – even Roo tried to smile. There was time to do something before dinner. The covered market in Kihei's Kalama Village was open until about seven o`clock and it would be good to get out for a while, so I suggested we go. I was surprised when everyone agreed and we walked straight out of the door with brollies and ran to the car.

Kalama Village is a unique shopping area built amongst lush tropical plants and palm trees with something like forty shops and a dozen restaurants. It's the best place for souvenirs, or a special momento and the best thing is that most of it is under cover. The rain was hitting the tin roof like a machine gun when we got there and everyone was having to talk loudly to be heard. It was here on an earlier trip, that we bought the photographs I have in my bathroom at home and I don't know how many Hawaiian island crafts and other lovely bits too. Strolling around in the warm breeze safely away from the pouring rain was soothing and Roo lightened up even more. Harry bought some tropical scented soap (for a lady I hoped) and I hinted that I had fallen in love with a tiny box with a mermaid painted on the lid. *"It would make a wonderful Birthday present for someone."* I said. Roo had been looking through a set of whale photographs on the stall we'd bought my bathroom ones and gasped so loudly when he pulled one of them out that it made me jump. *"What is it?"* I shouted. *"Look, it's that pod"*, he said. What a coincidence! It was a photo of those young whales playing around off Lahaina. We told the owner we'd also seen them and he said that in twenty years of photography, he'd never been able to capture such a charming display of 'whalery'. Of course, we had to buy it and Roo was like the cat that got the cream. He'd missed the opportunity of taking the photo himself, because he was being miserable at the time and felt exonerated by coming across the one on the stall. The other thing that might have helped his mood when we arrived back at the apartment was the cheeky smile he had on his face while he stuffed a small, square-shaped object into his carry-on bag.

It was STILL raining. I cooked a very unimaginative dinner. Dead cow for Roo and Lukey, Dead chicken for Harry and a spiced pasta for me that was a bit TOO lively. The four of us watched some TV and went to bed absolutley done-in. We'd been up and down a volcano, seen a Huey and the Doctor, found a special photo and I hoped Roo had bought my Birthday present. By the look of the protuberance in the side of his carry-on, I might have been right.

DAY SIXTY-Five: "Hey-Ho"

Spoke to Mum. Laurie and Josie had taken her out for dinner last night. Otherwise nothing to report. Thick cloud covering the sky made the ocean as flat as a pancake and it was easy to spot two whales showing off in the water. They slapped around for a long time – breaching every now and then showing their lovely tails before diving beneath the surface. It's impossible to have too much 'whale'. So another dull day, weather-wise. We'll go out for dinner tonight. Alyssa, the American girl from Minessota the boys met here three, or four years ago was arriving today and they were looking forward to seeing her, if only for a few days. We investigated the weather in Vegas on Google, which forecast 91 degrees and sun. New York however was much cooler at 54 degrees, similar to London. It will prepare us for the shock!

Roo is much better and is annoyed with himself for being so miserable yesterday. My calculation of his illness to date is: Physically = nine out of ten and Mentally = five out of ten. Let's say we're making progress.

The boys hopped over the hedge to our beach and played 'bat and ball'. It was odd to see them enjoying something so simple, but the laughter drifting up on to the lanai meant they were having a good time. I fussed about a bit and when we were clean and tidy sat down to read a book on the history of Pan Am the now defunct airline. It may sound an odd choice of reading material, but it was very interesting, so if you ever need to know anything about one of the first transatlantic corporations that lasted nearly sixty-five years, do let me know.

Roo dozed.

Soon, it was time to feed everybody again. I was so good at triple-decker sandwiches by now, I thought I might open a snack bar of my own somewhere. A café with Hawaiian influence perhaps, maybe even with grass skirts. After Luke had had seconds of the triple, we went to have that game of mini golf we'd promised ourselves. It was worth waiting for and as good as ever. Plenty of laughing and being daft. Lukey won, of course and Roo actually seemed sorry to leave.

The mini golf course being the last thing on our list of things to do made me realise just how soon we'd be leaving Maui. Five days in Vegas, three in New York and that would be it. The end of the trip. We had enjoyed ourselves – even with Roo's sad moments and there would be plenty to keep us busy back in England. Harry would be moving into his first home (although he insists Langley will always be home too). Lukey plans to do a few things before Uni and try for the RNLI Beach Lifeguard qualification and Roo will have a go at the volunteering job at Duxford. I can't say I'm looking forward to editing the May Parish News, or the zillion court sittings I'll have to do to make up for a three month gap, but how can I complain?

By the end of the trip I would have been a passenger on fifteen aeroplanes, several seaplanes, a submarine and two cruise ships….. seen Bali Hai, driven up and down a volcano, sipped champagne outside Syney Opera House, held a Koala and lost count of the number of whales I'd seen and Roo and I would have spent three wonderful weeks with our baby boys.

Lukeys ears didn't hurt as much, so I presumed they were on the mend. He walked around the apartment with his head on one side while the drops did their job on his left ear and then dealt with the other, but was deaf as a post while he did it so he didn't hear me say, *"Let's have dinner at the White Restaurant"*. Harry was already raring to go and sat waiting with one eye on the TV and Roo and I joined him a few minutes later.

Lukey still had his head on the side as if he were listening intently for something and seeing us all sitting there said innocently, *"I'm hungry"*.

'The White Restaurant' isn't really the proper name, but it's what we've always called it because the building is white and it was easier to call it that when the boys were small, so they could picture where we were going. Off we went as quickly as possible to resolve the extreme hunger of the youngest member of the family. He must have hollow legs.

The restaurant had changed hands since the last time we ate there and had a completely different menu matching the odd music playing in the background. Gone was the Colonial look of the place. Now it was all chrome, black and white tiles and up-market furniture. We asked for a table on the verandah. At least the view was the same. It wasn't a pretty view, but it was an interesting one of the main thoroughfare through Kihei. Traffic passing by included a Lamborghini and a Ferrari (both could be rented by the day) and a gaggle of Harley riders - members of 'Street Bikers United' no doubt with their long hair, beards and bandanas. They might look a bit threatening when they ride together, but their organisation works on behalf of all bikers in the State of Hawaii promoting motorcycle safety. The Harley Davidson's they ride are fabulous and their owners really look the part. Some are known as 'Coots on Scoots' because they're a little older than you'd expect.

I'd remembered to put in just ONE contact lens, so I could see what I was eating, but not bump into things. I was still getting used to this concept and the boys thought it hillarious when I had to close the naked eye to read the menu. (I was sure I would get used to it and be able to make the adjustment the more I practised). But the menu was a bit of a disappointment. The wholesome food had been replaced by 'Posh Nosh' and I had to read the menu over and over to find something simple. Nothing is forever of course. Perhaps if we're lucky enough to return to Maui another year, it might have changed hands yet again back to the traditional eating place it used to be. We all hate Nouvelle Cuisine. It's just an excuse to charge more for a blob of food in the middle of your plate. Lukey had to have two main courses to fill him up and two slices of toast before he went to bed. Roo said he wasn't feeling well and went to bed with two headache tablets. I felt fine, but did the same.

At least I wasn't being driven to drink (too much).

DAY SIXTY-SIX:

"Interesting Facts and Unusual Happenings"

We discovered that the weather had been affected by Kilauea – the volcano on the Big Island of Hawaii. It had been erupting for some time and had caused what's known as 'VOG' (volcanic fog) - the thick mist and rain we were being subjected to. I don't think even that could have caused the torando though. The southern tip of Maui is supposed to have only 10" rain a year, but I reckon on this trip – our seventh – it had fallen all at once. In a funny sort of way, I was glad there was a reason for the unusual weather. Not much can be done about an erupting volcano and for a change it wasn't a manmade problem.

Although it was drizzling and overcast, it didn't stop the boys sitting on the beach with Alyssa. With frequent giggling and loud chatter, they were hardly interested when I shouted to them to say we were going out. I'd noticed an advertisment for a new art studio and thought we'd have a look.

The nice chap running the place was originally from Banbury in England, but didn't remember it at all as he was tiny when he with his family left for a new life in Hawaii.

347

We didn't like to ask why his family had decided to move from Oxfordshire to Maui, but guessed it was something to do with the hippy times in the 60's. He had friends in the UK though, who regularly sent jars of Branston pickle for his daughter, who is addicted to it. We bought a couple of prints and wandered around looking at the original work some of which were so good they could have been photographs and then leaving the studio popped into 'Hilo Hatties' a store selling Hawaiian clothes and stuff you don't really need, but think you do.

For a change, we were having a Chinese Take-Out for dinner, so back in Makena, I spent the remainder of the afternoon searching the ocean for whales. It didn't take long to find one. A huge chap (could have been a lady), was splashing around in the water just off Molokini – that partially-submerged crater with all the fish in it that I told you about earlier. For once, there wasn't a boat in sight and I may have been the only human to see him, but one minute he was there and the next he had made a dive with hardly a water ripple from his huge tail. Watching the area anxiously calculating the amount of time he was down, I wondered what he was doing down there. Whales have very efficient lungs. Of course, it might be due to the fact that each lung is the size of a small car and also because they have special blood with an oxygen-holding substance, which is why it's almost purple in colour. They usually have to surface for a breath after no more than fifteen minutes and when they do, they blow a huge stream of water through their spout and start the slapping process all over again. I had often wondered if whales slept and if they did, where? On a boat trip we took a few years ago, there was an on-board

Oceanographer who told us that they don't sleep, but like to doze and have the ability to switch of half their brain to relax. How handy that would be for us humans if we were able to do it. Just think how much ironing we'd get done during the night, but that's only half the story. I'll never forget the boys' faces when they came running out of the water wearing snorkels having heard whales singing for the first time. They couldn't believe it and dashed back into the water to listen for some more. Not many people can say they've been sung to by a whale.

It was just under twelve minutes before he surfaced. I was quite relieved. What had he been doing? We know they don't feed while they're in Hawaii and one theory is that they stay underwater because there are no distrubing sounds. I can understand that. Whales may be big, but they're very gentle creatures and obviously like a bit of peace and quiet from time-to-time. I doubt they dive purely to look at what's there, so it's as good a reason as any.

Harry and Lukey had been to Alyssa's apartment and had been chatting with her family. They came back starving hungry, so Roo ordered the Chinese while I cooked the last of the prawns with ginger and pineapple and threw in anything else half-decent left in the fridge to add to the meal. Real Gordon Blurr. Jamie would be proud of me. It's strange how Chinese food can be so different in other parts of the world. In Hong Kong, the food was more western and similar to the type we get in England (apart from those moving objects in that pan), but here it had an Asian influence. Lukey ate it without tasting it, I think. While we were eating, we heard something rooting around in one of the bedrooms and for one awful moment I thought it might be our mongoose. It was when we'd nearly finished that Harry couldn't resist investigating and found a cat. It was a very friendly cat. She stayed the whole evening tucked up on the sofa, until in typical cat-like manner and for no apparent reason, she looked around briefly, sniffed the air and decided to go elsewhere. They're all the same.

The boys had arranged to go out with Alyssa, which meant that Roo and I would be alone after dinner. Roo had been exceptionally quiet and moody, so I knew not to expect a scintilating evening of social intercourse – indeed intercourse of any kind and it was only eight o`clock. Too early for bed – to sleep. I knew I should have got on with the packing, but couldn't bring myself to do it and found myself peering out of the lanai doors. The sky had cleared apart from fluffy, fast-moving clouds and in between were those massive lumnious balls of plasma. The lure of the twinkling was too tempting to ignore and as if spellbound, I was led out onto the lanai to star-gaze. I must have stayed out there for more than an hour and when I dragged myself away, I found Roo in a deep sleep on the sofa with that cat who must have crept in behind me. They did look funny together. The cat had automatically curled herself up and lay cradled in Roo's arm. It was just like being at home. But then Maui is like that.

Increasing the volume on the TV woke both Roo and the cat, who disappeared out of the lanai doors the minute she stirred. *"Did you know that cat was asleep with you?"* I asked. *"Huh?"* Roo said.. *"Never mind"* I told him, but his eyes were closed almost instantaneously and he was asleep again. Flicking through the TV channels, I came upon something-or-other and started to watch it, but hearing the front door open switched it off and looked at my watch. It was only ten o`clock and the boys were back. They weren't back. It was Lukey alone. They'd all been ID'd at a Bar and of course, Lukey at nineteen, hadn't been allowed in. He didn't seem to mind and said he'd wait up for Harry to let him in the apartment gates, which would be locked at 11pm. It was a shame for him but at least I would have some cognitive company. Roo perked up enough to watch the tail-end of a film and stayed up until midnight. I left Lukey to the TV and his security guard duties shortly after. Before I flopped into bed, I finished our packing but was worried about the boys' stuff, which was all over the place.

It was 4.30am when there was a comotion in the hallway. Even Roo was woken and I was there like a shot with a bleary-eyed Lukey. Harry fell through the door laughing uncontrolably between hiccups into Lukey's arms. How he let himself into the complex was a mystery because Lukey certainly hadn't opened the electric gates for him at the front. He reeked of alcohol and his arms were covered in something written in black Biro.

Desperately trying to focus with one eye closed, he said in a long drawl, *"I've had... a wuvverly time. I ... lerv Aryssa"*.

We weren't quite sure what to do with him. Sticking him under a cold shower would be cruel, but would help the smell and might remove some of the Biro. On the other hand, we were intrigued to know what the writing said. Maybe it was something important. Instead of the shower, we put him to bed half-dressed laying on his side packed out with pillows to his back, so he wouldn't suffocate should he be sick. I was always awake at 5.30am.when the sun rose anyway, which wasn't far off and I knew Lukey would have one ear open now that they were better. So less than an hour later it was light outside – the cue for me to rise.

I crept into the boys' room to determine Harry's state of consciousness. He was breathing deeply and although his lips were pale, fortunately they weren't blue and the bowl beside the bed was empty. I wasn't sure if that was good, or bad. He would feel ghastly when he woke up. Lukey was still out cold and looked incredibly pink in comparison.

Closing their door behind me, I did what I always did every morning at the same time, come rain, come shine in Maui. I sat on the lanai with the dickies tweeting at me and looked longingly out to sea.

It's the most wonderful time of day. Fresh, clean and always breezy, it woke me up and made me feel alive. I think it's something to do with ozone or sunlight – or maybe both those things. Whatever it was, I wished I could take it back to England with me.

DAY SIXTY-SEVEN: *"Last Day in Paradise"*

Lukey and Roo were up for breakfast by 9.30am when I'd already enjoyed four hours of daylight. They both complained of the broken nights' sleep and Lukey said he felt quite unwell. *"Not half as much as Harry will feel later"*, I said under my breath.

Roo wanted to make breakfast and said he would make bacon butties. Encouraging his enthusiasm, I showed him the 'American' bacon, reminding him that it was nothing like the stuff back home and that it had to be watched with the utmost watchery because it cooked in seconds.

Fifteen minutes later, the three of us we were crunchng our way through toast and cereal out on the lanai, because the bacon was burnt to a crisp. Even the dickies din't want it and I really couldn't blame them. I had to give them boring old naked bread and I'm sure if they could have sent a letter of complaint, they would have. Lots of Red Hats, but no sign of the mongoose, or the cat. Probably a good thing with so many dickies around. A beautiful day. Perhaps the wind had changed direction and moved the VOG to another island. It was their turn, I would say.

I hated the thought of leaving Maui. The weather at home was foul and having to wear sensible clothes and shoes again would be weird. Roo wasn't too bad and actually talked to Lukey about Harry's high jinks. *"What was with all the Biro?"* Roo asked. *"I have no idea",* Lukey said in the superior way he often does. *"Perhaps it's telephone numbers, or even Tatoos",* Roo said.

We needed to make most of the time we had left – just one last day on Maui.

Kahoolawe and Molokini were as clear as a bell and so was the wind farm. It looked as though the final few hours weather-wise would be good. We should take it all in to remember on a grey day back in England. Meantime, I hoped and prayed that Harry wouldn't hold us back by his alcohol-induced antics and began to wonder how he would be when he eventually surfaced. That prospect was bad enough, but I also had no idea what was in store from Roo. The closer we came for the move to Vegas, the more unpredictable his behavious might become. It was like sticking my hand in a Tombola. I had no idea what I'd pull out.

All I had to do was iron a few bits, close the cases, make sure the boys were ready to go, check the tumble drier and have one final sweep of the kitchen. I'd hate to leave it looking like a tip. We'd booked a table out on the terrace at 'Tommy Bahamas' – one of the poshest restaurants in Wailea for our last night, which meant I wouldn't have to cook again until we arrived back home. I was really looking forward to it. Dressing up … the food … the atmosphere … but not the bill.

Harry materialised at last like a zombie from a film called, ' *Harry, King of the Zombies'*. He looked terrible and swaying a little, mumbled that anything after nine o`clock last night was a total blank in his mind. Unable to explain the Biro scrawled all the way up his arms, he had no idea how he and Alyssa had gained entry to the resort. They were sure no one had pressed the button for them, so they must have scaled the twelve foot gates without being detected by the Security Guard. Harry said he thought he'd had a wonderful time and hadn't done anything he shouldn't have, to or with Alyssa, but was pretty sure he didn't love her.

The way he looked at that moment, had he slipped into a coma for the next four weeks, I wouldn't have been surprised.

The weather stayed fine and and I tried not to clock-watch. The dickies somehow knew we were leaving the next day and ate every scrap of food I gave them. I kept a constant vigil for whales, until I saw what might be the last one - the big one I saw yesterday perhaps. It was quite far out, so it was difficult to recognise its tail.

Not that I was an expert, of course, but these were my last few moments on the lanai and I tried to suck in every single second. Willing the whale to breach for me just one more time, I couldn't be disappointed with the performance it gave. It didn't breach, but what it did was to rise up majestically and slowly disappear beneath the water. I could have cried. It was if he – like my dickies - knew I had to go and was saying goodbye.

It was time to be busy. With the thousand things I mustn't forget going through my mind, I began to collect up the remnants of breakfast, but the perfect excuse delayed me. A wedding! It was a very simple one - bride, groom and Minister, with the three of them in white, standing barefoot at the waters' edge for the brief service. There wasn't a flower in sight and there really wasn't need for any. The breeze caught the brides' flowing Holoku and tousled her long dark hair and the Minister reading from his Bible looked up at them both every now and then, finishing as usual, with the sign of the cross. It was very romantic. The magic of Maui is difficult to describe, but if anything can sum it up it's a scene like that. The newlyweds left the beach, with the groom carrying the bride in his arms and the Minister following. It was a real finale for me and the best wedding of all. But I had to get on with things and reluctantly left the lanai. The boys were already in the pool. I was surprised Harry felt well enough to swim and wondered if it was a good idea. As long as he was with Lukey he would be okay though and the water might even rehydrate him through osmosis. It would also soak off that Biro.

Roo wasn't in panic mode – yet. He asked me if I wanted him to do anything and I knew I should say *"Yes"*. What could I get him to do that wouldn't worry him, OR me? *"If you collect everything up from the bathrooms and put it all on the dining table, then we'll know those areas are clear"* I suggested. I think he wanted me to say, *"No. You sit down and leave it all to me."* But several journeys later, he'd deposited a clonglomeration of toothpastes, shower gels and personal items unceremoniously onto the table. Then he sat down. At least he'd offered to help for once, I reminded myself.

The boys came in after their swim. Harry looked much better, but the Biro was still visible. It would probably be a while before it was all gone and would be a reminder of 'the evening' for some time yet. It was actually quite funny if I didn't think about what could have happened. I also wondered how Alyssa was feeling.

I'd kept back some cheese and ham and made toasted sanwiches for a change and we took them outisde to eat. Lukey had finished his before he had a chance to sit down and turned circle to make himself some more. How he stays so slim with everything he eats is a mystery to me.

Our last day was flying by. After lunch, we stole some time for a final walk on the beach and found some driftwood looking as though it had been carved into the shape of a seahorse. Roo picked it up to take back to the apartment, where we'd leave it as our contribution to the collection already there. Harry thought sitting in the Jacuzzi for a while might remove the remainder of the Biro. I reminded him that there was still a lot to be packed (the clothes on the floor of their bedroom, for example), but he assured me that it was all under control and off he and Lukey went.

Roo decided to have another shower, but was back in less than a minute soaking wet with a towel round him. *"Where's the shower gel?"* he moaned. *"Where you put it"*, I moaned back grabbing it from the table and throwing it to him. Not much more to do. Good – there would be time to sit outside before getting dressed for dinner. I poured myself a glass of wine and nipped out onto the lanai hoping I hadn't been seen. It was a bit early for booze.

The sun was on its way down and now that the weather had cleared, the light on the ocean was beautiful.. I thought the waves would have come up to my waist had I been in them, so an estimate of their height was around three feet - big enough to have a blue tinge in the curl. The noise as the surf crashed onto the beach was quite intoxicating. It was nothing to do with the glass of wine. With the retreat of the tide came the sound of the ocean being sucked back across the sand and then silence, until it was repeated all over again. Had I been into meditation, I would have been asleep by now.

The beach was empty of people until two hula girls and a photographer appeared. The girls weren't wearing very much at all and I wondered what was going on, but it didn't take long to realise that it was a photo shoot – probably for next years' calendar. The girls' skirts were made from palm leaves and their abundant leis managed to cover their top half matching their headdress and ankle adornments. All very pretty. They rolled around in the surf, posing and posturing in turn and then together, as the photographer captured the mood of the moment, until the sun was low in the sky creating pink hues.

I dashed in to replenish my glass and walked straight into a sweet-smelling Roo. *"Bit early",* he said looking at my glass. *"Sunset".* Was my excuse. And what a sunset it was. You must be sick of hearing about all the sunsets I've mentioned in my journal, but as this will be my last Maui one, please indulge me with one last description….. *Pink-tipped clouds were framed by tufts of purple 'brush strokes' in an atmosphere of clear blue from God's own palette.* That's all.

Although I say it myself, I looked quite nice. We'd all made an effort, but the boys did have to telll Roo that he needed to change out of what he thought he was wearing. His second choice was more acceptable to them both and we left the apartment for 'Tommy Bahamas' to have our Last Supper. The restaurant was its usual busy-self, but as I'd insisted we book a table, we were taken straight outside to the balcony . It was difficult to see the menu by the light of gas lamps – or was the difficulty due to the ONE contact lens? Anyway, anything on their menu is good so I ordered the fish of the day.

The food was excellent as was the musician strumming his guitar and singing as if his life depended on it. We were all in a good mood – even Roo, who was showing no signs of panic about the impending move first thing in the morning. I couldn't fault our time together as a family. There hadn't been any arguments, or upset and the boys had been so good with Roo giving me the support I so often lacked at home. I felt blessed and grateful all at the same time.

DAY SIXTY-EIGHT: "Time to Go"

I wasn't so much 'up with the Lark' as 'up with the Cardinals, Mynahs and other peep-peeps', because they were all waiting for their breakfast at 5.30am. I cooked oodles of bacon (the uncrispified version) for sandwiches once the others were up and gave the dickies everything left over. They loved it. I hoped they wouldn't be too confused tomorrow morning when I didn't appear with food, but maybe the apartment would be used by another bird-loving occupant. If not they'd have to make do with worms.

Some time during the week, the boys had met one of the Makena Surf *'ladies wot does'*. She owned an old Camero and was restoring it on her day off. Probably a bit older than me, she had two jobs working as a maid six days a week and did renovations on the car on the seventh. She put me to shame. The red Camero sounded wonderful with its engine running and the boys were very impressed that something 'so old' could look so cool.

How the boys managed to get the luggage into our rental car though I'll never know, but they pummelled it and pushed it into the back and slammed the door shut. It clicked open twice, until they both leaned on it and held it down for a moment, as if they were suffocating something inside. It did the trick.

We really were leaving. From where the car was parked, I could see the beach and the blue of the ocean meeting the lighter blue of the sky. I wished I had appreciated it all even more than I knew I had, but it was too late now. Hanging it out for a few more seconds, I had no alternative but to accept the fact that it was time to go.

Within half an hour, we were at the airport and had returned the car, minus our luggage. It was all going too quickly. In less than an hour, we had dropped our suitcases and were riding the escalator together taking us up to Departures. The boys were laughing and talking about something un-Hawaiian and I wanted to shout at them saying, *"Don't you realise we're leaving?"* At the top of the escalator, I stopped and looked back longingly. I was being pathetic now. The flight was called and we trooped onto the plane for the hop across from Maui to Honolulu. As we rose into the air, I didn't know whether to look out of the window, or not. My heart got the better of me though and as I sipped the last native Mai Tai, watched Haleakala dreamily drift out of sight behind the clouds and in an instant, Maui was gone. Twenty minutes later we swept past the military aircraft and navy ships floating around Pearl Harbour once again to land in

Honolulu and with little time between flights, headed straight to the gate for the next one. If I wasn't making triple- decker sandwiches, I was getting on and off aircraft, it seemed. Roo hadn't had time to be worried, or upset.

The 767-300 taking us to Las Vegas dwarfed the planes sitting either side of it and on board we were greeted by yet another gorgeous cabin crew wearing leis and flowers in their hair. The perfume of the Plumeria permeating throughout the cabin was exquisite. Once in our seats, Roo didn't look too concerned, so I sat back to enjoy the typical 'pyoingy' ukelele music playing in the background and had a look at the menu for the flight to mainland USA.

During the five hour journey, the window shutters are kept closed. There's nothing to see but ocean and we would be flying much too high to see a whale, or even a large ship so people snoozed or watched their screens in between being fed and watered the Hawaiian way.

The trip was as smooth as a whistle. You wouldn't have known you were in the air. Roo slept constantly – his way of coping of course, but I nudged him awake when dinner was ready to be served. He said he wasn't hungry and closed his eyes again, but I nodded to the flight attendant when she came with his meal and nudged him awake again.

Our trays were covered in a white linen cloth presented with a fresh orchid. A charming, very Hawaiian touch. Roo didn't make conversation and only picked at his meal, but I had no trouble polishing off mine, which I knew had been created by Beverly Gannon, one of the best chefs in the islands from 'Joe's Bar and Grill' on Maui. Anything 'Maui' was more than fine and dandy for me.

Moving through another time zone meant that Vegas was three hours ahead and when everyone opened their window shutters for landing it would have been difficult to miss the million-trillion lights of the city in the distance as it was 11.30pm. We touched-down like a feather landing on a cloud, in spite of the plane's enormity and before the clock struck midnight had retreived our luggage, found our driver and were on our way to 'The Strip'. The boys were staying at The Hotel (at Mandalay Bay) and we would be next door at the much quieter, Four Seasons *"to give them some space"*. (Well, that's what I told them anyway).

By the time we had checked in it was almost 1am. We waved the boys off and watched them go through the connecting door to the other hotel, hoping they'd be alright on their own. I told myself off for thinking they wouldn't be and followed Roo to the lift. It was strange to be without their company and I missed them already, but we'd see them for breakfast. We ordered sandwiches from Room Service and ate them in bed.

Really good for the digestion.

DAY SIXTY-NINE: "Viva, Las Vegas!"(-7hrs GMT)

We meant to get up early, but the beds were so comfortable and the suite so cosy, it was 11.30am before we surfaced to meet the boys for what would now be 'Brunch'. They had slept well, but admitted they hadn't gone to bed until 5am. Naughty them. The lure of the hotel and casino was just too much and they had felt the need to investigate every part of it before turning in. This was day one. With a few more to go, they were intent on making sure their time here was well-spent. Each visit in the past had viewed them as different people. Now they were young men, it wasn't only them seeing Vegas in a completely different light, it was also Vegas seeing THEM in a completely different light. I hoped I had done the right thing by making it part of the trip and wasn't sure they should be doing 'man' things yet; especially with Lukey being so young. I consoled myself with the thought that they'd be ID'd everwhere they went and that would clip their wings a bit.

Roo was seven out of ten. Not bad at all, apart from one flood of sadness that made him burst into tears. It came quite suddenly and made me sit up with a bit of a shock. We'd been lounging round the pool surrounded by people when it happened and they must have thought I'd said something terrible to him. It lasted about ten minutes and came out of the blue. How could it happen when he was in a fantastic place, with beautiful weather, beside his fabulous wife? I haven't the faintest idea. But that's depression for you. It's sneaky. Before you know it, it's there like some vile monster waiting to pounce on an unsuspecting person hoping to devour them and it will - if you let it.

I had to do a bit of surruptitious speed-counselling to get him over the worst and then suggested he went for a stroll. As he stood up, a lady on the next sun lounger gave me the look of death – as if I'd just told Roo that I was running away with a croupier from the casino. It's at moments like this, that I want to shout through a loudhailer, *"Do you know what it's like living with a Depressive!!?"* Of course, I just smiled at her sweetly instead.

While Roo was wandering, the boys appeared before me. Excitedly, they said they'd booked themselves seats at a Burlesque show later that evening. It seemed ridiculous that at nineteen, Lukey could watch a steamy show containing scantily-clad girls, but couldn't buy himself an alcoholic drink. I expected it would be alright. Wouldn't it? Noticing the boys talking to me, Roo ceased his circumnavigation of the pool and came back. I could see he was really trying to pretend that nothing had happened to him and to appear in complete control. *"What's this?"* he asked in a shaky voice.

Taking his arm, the boys led him away from the poolside and the three of them stood in a huddle. They obviously felt the need to tell someone about the finer details of the evenings' entertainment and the chat culminated in 'throatty' laughter. I didn't think I wanted to know the finer details and pretended to read my book.

The 'look of death' lady glared at me again. I couldn't do anything right in her eyes.

We'd hired a Jeep and thought we might as well use it to drive down to the other end of 'The Strip'. The ride along the four mile road could take anything from half an hour to an hour and a half, depending on the traffic, but doing the trip slowly meant we would get to see everything in greater detail. It would be a cheap night out and a very entertaining one with so much to see, hear - and smell, if we turned the air conditioning off and wound the windows down.

There is a free monorail running behind the hotels, but then you don't get to see everything going on. And boy, is there a lot going on!! The dazzling lights alone are amazing. I don't know if anyone has ever calculated the amount of lightbulbs, but the beam from the top of the Luxor Hotel pyramid has a 40billion candlepower – and that's just one light!

Nineteen of the world's twenty-five largest hotels as far as capacity is concerened, are here with a total of more than 67,000 rooms. The first casino built in 1931 was a favourite place for the men constructing the Hoover Dam to let of steam. (I'll tell you about the Dam later), but a Jewish-American chap known as 'Bugsy' Siegel, a Vegas gangster involved with Italian-American organised crime was behind a lot of the early development. He was murdered in 1946, but I wonder what he would say if he could see it now!

Las Vegas was the first American city to have legalised gambling … one of the first cities to stop the 'colour line' of racial segregation … maybe the only city with a street that can be seen from outer space … and the first (and only) city to make atomic testing a tourist attraction! There are no clocks on The Strip, because time doesn't really matter in a city that definitely doesn't sleep.

'The Rat Pack' was the nickname of a group of famous actors and singers who frequented Vegas in the 50's and 60's and included Humphrey Bogart, Frank Sinatra, Dean Martin, Sammy Davis, Jr., Peter Lawford, and Joey Bishop. It was mainly a male-dominated group, but a few ladies were allowed to join this elite clan, such as Lauren Bacall, Angie Dickinson, Marilyn Monroe, Ava Gardner, and Judy Garland. The fact that they were all beautiful had nothing to do with it, of course.

Elvis performed here for the first time in 1956 when he only twenty-one, advertised as 'The Atomic Powered Singer' and obviously filmed 'Viva Las Vegas' here. There's a museum dedicated to his memory and a very convincing Tribute Show.

The US Air Force Base at Nellis just outside Vegas grew during WWII and is now a key military installation flying jets such as F16's and the 'secret' Area 51 is only eighty-odd miles away. With all this information I'm giving you, I'm sure you realise that Las Vegas has much more to offer than gambling and light bulbs. What with famous boxing fights taking place, massive convention facilities, spectacular shows and top-notch singers, outrageously-themed hotels, Lake Mead, the Colorado River and the Grand Canyon, there's something for everyone. (I really deserve to be paid by the LV Chamber of Commerce for my advertising skills). Marriages can take place in the blink of an eye (there's even a Drive-thru where you're married in your car) and if you live in Vegas you can divorce your new other half six weeks later.

There's no need to spend a huge amount of money in Vegas. Visiting other hotels doesn't cost anything and is real entertainment. Some of our favourites are The Luxor (more Egyptian than Egypt and in colour), The Mirage with an exploding volcano, The Venetian, which has its own Grand Canal complete with gondolas and strolling performers, The Bellagio's dancing fountains and Caesar's Palace, which is a favourite with Harry and Lukey for its cocktail waitresses (nearly) wearing (very) mini Togas.

The themes go on and on .... Paris with its own Eiffel Tower, New York/New York (yes, it does have a Statue of Liberty), etc., etc.....

Eventually reaching the end of 'The Strip', we came to Freemantle Street, which is the oldest and original part of Las Vegas. Some of the shops and Revue Bars have been covered with a vast canopy the length of five football pitches, housing an amazing light show of spectacular technology on the hour, every hour. It's a 'must-see', although this area is probably not the best place to linger if you don't want to mix with the drifters from out of town.

We needed to have dinner somewhere and were keeping an eye on the time so the boys weren't late for their Burlesque Show. The general concensus of opinion was that heading back to their hotel to eat was the best idea and afterwards, they could dash off to their room for a wash and brush up. The balmy evening air combined with the extravaganza of the scenes we were passing on the way back along 'The Strip' couldn't help but make us feel carefree and content.

Dinner was good, with an atmosphere of anticipation on both the boys' and my part. They were living in hope of an eye-opening experience, while I shut my eyes at the thought of what they might experience. It was hard to think that my baby boys had turned into big boys now and I'm sure Roo would have gone with them if he felt he could have. The shock might even have helped his depression! I can't remember Harry ever eating so fast – he kept up with Lukey and neither of them had a pudding. They were standing up, ready to go, the second the cutlery hit their empty plates, leaving the table with hardly a *"Thanks for dinner. Bye, bye"* a second after that to go and change their clothes.

It was still early and as our hotel didn't have a casino (God forbid, at 'Four Seasons'!) we wandered around the one in the Mandalay Bay. It was huge and the constant noise from people feeding the slot machines, the "ching-ching-ching" sound of coins dropping and bells ringing every now and then attacked your senses in every way, but it was still exciting and quite contagious. The casino covers 135,000sq feet and sits amongst a tropical setting of waterfalls and palm trees with clever lighting tricking you into thinking it's daytime (there are no windows).

You know I'm not a gambler. I'm a black and white person who doesn't take risks in any grey area, but Roo plays Black Jack occasionally – at least for a whole ten minutes until his money has gone. As I've said before, the only thing I've ever won was the prize for bandaging, so why would I risk losing money to a slot machine? However, Roo seemed interested in a particularly bright, flashy, lighty thing and slid a $5 note into its hungry mouth. Two seconds of "ching-ching-chinging" later and it was gone. That had to be the fastest way on the planet to lose $5. It would take longer to burn with a match.

It was sheer coindcidence (honest) that we found ourselves outside the entrance to the Burlesque Show the boys had tickets for. A second, or two later, they bounced up looking clean, shiny and quite the Men About Town. We watched them go in and went to bed.

DAY SEVENTY: "Nascar"

We'd ordered breakfast for 8.30am and it arrived on the dot. A nice young chap wheeled in a table covered with a Damask tablecloth, complete with a vase full of pretty yellow daisies, Eggs Benedict for me and eggs and bacon for Roo. The lapsize napkins had been starched so much, they stood up on their own and the freshly-squeezed orange juice tasted even better from the chilled cut glass tumblers the chap produced from the fridge beneath the table. Lovely.

Today was the day the boys were to drive NASCARS. I had no idea what it was when they mentioned it the year before, so I investigated, thinking that anything to do with cars would be okay and for once, it would solve the dilemma of Christmas present-giving. NASCAR racing began in 1948, using four-door American-made cars like the Ford Fusion, Dodge Charger, Chevrolet Impala and Toyota Camry and have fenders to allow side-to-side contact between competing cars without causing a crash. The cars that race professionally have V8 engines differing from the norm by generating more than 750HP, rather than 400HP. Apparently this sort of racing with the brightly-coloured cars and the sound of the engines has a real following from young and old alike. The Las Vegas track right next door to Nellis Air Force Base offered the novice racing driver the chance to drive a 600HP V8 stock car around eight laps of the circuit and when the boys opened the envelope containing the tickets they were delighted. It seemed like a good idea at the time, but now I wasn't so sure.

Meeting the boys in our lobby at 9.30am, I was anxious to know how the evening at the Burlesque Show had gone. Lukey grinned and studied the floor avoiding eye contact, but Harry whispered softly, *"It was a bit rude, Mum"*. Obviously reluctant to spill the beans, I wondered if they'd tell their Dad more and left it like that for the time being. Perhaps I'd rather not know what the show contained. At least they were where they were supposed to be now and we hadn't had to go looking for them backstage, or down a dark alley somewhere – or worse ……. get them bailed.

Driving for half an hour out of Vegas into a bit of desert, we followed the signs to Nellis first and eventually those for LV Speedway and along the way we saw several F16's doing acrobats and somersaults high up in the sky. The crackling noise the jets made as they passed immediately above us was deafening and the dives they made in and out of one life-threatening turn after another scary. With their escapades holding our attention it wasn't long before we were at the track. It was then that I realised exactly what I'd bought them last Christmas.

One thing I never get used to in America, is the amount of space they have and Las Vegas Motor Speedway certainly takes up some of it in a 1,300 acre complex, consisting of 1.5 mile oval with seating for 107,000, a 3/8 mile paved oval called the "Bullring", a 2.5 mile road course, a 1.3 mile road course, a stadium truck racing course, a 3/4 mile kart sprint course, a 10 mile off-road course and a quarter mile drag strip also known as 'The Strip' sometimes opened for locals to drag race in the Midnight Mayhem Programme, designed to get boy racers off the streets.

It's huge. To get to the Driving Experience Office meant passing through a tunnel beneath the track – a bit like Heathrow, where the access tunnel crosses the runway. On the track above us, half a dozen brightly-coloured saloon cars drove at speed, with barely an inch between them. *"Phew! Look at them"*, I said naively. *"They must be in a race".* The noise outside was deafening, but the silence inside should have triggered my understanding.

At that time however, it still hadn't dawned on me that this was what the boys would be doing. When we reached the parking area though, I had become suspicious enough to say, *"Who's driving those, then?"* Pointing to the gaggle we'd just seen. No one answered me and I began to repeat my question, *"Who ...."* but Lukey interrupted me by pointing to a portacabin and turning to Harry said, *"That's where we report for the safety briefing".*

SAFETY? Hang on a minute. Weren't they just going to 'toodle' around the circuit to get the feel of things? They couldn't possibly be driving fast. It wouldn't be allowed. They weren't racing drivers.

By this time, they were inside the office and the look of horror on my face warned Roo that I was about to throw a wobbler and he took hold of my arm keeping me from going after them. *"They'll be fine"* he said. *"Of*

course they will, because they're not going in those cars."
I yelled. But just then, the boys left the office and walking towards us, Harry said, *"We're miles too early. The lady suggested we visit the Shelby Museum and Body Shop down the road and come back in an hour."*

"Over my dead body", I thought.

We piled back into the Jeep and I wondered what on earth I was going to say. It had been ME who had bought the 'Experience', but I swear I had no idea that they'd be able to drive as fast as that. If they had an accident I'd never forgive myself.

The Museum was literally round the corner and as we went in, I wracked my brain to think of a reason to cancel their present. They'd be cross, of course, but would appreciate my fears and accept the ruling. They loved their mummy and wouldn't question her judgement of a dangerous situation. After all, what were mummys for?

The Shelby Company, founded by racing driver Carroll Shelby modifies/converts (not sure of the correct term) cars into what can only be called *'Grrrrr...'* Their small museum holds some of the cars they've tweeked from 1962 to the present day and if you love a sleek, sexy beast of a car, you must visit and see for yourself. I left Roo and the boys drooling over them and went outside in the sunshine to concoct my speech. Two more (or maybe the same) F16's were up there making a helluva racket and I shielded my eyes to watch their cavorting while I thought. It was quite simple. They would see sense now that they knew how dangerous those cars were and would probably be glad I had provided them with an excuse not to go.

Ten minutes later, Roo and the boys joined me outside raving about the Shelby's, but before they had a chance to get back into the Jeep, I began my lecture on the 'perils of the track' and was still rambling on when we parked outside the portacabin once again. *"So you see my point, don't you?"* I declared. *"Yes, Mum"*, Harry mumbled. *"Of course"*, Lukey muttered, as the two of them left the car and walked into the office. I stared after them while Roo just sat there. *"Well aren't you going to do anything?"* I yelled. *"Yes, I'm going to the Wal-Mart up the road"*, Roo whispered. *"Why don't you come with me?"*

Even the contents of Wal-Mart couldn't stop my thoughts of mangled metal and tangled wreckage – and they were only attending the safety talk at that moment! I turned round to see where Roo was and my heart sank. His colour was dreadful and that bucket of water had been chucked over him again. *"Wassup?"* I asked. He was trembling like a junkie needing a fix and hanging on to the trolley for dear life. Meandering over to him without appearing alarmed, I stood looking at him for a second or two because deciding the best course of action to take in these situations is sometimes difficult. We could ditch the trolley, walk out and sit in the car until the attack passed or we could try to get through it and feel we'd got one over on it for a change. I decided on the latter.

"Oh, it's just one of your panic attacks", I said reassuringly. *"You secretly don't want them to drive those cars either!"* I added.

The joke seemed to help and he actually smiled, but the next fifteen minutes was a real strain. There I was in a Wal-Mart on Nellis Air Force Base in the middle of the Nevada Desert, struggling to cope with my husband's major panic attack and with my baby boys about to risk their lives in cars that I might just as well have handed to them on a plate.

Just then, an F16 streaked somewhere above us adding to the madness of the moment.

Of course, Roo survived the attack in Wal-Mart and once I'd prised his fingers from the trolley we returned to the race track.

He'd improved enough to start sorting out his camera, but fiddled with the camcorder at the same time and found himself in a right 'two and eight'. The palaver seemed rather out of proportion. Half of me wanted him to film the boys driving and the other half didn't – just in case something dreadful happened.

All those involved seemed very professional though and I tried to look as relaxed as everyone else – but surely the other mothers had to be acting.

The boys appeared wearing fireproof suits and helmets hardly resembling my little boys at all. I felt dizzy and couldn't move my head. I remembered Harry's amazement when we bought him a plastic Police car for his second Birthday and Lukey's joy when he was allowed to sit in it at the same age, even though we said it was only for "big boys". Just then, my motherly thoughts were interrupted by someone mentioning 160 miles per hour and holding my breath, I scoured the area for a suitable vomit bowl.

Lukey's name was called over the PA and like a big, little lamb ... and with the spectators clapping and cheering as though they'd known him all his life ... he followed the Marshall to a beastly-looking red and yellow monster–of-a-car with the number '54' on the side. I was a bit bemused when he entered through the window and not the door, but assumed this was normal. Desperately wanting to rush over and say he couldn't go without me sitting beside him, I stood firm knowing that he would never forgive me had I done so – and anyway, I'd only have been able to slide half of me through the window (and out again). The noise was deafening as Lukey started the engine. The pace car drove in front of him and he was off! I watched as much as I could, but he was soon out of sight until thirty seconds later when he roared past the viewing area. Roo was madly clicking the camera with one hand and eye and camcording with the others. I just wanted it to finish safely and couldn't care less about photographs. Lukey was only half-way through his eight laps, when Harry was called, which meant they would both be on the track at the same time. I didn't know where, or which way to look first and was surprised that I hadn't suffered a cardiac arrest by then. The relief I felt when first Lukey popped through the window of 'number 54' and then seeing Harry pull up to the Finish line unscathed was enormous; but it would be Thursday before my pulse returned to normal.

The boys were delighted with themselves. Harry's top speed was 127mph and Lukey's 120mph. They both looked flushed with the excitement of it all and I could hear their nervous laughter as they went to change out of the fireproof suits. That was quite enough speeding for one day – it was back to the pool for them to recuperate and the coronary care unit for me. The DVD of the experience from the drivers' angle would be something to study at home, but they were already disappointed that they hadn't driven faster and assured each other that their speeds 'next time' would be completely different now they had the hang of it.

We left Harry and Lukey 'cruising' the Mandalay Beach – as all good racing drivers would after a race and Roo and I sat in the quiet of Four Seasons allowing relief to return me gently to earth and my blood pressure reading to a more normal level. I would definitely make sure that their Christmas presents next year were more mother-friendly and vowed to study interesting gifts on the Internet in greater detail before hitting the 'purchase' key in future.

We all wanted to see The Wynn, the hotel which had replaced the famous 'Desert Inn' and was the most expensive hotel and casino ($2.7b) in the world at that time. Instead of using 'Paris' or the canal at 'The Venetian' as a theme, the focus of this hotel is a rather intriguing, *'The Dream'*.

The entrance wasn't the grandest of entrances but once inside a tree-lined path lead us into the 217acre hotel, housing a 150' man-made mountain with waterfall dropping into a three acre lake. It would have taken a couple of days to see the whole hotel and its interpretation of oneirology, so without time for that we nabbed a table in the bustling buffet restaurant. The room was painted in colourful hues of pale green and lemon with fruit and flowers piled high on four huge tiers reaching about fifty feet to the ceiling. It was most odd. I've never had a dream involving fruit, or flowers. But there you go. Wherever you looked there was ... *flowers and fruit ... fruit and flowers ... flowers* ....

My baby boys were all tuckered out – as racing drivers and baby boys often are and they left us as soon as we'd eaten and were back in our neck of 'The Strip', but before Roo and I went to bed, we watched a very jolly programme about a meteor strike.

I hoped to dream about something else. Flowers and fruit, perhaps.

DAY SEVENTY-ONE: "Ready? Aim …"

Roo woke up with a start, sitting bolt upright and immediately crashed down on the pillow again with a massive sigh. I knew we shouldn't have watched that 'doom and gloom' film last night. A speedy pep-talk seemed to do the trick though, after which he got up and showered returning twenty minutes later looking much improved.

In spite of the exciting and memorable day yesterday (in more ways than one) the boys planned to go to a gun shop today – to shoot guns (amazingly).

You were thinking I was going to be a spectator weren't you? Well you would be wrong, because I had promised the boys (who are terrific clay-shooters) that I would do my best to fire a machine gun. It amused them somewhat to think that *'Medical-Mew-Mew-the-Magistrate'* (their name for me – not my official title) could do something as mad and dangerous, but knowing I will try most things apart from bungee jumping, skydiving, or anything to do with whisky we went straight to the 'shop' after breakfast.

In a country where citizens have "*the right … to keep and bear arms*", gun ranges are commonplace. Most law-abiding and sane people have no wish to use a gun on their fellow human beings and as a mother and Magistrate I wished guns didn't exist at all, but these places are perhaps the best way for some to satisfy their curiosity by shooting at a picture on the wall in a secure purpose-built facility.

In a side street off 'The Strip', the range was an ordinary-looking building, but quite rightly gaining admittance was as hard as getting into Fort Knox. (I've never tried and can only assume, *but surely* ….). When we were eventually allowed in after speaking through the entry phone, confirming our appointment and being 'eyed up' through the CCTV, we could see that this was no happy-go-lucky adventure playground.

Once inside, we stood in the corridor while the front door was locked behind us and another door unlocked to let us through to the range itself.

Viewing the array of firearms housed on the wall behind the long counter, which also acted as a barrier, I suddenly felt a bit worried about handling a real weapon and had to steel myself for the experience.

I know we hear too often about shootings in America and it might all sound a bit flippant, but stringent rules must be followed to allow them to offer this service to the public, with only a qualified Rangemaster able to give firearms instruction and a Certified Armourer to distribute the equipment.

Our Rangemaster, who was the size of an adolescent hippo, delighted in giving us our safety briefing and obviously loved his job. He had our attention instantly and after choosing our weapons and donning ear defenders he led us to the actual shooting range – a long corridor with several cubicles and we crowded into one that was empty. The noise from the others firing at their targets was awful even with the big ear covers and at first, I wasn't sure I would be able to handle it all.

Standing with the Rangemaster beside him, Lukey faced his target - a life-size photograph of a well-known terrorist hanging several meters away. It was impossible to hear what was being said, but with a nodding head and with his serious face on, Lukey slowly squeezed the trigger of the Beretta and the bullets all hit the picture until the barrel was empty. I'd never been so close to a hand gun before, let alone watch my son fire one and found the whole thing quite surreal. It was Harry's turn next. He'd chosen a Glock hand gun and with the same careful aim hit the target as if it was all true.

Itching to try something else, they made another visit to the Armourer, returning with machine guns: AK74, MP5 and an S.A.W. This was getting a bit weird now.

When it came to my turn, I have to admit that I did look peculiar standing there holding an MP5, but it amused the boys and I kept my word. My aim with the sub-machine gun wasn't as good as theirs but studying the picture of the terrorist I had shot at, the Rangermaster said, *"Well, he won't be making any little terrorists!"* which would have been marvellous – had I not been aiming at his head. However, the men around me decided I was not one to be messed with. It would take me a while to recuperate from my new experience and I decided that it was probably one I would not choose to repeat.

With more than enough activity for one day, it was back to the hotel pool. I was counting the hours of sunshine we had left – approximately ten, excluding tomorrow, because we'd be driving all day.

All day in the Nevada Desert. Another crazy idea of mine organised over the Internet.

Yes, I hear what you're saying. Me and that 'purchase' button!

Apart from the funny five minutes first thing that morning, Roo had been fine. Forward-thinking had definitely helped to re-programme his thoughts and his sadness hadn't been excessive. His panic attacks were horrible, but usually didn't last long and we both sort of pooh-poohed them trying not to include them in his overall condition. They seem to occur abruptly, reaching a crescendo around ten minutes later and slowly subside.

I'm sure anyone can suffer a panic attack, given the right conditions. I think I had one myself once for no apparent reason it seemed. I was shopping alone in a supermarket and was suddenly enveloped in intense fear. It was most peculiar and I remember hanging on to the trolley just as Roo did. I blame the artificial lighting in some of these stores, it seems to affect a lot of people in a very detrimental way, but maybe I just wanted an excuse for it happening. I do remember how frightening it was though and hope it doesn't happen again.

There were a lot of very strange people around the pool. They weren't all skinny and been 'done' this time, some of them were enormous – making ME feel skinny. But most of them were so rude it made my toes curl.

There was not one 'please', or 'thank you' to be heard from our companions, so each time Roo and I were served, we made a point of saying these niceties as loud as we possibly could. Not that it made any difference; they didn't take the hint.

I'm no anti-capitalist, but there was such an obvious division between the guests and the staff, it made me squirm. There was me - wearing a $10 sarong from the market in Hawaii and Roo looking his delectable-self in a pair of M & S swim shorts. But beside us, a lady wearing a Chanel bathing suit expected the waitress to fetch a bowl of water for the small dog (wearing a sparkly collar) peeping out of her Gucci handbag. When the bowl arrived, the owner of the dog complained because the waitress had spilt a little of the water on the floor and of course, there was no 'thank you'.

Is it me?

Roo said the potty pool people were making him feel miserable and he needed a change of scenery and would try to find the boys next door, which would be like looking for a needle in a haystack. It didn't matter if he found them, or not - the walk would change his mood and might stop it degrading into something worse.

Miraculously he discovered Lukey quite quickly sitting all alone and forlorn-looking beside the pool with the pretend beach. Roo asked where Harry was and without saying a word, Lukey pointed to the Jacuzzi.

Harry was there, alright – bubbling away with a very pretty blonde girl beside him. Lukey was already disgruntled, because Harry had arranged to have dinner

384

with a friend who just happened to be in Vegas, which meant that he would have to spend the evening alone with his mum and dad. With a promise to try not to look like his parents (it would be easy when he towers above us both), we hoped that taking him to Caesar's Palace to eat might make up for it.

Back in our suite, I rang Mum. Nothing cheery to report. The weather was dreadful. My sister was miserable. Mum hadn't been outside for days because of the weather and the forecast was cold, wet and windy. I was really glad I'd 'phoned.

Looking at the clear blue sky, I felt terribly guilty until Roo appeared wearing nothing but a towel having had a shower. He turned to say something to me at the same moment the towel fell to the floor. It put the whole thing into a different perspective and I laughed until my stomach hurt.

With Roo in a less-distracting outfit, the three of us jumped into a cab outside Four Seasons, discovering that the driver came from Oahu in Hawaii. We jabbered on and on about the islands and how much we loved it and he did too. The thing was, he could earn three times as much in Vegas as he could in Hawaii and went on extolling the virtues of being able to send money back home and still enjoy twice-yearly visits. We agreed with him and said how sensible this was, but secretly felt that it couldn't possibly match being there all the time though and of course, he knew this in his heart too.

Driving past the jaw-dropping fountains running down the middle of Caesar's Palace forecourt, we stepped out onto the impressive mosaics that greet you at the entrance. Once through the front doors, visitors are instantly transported back to Biblical times making it easy to believe that you've stepped into the Roman World. I was hoping however, NOT to bump into Yule Brynner on the set of 'Westworld'.

Lukey's eyes though were more on the tiny togas the bar waitresses were almost wearing rather than the architecture.

It was too early to eat, giving us the perfect excuse to wander around the marble halls with their huge columns and arches and watch the ceilings cleverly change from sunrise to sunset, as they do every three hours. The 'animatronic' displays are a bit freaky, but terribly clever and Michelangelo's "David" – being only a few years old, looks the way it would have brand new. If the stores weren't there, you'd think you'd fallen out of a time machine, but Cartier, Luis Vuitton, Bvlgari, De Beers, Tiffany and Gianni Versace say you haven't.

Planet Hollywood was good for burgers and the movie memorabilia they have always entertained, so we grabbed a table there. Lukey wasn't sulking about Harry not being with us and was actually being quite sweet. The flat-screen TV's placed strategically around the restaurant kept our attention while we waited to give our orders and the props from scary movies were a talking point for Lukey while we ate. It was a good job he was talkative, because Roo was doing his impersonation of a mute once again.

Leaving Planet Hollywood, we needed to walk off our supper and I reminded myself not to forget to collect the diamond ring my secret admirer had bought me at Bvlgari earlier. Every high-end shop you could think of is here at Caesar's. I can't possibly imagine how they all survive, but they seem to. Maybe from lucky people at the Roulette table, or lottery winners, who knows? Some people though seem to have money to burn. I was content to go next door to West of Santa Fe to buy my sister something Indian (the 'Red' kind) and didn't bother to pick up the diamond ring after all. I was sure my secret admirer would find another gorgeous creature to give it to.

I could have stayed for hours just wandering – and me who hates shopping! Lukey was happy to window-shop too, but Roo was in a funny mood and looked bored stiff. He sat on a bench for a while and then walked on a bit further and sat on another bench and in the end I decided it wasn't worth pushing him when he was SO NOT enjoying himself and the three of us walked back outside to where the real world was.

The warm evening breeze would have been nice to walk in, but one look at Roo made me realise that it would be better to go back to the security of our hotel. Anyway, it would be silly not to take advantage of our suite, which would hold 100 people and returning first to Lukey's floor found that Harry was already back, which pleased Lukey.

Roo and I watched a bit of TV …… I say 'watched', when in fact Roo simply stared at the screen. I hated seeing him as despondent as this. I've asked him what it is that goes through his mind on these occasions and he says that's the problem – *nothing* goes through his mind.

We would need to get a good nights' sleep before our trek tomorrow, so maybe an early night wasn't a bad thing. Roo was asleep in an instant, while I was wide-awake. I listened to his breathing while I lay there hoping that he'd be okay tomorrow. Maybe the trip into the desert will stimulate him – or maybe I could conjure up another angel to help him with his struggle.

Secretly though, I knew I was really running out of ideas, or the enthusiasm to continue the struggle, which scared me a bit.

DAY SEVENTY-TWO: "Into the desert to Walk the Sky"

I was up a bit earlier than usual after a restless night. Roo had slept well though and seemed much happier than he was yesterday, but with a long day ahead of us I wasn't too optimistic. He said he was hungry, which I thought must be a good sign when right on cue another delightful table on wheels arrived with more of those sunny yellow flowers. (I couldn't resist their Eggs Benedict again but would be 'egg-bound' if I wasn't careful). Roo had finished his fry-up before I was even half way through mine, when the lovely chappee on the Reception desk rang to say that the 'Hummer' (Humvee: a 4-wheel drive Army version of a Jeep), which we'd swapped with the smaller Jeep, was outside waiting for us. I hurried to finish eating and ten minutes later we were downstairs to see the enormous thing we'd hired to take us through the desert to the Grand Canyon.

I could have done with a ladder to get in it and in spite of my seaplane and small boat training found it difficult to haul myself into the seat. I did it, but not very gracefully. The Hummer is a bit like a small Tank but amazingly easy to drive and a lot of fun. It was comfortable and being so high off the ground meant that we all had a marvellous view of everything we passed. Once on the road, we drove through Boulder City and had to agree that it was a super little town, with lots of green, open spaces and neat rows of attractive houses. It looked like a nice place to live if you worked in Vegas.

Lake Mead and the Hoover Dam were in sight now. The lake had been created to house the water to run the turbines in the dam and took five years to build, with great loss of life. In 1931 there was no Health and Safety Executive. Photo's in the Dam Museum show men climbing wooden ladders and hauling buckets up ropes and a few poor souls even ended up in the concrete as a permanent monument to the structure. We stopped briefly, but had 'done' the Dam and Lake Mead on previous trips and wanted to get on to the Grand Canyon. We'd done THAT before – well, we'd flown over it and looked into it, but driving there would be a different experience.

Roo had shown no signs of anxiety so far and we trucked on in jovial mood, until the terrain became rocky and desert-like, with Joshua Trees (resembling enormous cacti) and Brush – the stuff you see flying past the Saloon in cowboy films. Every now and then, I pointed to the rocky hills shouting, **"INJUNS!"** The three of them thought it was amusing at first, but after a while ignored me so I shut up and we continued in silence.

Killjoys! They had no sense of adventure – especially as I thought I really DID see some! The route to the Canyon took us through some pretty strange territory. We passed through an area of flat desert and cacti, which had become a sort of Homestead where people were living in big RV's and smaller motor homes. Corrugated shacks and wooden huts dotted between them appeared to have been there longer, but none were in good shape.

It looked like the aftermath of a nuclear war, with the inhabitants being the survivors. No electricity, water, sewage works or obvious medical help seemed readily available, but we counted nine hut-like churches and a small school. We wondered what could have happened to these people for them to exist in such a place, but it must have been a very close-knit community with religion figuring quite heavily in their lives. I found it all a little unnerving and hoped we'd make it back through there before dark.

The driving instructions from the satnav told us to turn right suddenly and we missed the road to the Canyon. 'Road' wasn't exactly the right word for it and from then on, it looked as if the Hummer would really be useful. The next fourteen miles was a sand, dust and rock track cut through a forest of millions of Joshua Trees.

It was Harry's turn to drive and he thoroughly enjoyed manoeuvring the Hummer round the hairpin bends and sliding to a 'broadside' in the dust.

The track ended abruptly at an airfield where the sky was suddenly full of helicopters and light aircraft taking off and landing and although the canyon wasn't in sight there was an atmosphere of excitement and anticipation from the people waiting for their chosen mode of transport to take them to see this extraordinary sight. In equal amounts were visitors who had already been there, wearing their tell-tale souvenirs. You know the sort of thing such as the Tee shirt saying, 'My Mom went to Vegas and all she got me was this Tee Shirt'. The irresistible stuff that ends up at the Scout's Jumble Sale.

This time our interest was with the new 'Sky Walk'. We wanted to *"Walk the Sky"*, as it's known. Leaving the Hummer at the airfield we caught a visitors' coach, which ferried people to and from this feat of engineering at the edge of the Canyon built right opposite 'Eagle Point'. You don't need to use your imagination – it really does look remarkably like an eagle with wings outstretched naturally hewn in the rock by the weather. The 'Skywalk' has been built on Indian land of the Hualapai Tribe, giving them a significant share of the profits and is literally an enormous 40` glass horseshoe strung out across the canyon 4,000 below. Jumping off it, it would take fifteen seconds to reach the bottom in a freefall suicidal nosedive and you'd hit the Colorado River with a bit of a splash. This is, of course not recommended.

The glass viewing platform gives a bird's eye view of the drop and a completely different perspective of the canyon. It weighs 1.2m pounds and can hold the weight of 700 fat men, or 699 and me. Buzz Aldrin was the first person to walk on it, which might have made up for the fact that he was the second person to set foot on the moon. The Grand Canyon itself doesn't need describing. Most people have seen photographs at least of the spectacular gorges and sheer drops, but the colours in a photograph don't do it justice. The pinks, reds, oranges, greens, blacks and greys have to be seen with your own eyes to really appreciate the spectacle and enormity of it all.

Several Indians (real ones) in native dress stood outside the visitor centre looking on proudly as we all 'ooh'd and aah'd' when the Skywalk was in sight. We would pay to go out onto the platform and while on it, have our photo taken with the Indian Chief. Before we did this we were told to put all our belongings into one of the lockers provided as cameras, telephones and other hard objects would damage the glass if they were dropped on it and litter the canyon with junk, should they slip over the side. It was a good idea and I could see the logic. Free from our bits and pieces, the next thing we had to do was don plastic overshoes; again so we didn't scratch the glass with shoes. Then we were ready to 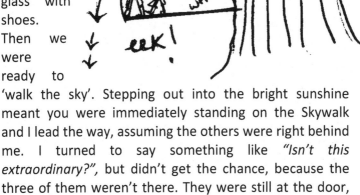 'walk the sky'. Stepping out into the bright sunshine meant you were immediately standing on the Skywalk and I lead the way, assuming the others were right behind me. I turned to say something like *"Isn't this extraordinary?"*, but didn't get the chance, because the three of them weren't there. They were still at the door, rooted to the spot. Harry was hanging onto the side rail unable to move in any direction and had his eyes tightly shut (crazy, when he can fly a plane). Lukey wasn't exactly happy either and Roo (who has trouble climbing a ladder) was in a state too.

It was quite comical, but I stifled a chuckle and walked back to see if I could help. Harry wouldn't be coaxed from his grip on the rail and the other two were mumbling *"Ground Rush"* and *"Woh … dizzy"*.

Fortunately, there were very few people around and we could stay there all day if we wanted as there was no time limit, but we'd driven all that way and I knew they'd be disappointed later if they didn't do it. Just then, an attendant came up to us and asked if he could help. He was very kind and said a lot of people have trouble stepping out onto the glass at first, but once you get used to being up in the air with nothing apparent between you and a 4,000 foot drop, it was fine. Harry still hadn't opened his eyes and continuing to hold on for dear life, his knuckles had turned white.

Apart from standing in the blistering heat, I could have stayed all day, but obviously we'd need to move on sometime and would also have liked a change of view. Roo and Lukey gripped the side rail and looking straight ahead, rather than straight down through the transparent glass edged their way slowly, but surely around the Skywalk. With the attendant walking backwards in front of him, Harry, with his right hand gripping the rail and the other clinging on to me, inched his way along but still couldn't open his eyes.

At the halfway mark – the bend in the horseshoe – he did manage to take a peek but as soon as he saw the canyon through the glass, he quickly closed his eyes again. Then our soft-shoe shuffle was interrupted by a young boy jumping up and down on the glass, shouting, *"I can break it, Maw"*, but fortunately, after receiving a clip round the ear from 'Maw' ceased this activity. Bless him. The exit door was in sight and standing there waiting for us was Brown Bear in his glorious head dress. Harry managed to keep his eyes open for the photograph, but now whenever he sees it, can't help groaning.

I was delighted to have had the experience but once was enough for Roo and I. However, Lukey behaved like a real brother, by holding Harry's arm and taking him round once more; this time he kept his eyes open – well, at least for some of the time.

Waiting for the coach to take us to another part of the canyon, we sat at the very edge of the cliff side and had a drink, marvelling at the view and giving Harry some time to recuperate from his ordeal. The Grand Canyon is sacred to the Indians and they must hate our intrusion but the Skywalk will be given to the Tribe in 2028, once the builders have recouped their expenses, so at least they'll benefit financially eventually.

At our next stop, it was possible to see right down to the bottom of the canyon and the muddy Colorado River snaking its way through the sheer rock face. This enormous area was below the sea a few million years ago and fossils, shells and fish skeletons have been found in the rock to prove it. If you get the opportunity to go to this part of the world, you must. It's an amazing place.

Back to the Hummer and air conditioning. We looked and felt quite grubby by now and were looking forward to a long shower and dinner. But first, it was back to the dirt road. The journey was fine to begin with but a couple of real cowboys passed us at speed in a pickup truck, causing a complete dust-out with nil visibility. It was like a Pyroclastic Cloud had been dropped on us as the Hummer was instantly covered in a thick layer of desert. Coughing and spluttering, there was no alternative but to make an emergency stop. I bet the cowboys laughed their heads off knowing what they'd done to the annoying and unsuspecting tourists. We had to wait for the dust to settle and regain our composure before we could continue our journey.

The sun was dipping by the time we reached that strange shanty town where by this time the shadows made by the Joshua Trees did nothing to give you confidence. I think we were all glad when we came out the other side unscathed and by the time we reached Las Vegas it was 6.45pm. The Hummer was filthy. The windscreen was plastered with remains of a hundred large insects and caked on mud from using the washers. Goodness knows what the rest of it looked like when we pulled up outside the Four Seasons.

The valet shot out to park the car as usual, but hesitated the closer he got. We must have looked like the Beverly Hill Billies when we decanted. Even funnier, were the looks on the faces of the dozen or so people standing in the entrance wearing their Armani jeans and Swarovski-peppered belts, but with our noses in the air we swept past them an headed for the shower.

Looking a little more presentable, we drove the Hummer to the Bellagio in spite of its state, where we were going to eat and pulled up beside a Bugatti Veyron – a car with a price tag of around two million pounds. We shot out of the Hummer and moved away from it as fast as we could, looking back saying, *"Look at that disgusting Hummer, what type of person could have been driving that?"*.

We could have been eccentric millionaires like the Beverley Hillbillies, of course.

The Bellagio is superb, but not much like the town on Lake Como in Italy it was named after and is supposed to resemble. But it does have pristine, finely-manicured, colour co-ordinated gardens inside and out and even an indoor greenhouse full of butterflies. The piece de resistance however, is the ten minute show of dancing fountains at the front of the hotel, which has water shooting all over the place in time to music. It's an amazing spectacle with the finale being a jet of water exploding 100 feet into the air.

After dinner the boys went for a last meander along 'The Strip' and Roo and I found ourselves in the cocktail lounge at Four Seasons. Roo had been reasonable all day but then he hadn't had time to be miserable. If he thought he could be entertained like this all the time though, he had another thing coming. I was edgy about leaving the next day and how he would cope with it, especially as we had to vacate our rooms at noon and wouldn't be leaving for the airport until 7.30pm.

But for the moment he was fine and chatted away to the bartender, another Hawaiian who had lived in Las Vegas for twenty years and didn't miss Hawaii at all. I was missing it already.

Once I knew the boys had returned safely, it was time for bed. Reflecting on the day, I thought it had been a good idea to have the Hummer, but the rental company would need to steam clean it and I was thankful that we didn't have to hand it back personally.

I tried to order a dream about Bali Hai, rather than flowers, fruit, or fountains, but was so tired I don't think I dreamt at all.

DAY SEVENTY-THREE: "New York, New York"

Roo hoped to go to an Antique Fair just off 'The Strip' today and I kept my fingers crossed that he would feel able to, without the need to drag me along for moral support.

I wasn't surprised though, when before he'd even crawled out of bed, he said he couldn't go and any attempt at cajoling him into making the trip fell on deaf ears. It was disappointing, because I had hoped it might go some way to improving his confidence if he went alone and suggesting I went with him would completely defeat the object. Probably for the best though. It would have been nerve-wracking for both of us if he'd gone.

We stayed in bed until 9.30am when our last breakfast table arrived. Using my sensible head, I had ordered mushrooms, tomato and vegetarian sausage, rather than the usual eggs. Travelling and a change of climate might have a detrimental effect on my digestive system and I would hate to sit in the loo all the way to New York. I do wish other travellers were as considerate.

I was thinking about offering lessons in organisational skills on my return to England with a major part concentrating on packing a suitcase. It took me less than an hour to pull out the clothes suitable for the cold weather in New York and stack the remainder in fifty pound lots. Truly, I was now an expert. While I was doing this, Roo had taken a long shower and showed no sign of panic but I steeled myself for a nosedive once we left the suite and the seven-and-a-half hours without a base.

The boys knocked on our door at eleven o'clock with their bags and we waited together until it was time to vacate our lovely suite at noon. With travelling clothes at the top of our luggage, we would be able to shower and change at the Spa beside the pool later in the day and feel fresh for the flight. The Concierge would store our suitcases until we were collected at 7.30pm.

Roo was behaving astonishingly well. Even the boys mentioned it, but the three of us were very surprised when he said he would go to the Antiques Fair after all. In a bit of a panic, I offered to go with him, but he was adamant that he wanted to see if he could handle it alone and courageously went off in a cab.

Harry and Lukey deposited our luggage with the Concierge and we headed for the pool, where I would wait for Roo desperately trying not to watch-watch. It suddenly occurred to me, that it was quite possible that I'd never see him again as I had no idea where he was going. *"An Antiques Fair"*, he'd said.

Well, I suppose there couldn't have been too many Antiques Fairs on in Vegas that morning so that would narrow it down a bit, but I did moan at myself for being so flippant at the time and not even asking for the address.

But there was no problem. Less than two hours later, he stood at the end of my lounger, casting a shadow across my top half. He was a little shaken up – I think the fact that he'd actually done something so brave had rather shocked him into a sense of achievement and he looked quite proud of himself. *"How was it?"* I asked nonchalantly. *"Well – different"*, he replied and with a relieved look on his face – and mine, lowered himself into the lounger beside me.

"Aaah", he said, with a smile on his face, *"Now I'll soak up the last few rays of sunshine and go to New York looking fit and healthy"*. Of course, a whole twelve minutes passed, before he dashed off to the shade on the other side of the pool.

I was delighted with his achievement. On the rare occasions that something positive happens, I feel 100% optimistic that our lives will return to some sort of normality one day and continued to read my book with a smile on my face, although the subject was a gory one. It was a good job the lady from yesterday wasn't around, she would have definitely assumed from the title on the front cover that I was a sadist.

After a while though, I put my book down and between a bit of pondering and forward planning I thought of home. I hoped that my next telephone call to Mum was more pleasant than the last one and that she and my sister would sound a bit happier than they had in the call before. Surely the weather had to improve there soon, which would brighten everyone's mood – even my sister's.

At least I wouldn't have to suffer one thing that was always hard to bear after a sunny holiday - the lack of natural light in the Operating Theatre. Now that I was retired from paid employment, I wouldn't miss long shifts, artificial lighting and air conditioning and yearn for my next break with blue skies and fresh air. I don't think we appreciate how necessary it is to be exposed to daylight. It's really important to our health and behaviour and especially so, if the nature of your work is stressful. But someone's gotta do these jobs and in spite of the unnatural environment, I had so loved mine.

Continuing to ponder, home was still on my mind. As well as writing my diary each day, I'd made copious notes on all sorts of interesting things we'd seen, especially about plants and food. I doubted the medicinal 'Noni' plant would survive the English climate, but knew I could buy the ingredients to cook up Fijian Coconut Chutney – a must to make for the next church Produce stall. In fact, I'd collected enough recipes on our travels to write, "*Around the World in 77 Recipes*".

Seeing so many different cultures and customs in a relatively short space of time, it was amazing to see how we all manage to get on with being human in our own way. We might eat and drink different things and have strange methods of communication, but the majority of us demonstrate our humanness with kindness and mercy and there does seem to be a global change in attitude towards depression and mental illness. With 12% of the population of the world – *around 450 million* – or one in four of us being affected by some form of psychiatric disorder at some time in our lives, even in far-flung places such as Fiji, taboos are being broken down and what was once shameful in many societies is now seen as a more acceptable illness.

If you'd told me a few years ago that I'd be campaigning for better understanding of this subject I wouldn't have believed you, but I have to admit that I've been hugely affected by Roo's depression. His constant battle to keep his head above water is also my battle. Every now and then, I have to remember to take a step back and regroup to stop myself being sucked down too, because a never ending call for help and attention is often very draining.

Harry and Lukey popped up in the nick of time saving me from feeling sorry for myself. They always seemed to be there for me at the right time. I wondered what happened to that blonde in the Jacuzzi, but she hadn't been mentioned since and I thought it best not to ask. Suggesting we eat at the pool, Lukey said, "*YES!*" before I managed to finish the sentence. I had no need to remind the boys to add 'please' and 'thank you' when the waitress took our order and although the lady with the little dog was absent I'd like to think that our present companions had taken note of our politeness.

It took longer to cook the food and deliver it to us than it did for Lukey to consume it and I panicked a bit knowing that he would be looking for another distraction, so I was surprised when he sat quietly on the end of my lounger without asking for a suggestion. There were several options to pass the time but when Roo offered to pay for another visit to the shooting range they were dressed in a flash and disappeared in a puff of smoke. Roo went inside to 'phone his friend in New York, which meant that the three of them were being entertained. I didn't mind being left alone at all – especially when I decided to compensate myself by ordering a Mai Tai. It was quite a good one, but even with the blue sky and a palm tree waving above my head it was nothing like a Maui Mai Tai.

Half the pool and gardens were in shadow and almost empty, but sudden riotous laughter and the clinking of beer bottles interrupted the peace. Hiding behind my sunglasses, I sat up to see what was going on. The smart, suited and booted bunch of chaps at the bar just had to be on a stag weekend and seemed to be drinking for America, but they were enjoying themselves and that's what it's all about in Vegas. It's a bizarre place full of fantasy and fiction. A town surrounded by incredible geographical sights and features together with magnificent manmade examples of courage and achievement. You can get married and divorced at the stroke of a pen, see a show so dazzling you'll never forget it, be quickly parted from your money in a casino and see a wonder of the natural world all in the space of a few hours.

You either love it, or hate it.

An hour passed and thinking I had better make sure that the bartender's interpretation of a Mai Tai was almost correct, ordered another. I was half way through it when the boys skidded to a halt at the poolside. Assuring them that the empty glass they could see was nothing to do with me I diverted their attention away from the table by asking how they had got on. They'd had a wonderful time saying it was a real finale to their time in Vegas and that they'd despatched several more terrorists to paradise. Their timing was perfect. All that was left to do was shower and change in the Spa, before being collected and taken to the airport.

It was simple to extract our travelling clothes from the top of our cases in the Porter's Room and gathering up Roo along the way, we wandered through the peaceful, serene hotel to the Spa. The facilities there were glorious, with the smell of eucalyptus exuding amongst the calm surroundings. I may never have surfaced again from the separate ladies' section, where lotions, potions, big, fluffy white towels and everything else you could possibly need to refresh and caress were available but New York – our last port of call was beckoning.

We met up looking all shiny and new taking the aroma from the Spa with us into the cocktail lounge where Sam, our nice Hawaiian barman was on duty. He was delighted to see us and meet the boys too. He told us that Grissom from the programme CSI was a regular in the bar and that Tiger Woods was staying in the hotel at that moment. I don't know if the boys were particularly impressed, but out of politeness they *"Ooh'd and Aah'd"* anyway.

One drink later our ride to the airport announced its arrival and it was time to leave Las Vegas. We said goodbye to Sam, who behaved as if we were his long-lost relatives leaving him once more and piled into the sleek limo parked outside. We seemed to have accumulated an enormous amount of luggage and some of the smaller cases had to join us inside the blacked-out interior for the short journey to McCarran.

As the flight to New York was a 'domestic', we were able to check in at the departure terminal kerbside and by the time we had fought our way through Security, there wasn't much time to enjoy the lounge before boarding. The plane was brand new – just out of the packet – but the cabin crew were awful. The two 'older' Flight Attendants in our cabin hadn't flown on this particular type of aircraft before and didn't even know how to close the door! One of the crew from the flight deck had to come and deal with it, which did not inspire much confidence. However, we were fed and watered (reluctantly) and landed safely in New York, but vowed never to fly with 'them' (who shall be nameless for the sake of International diplomacy) again. It was nothing like the usual experience of being up the front of the plane and I dreaded to think how the poor souls behind us had been treated.

DAY SEVENTY-FOUR: "Nearly Home"(-4hrs GMT)

The driver waiting for us was an ex-Army Drill Sergeant. More than efficient and chatty and obviously still very fit from his service days, he lifted our luggage into the car in two swift goes as if it were filled with tissue paper rather than a conglomeration of clothes and souvenirs from seven different countries. It was only 7.30am and although we'd all snoozed on the plane, we felt jaded and irritable with the uncaring attitude from the cabin crew who had sat in seats behind us asleep! Just a few hours before, we'd been beautified in the Spa, but all we wanted to do now was have another shower and go to bed.

Battling our way through the morning rush hour, we were delivered to the Waldorf Astoria just a stones' throw from Central Park. The usual check in time was 2pm so we didn't expect our rooms to be ready. Not only that, New York was amazingly busy as our whistle stop tour coincided with a visit from none other than the Pope and the closer we had come to this part of the city the more Police we saw. I was sure they outnumbered the ordinary person on the street.

The foyer around Reception inside the hotel was buzzing with Cardinals in their bright scarlet cassocks reminding me of the birds of the same name waiting for their breakfast in Maui. Lesser Clergy of all kinds fussed around the more important of these Theologians, with hardly a woman in sight making the whole thing quite bizarre like a scene from a Ken Russell film. We waited patiently to be dealt with and while we waited, I pictured the receptionist typing away merrily on the computer and studying the screen, only to look up and say, *"Computer says No."* Fortunately, that didn't happen. One of our rooms was ready, thank God and the four of us flopped onto the twin double beds to sleep for a few hours. It was almost 12.30pm before we all woke with extreme hunger but before we could eat, I had to ring mum. The weather in England was a little better, but not enough to lighten everyone's mood, although my sister sounded brighter with the thought of our imminent arrival home. I was cheered up by this and with that job done, took the lift thirty-four floors down expecting to wade through the 'Sea of Cardinals', but they had gone. By this time, they were all at an enormous service being led by the Pope at the Yankee Stadium and the hotel was deathly quiet.

For some reason, we were unanimous in our choice of food type and asked the Concierge to recommend a good Chinese Restaurant. Unsurprisingly, we were told to go to Chinatown in Manhattan, which has one of the largest populations of Chinese people in the west. Outside the hotel, most of the Police had also gone to protect His Holiness but we spoke to a couple of young Officers who had been left behind 'on guard'. They were both from another city and had been bussed in the night before but didn't mind because they were on overtime. They even hailed us a cab.

We slid into the back of the _un_sweetly-smelling yellow taxi, only to find that the driver didn't know how to get to Chinatown! It was difficult to make out his accent but we thought he was from one of the eastern block countries. Roo wanted to try out his Rumanian, but thinking we might end up in Harlem he scanned the map, plotted the route and in very slow, loud English gave the directions to take us to Mott Street. It was quite a laugh! We were dropped a few blocks from the road we wanted though, which meant walking through a large part of this zany, crowded area.

Chinatown, New York is the biggest of them all in the US covering two square miles, right next to Little Italy. I was expecting it to be similar to Stanley Market in Hong Kong, but whereas that one centres more on clothes, this one is definitely more food-orientated. As soon as we left the cab the air was filled with the aroma of fish, noodles, cooked duck, incense and rotting garbage.

I had stepped into the gutter onto something unrecognisable, which attached itself to my left shoe and while trying to prise it off with a tissue realised it had once been a duckbill before being firmly flattened by a vehicle. How delightful. Welcome to Chinatown. Things dangling, things jangling, the shops were crammed so full of colourful wares, the excess spilled out onto the pavement increasing the capacity for a sale, because it was difficult not to stop and look.

Of course, each time we showed even a hint of interest we were descended upon by the shopkeeper and had to fight them off and more than once, the boys had to prise me from the grip of a tout whispering, "_You cuh_

wimmee laydee – see nice Gootchee hunbah. Velly chip."
You wouldn't have got me down that alley for all the tea in China (ha-ha).

Most of the shop fronts were simply decorated, while others had a typical Chinese appearance, Pagoda-style. Even the bank looked like a Pagoda. I had to stop and marvel at one of the open-fronted stores and its display of huge bowls of Chinese herbs in striking colours oozing the smell of spices, garlic and coffee, while behind them sat more displays of silk flowers and 'lucky' bamboo.

There's a monument here to the Chinese soldiers killed during the last war. That's something that had never occurred to me – the fact that the Chinese fought on our side and a statue of a Chinese National Hero, Lin Zexu, who did his bit to stop the opium trade in the nineteenth century. I don't think it helped much but there's also a thriving Chinese Catholic church, so some good must have been done.

Finally, we located 'The Peking Duck House' the restaurant we'd been recommended. It was half-full, mainly with Chinese who looked up at us mid-mouthful as we walked in, staring at us as if we were painted blue with green spots. We had really worked up an appetite so ignoring this, sat at a big round table and got down to the business of scouring the menu. In unison, the Chinese continued to scoop food into their mouths from the bowls under their chins but were, at least using chopsticks.

Live Lobster in Hot Sauce ... Sliced Jelly Fish ... Live (but Drunk) Prawns and Boneless Duck Feet just didn't do anything for me. Strangely enough, it didn't do too much for the boys either. Roo was simply staring at the menu and at first I thought he was 'having a turn'. Fortunately, he wasn't. Like us, he was looking for something familiar to order but with definitely no sign of a 'number 24' it looked like we would struggle.

One of the cute Chinese children on the next table kept turning round to look at us, in spite of the older woman amongst them – Granny, probably, speaking to him harshly but in the end she gave up and he leaned over the back of his chair to get a better look. We must have given him a very strange and stuffy impression the way we poured over the menu, or perhaps he was just curious at the way were talking. I don't know what it was but we certainly made his day.

Twice, the waitress sidled up to take our order and twice we said we needed a few minutes more until we finally settled for the conventional noodles, lemon chicken and rice, although I did let my hair down a bit by ordering soft shell crab, which wasn't exactly an example of living dangerously. The boys finished off their meal with fried bananas and walnuts, but the intruiging, '8 Treasures Rice Pudding' would have to be sampled another time. We may never know what precious ingredients had been hidden amongst the grains, I just hoped they were all dead before they were cooked.

I'm sure it was nothing to do with the food, but I could see Roo flagging, although he was quite jolly. Just to be on the safe side though, I proposed a cab ride straight back to the hotel. It was raining, anyway and walking around on those pavements wouldn't be very nice if they'd turned into one big slimy mess of goodness-knows-what. The cab driver this time was home-grown and taking the most obvious route, dropped us outside the Waldorf ten minutes later.The area was full of Police so we supoosed the service at the Yankee Stadium was over.

The boys went straight upstairs to their room, but Roo and I sat in the cocktail bar at a table very conveniently-placed for people-watching. Loads of Cardinals and other religious topknobs passed by, which still looked peculiar in the foyer of such a prestigious hotel, while Roo drank two glasses of fruit punch and being in Manhatten, I thought it would be appropriate to have a 'Manhatten', which is a really nice, gingerry drink.We talked about the day and the ghastly flight attendants and the fact that Roo had been quite good since we left Vegas.

DAY SEVENTY-FIVE: " Really, really the last day"

I'd woken several times during the night every time a Police car or an ambulance passed way below us sounding its siren. It's amazing how much you can hear even when you're on the thirty-fourth floor. Roo had slept well, apart from being disturbed by a couple of them and was bright and breezy when he headed for the shower.

Meeting the boys at the breakfast buffet, we made plans for the day. It was misty and a bit chilly but we thought it would be nice to walk in Central Park anyway and as the Natural History Museum was in that direction, visit that too.

All my cajolling and persuasion for the boys to use sunscreen in Hawaii and Vegas had gone out the window, when Lukey admitted that on the last day he'd sat for a while without slapping any on. He was itchy and irritable and his chest was quite red. I was cross with him and stormed off back to our room to get some antihistamine. *You can take a horse to water ....*

Harry wasn't himself either. He should have spent a long weekend in New York with his ex-girlfriend some months before, but sadly that didn't happen and he was obviously brooding. Pushing his breakfast around, he must have sighed a dozen times. He looked so sad. At this rate, our (nearly) last day wouldn't be a good one.

A short cab ride to the museum right opposite Central Park was easy – and the driver knew the way! Hooray!! The exhibits were jolly good, jam-packed with the usual and some unusual stuff and we also took in an excellent Imax film in the Planetarium on our Solar System. Goodness me, by the time we'd finished, we were on Natural History overload.

The non-drowsy antihistamine I'd given Lukey seemed to be making him drowsy somehow. The itching had stopped, but he looked a bit weird and said he felt light-headed, so before he flaked out we hurried to the exit. Once outside in the fresh air, he perked up enough to take that stroll through the park we'd promised ourselves and by the time we came out the other side he was fine. Roo was fine too. I was so surprised, but careful not to mention it.

We hailed a cab. The nearer we came to the hotel, the more Police we saw – two on every corner. I was sure they'd be glad when the Pope was gone. I could have kicked myself for thinking that Roo had been so good because it seemed the minute he left the cab, he changed. It was as if someone had flicked a switch on top of his head instantly turning him into that other person. The colour had drained from his face and he had that look of impending doom he gets when he's about to burst into tears.

Luckily, the boys were going for a wander and before they had time to see what was happening, I waved them off and rushed Roo back to our room where I made some PG. *"Where did that come from?"* I asked him. But before he could answer or drink his tea, he was asleep.

You see? There's no rhymn, or reason. No explanation or pattern to all this. It just comes out of the blue. It hits him without warning. It's the devil himself.

While he slept, I watched the tail-end of the Pope's service at the stadium on TV. It was very moving actually and then with another cup of PG, summoned up the strength to attack the packing – for the last time.

We were going out for our last meal of the holiday later on. It would be special not only because it was the end of our trip, but also because it would be a while before we were together again. Harry's birthday was on the 29th and we knew we couldn't see him on the day and would be the first time ever so we'd make a big thing of the evening instead – if 'Itchy Boy' and the devil would let us.

The hotel was still full of red, white, black and purple-frocked men who appeared to have enjoyed themselves by the flushed look on their faces. I was still wondering how their respective Diocese had afforded it all. The Anglican church has enormous financial problems, but perhaps catholics were more benevolent than us and donated more, like the Mormons, who give 10% of their income. That really is devotion. The Pope was leaving for Rome and listening carefully we could hear the Police saying, "Bye Bye Pope" and heaving a sigh of relief. Luckily, we wouldn't be flying out of JFK at the same time. Can you imagine getting through security?

The boys returned and we took a cab to Little Italy this time along a seriously potholed road, which didn't do my 4th vertebrae any good at all. The driver spoke good

Asian-American and took a direct route but he and his taxi smelt so bad the boys were heaving when we arrived at Mulberry Street. It's only Mulberry Street really that has retained its Italianism. The rest of the area, which was once full of European immigrants has been taken over by Chinatown, although the restaurants in this road look Italian and serve authentic food. The Italians worked hard enough to afford to move out of the area but apparently, it remains a Mafia enclave. I wondered if they got on well with the Chinese Triads.

Buildings are the tall, tenement type designed for maximum occupancy leaving no room for an emergency exit as well as a stairwell and have wrought iron fire escapes instead (you know - the ones that sort of swing down on hinges). Some of the roads have kept their cobblestones and look very nineteenth century English but there's definitely a Chinese influence there now.

That wonderful pizza smell was wafting through the air replacing the pong from the cab driver and increasing the moisture in our mouths. By now, Lukey had his **'URGENT! Food Required'** face on, so rather than wander around aimlessly, I stopped the others to formulate some sort of strategic restaurant-choosing process.

But oh, no ... Roo had gone wrong. "*Not now*", I thought, "*Not on our last night*". But he had. He was beginnning an 'angry' attack. The boys and I were content to go into the first decent restaurant we found, knowing that at the very least we'd be served really good pizza, or spaghetti. Roo, on the other hand in one almighty outburst insisted on visiting all of them and reading each and every menu in minute detail. He stomped off leaving us standing there like three lemons.

Terrific. The boys could see his crazy behaviour for themselves and there was no way of covering it up. I had no idea how long he would take to digest the contents of a couple of dozen menus and we watched him marching along the road like a nazi stormtrooper. Lukey's eyes kept drifting towards the open door of the restaurant beside us and I expected him to make a dash for it any second, but none of us had any intention of waiting there indefinitely.

The boys agreed to leave their dad to his own devices and allow him to goosestep to his hearts content for as long as he wanted. But in the nick of time and on the verge of doing just this, Roo came pounding back to us shouting, "*Well, I don't know —YOU choose!*"

The atmosphere in the restaurant was so good and the wine so delicious, I was able to calm down quite quickly. Unfortunately, Roo couldn't and sat at the table with clenched fists taking deep breaths as if he was blowing up a balloon. I was a bit upset, but determined to save the evening somehow.

I needn't have worried. With great food, wonderful service, the boys' good humour and totally ignoring Roo, we three had a terrific evening and by the end of it I had forgiven my dear husband once again. He'd stopped blowing up balloons and making ready for a fight and even tried to join in the conversation. As usual, I began to find all the usual excuses for his behaviour and convince myself that he would be better one day. Perhaps he was struggling with the thought of going home and dealing with the mountain of post that must be there. Maybe he was a real Jekyll and Hyde and had been experimenting with a potion all this time. If that was the case, let's hope it's the Jekyll side of him that would win.

Returning to the hotel, the boys wanted one last look at New York and wandered out into the night. I wasn't mad keen on them going but there was no way of stopping them, so to take my mind off their forray, Roo and I went for one last cocktail. Roo was completely calm now and tried hard to be nice to me.

I truly believe I was meant to marry Roo. The Designer sketching out his blueprint of life had made a mistake somewhere along the line, which for some reason wasn't possible to rectify. The only thing to do when the error was discovered, was for the Designer to steer the right sort of mate in his direction but it had to be a strong, stubborn and bloody-minded one to cope with the mistake. Remind you of anyone?

The boys returned having reached as far as Times Square. Harry had taken lots of photographs and would have stayed longer had Lukey not been so tired. The antihistamine tablets he'd been taking were definitely the non-drowsy type, but still seemed to have a spoporific effect on him. Harry had a G & T and then they both slid of to bed. I was relieved they were back safely.

Thanks be to God, or his Design Department.

"Home, Sweet Home"

It must have been a fire engine that woke me up. The blast from the horn went on and on and by the time it had passed, I was wide awake. By 7.30am I felt like I'd been to another one of those all night parties I hadn't enjoyed and hoped I hadn't picked up a cold or something worse. This wasn't the time to be ill.

The boys wanted to go to the Empire State Building even though it conjured up bad memories for Harry, as the last time he was there he'd suffered projectile vomiting after a Virgin Strawberry Daiquiri. He was much younger then but I'll never forget it. Poor little chap – it put him right off cocktails for years – virgin, or otherwise. They were also keen to visit the Chrysler Building, Ground Zero AND go shoppping but the thought of traipsing around New York filled me with dread. All I wanted to do was curl up in a blanket and watch a black and white film, so Roo extended our checkout time and I skipped breakfast to get some sleep instead.

After he'd eaten with the boys and seen them on their way with a map and plenty of cash for taxis, Roo came back to our room and dozed off too. What a pair! A real Derby and Joan, with not such an uneventful life. At least he would be calm and well-rested for the journey to the airport and I knew I'd feel better after catching up on some shut-eye.

A few hours later, there was just enough time to shower and dress before the luggage was collected. No more packing and unpacking. Yipee!

The boys weren't back yet but had left their cases 'packed' in the usual way. I hoped security wouldn't need to look inside. Roo and I took the elevator down to the lovely lobby and sat in squashy armchairs amidst chic dark wood and potted palms while waiting for the boys.

The Waldorf=Astoria (double hyphen) was built in the 1890's and when it was restored in the 1980's a vast amount of exquisite art was discovered, which had been hidden by those favouring the modernisation craze of the 50's - but thank goodness – it had only been covered up and not destroyed. Beneath a carpet in the lobby a mosaic entitled, 'The Wheel of Life' containing 148,000 little tiles was discovered, along with thirteen wall murals painted in oils lurking behind heavy curtains and the ceilings had been dropped to conceal ornate mouldings, gold leaf and wonderful Art Deco decorations. It must have been like discovering a mini Tutankhamen tomb.

At the front desk, you can't miss the two ton, nine foot tall mahogany and marble base holding a bronze clock with a small Statue of Liberty on top (and Queen Victoria on the side). It came from Chicago's 1893 World Fair and as well as the hotel icon, it's a handy meeting place too. One of the things I'd like to see everywhere is the rule they have at the Waldorf about dress, which says, *'NO tee shirts, tank tops, faded jeans, cut-offs, and casual hats permitted in the lobbies and lounges'.* Wonderful.

Harry and Lukey materialised. They'd done everything they wanted to do and at a much faster rate without Roo and I in tow. Being the Architect in the family, Harry raved about the Chrysler Building and Ground Zero had obviously been an unforgettable experience, but neither of them said much about it. When I asked why, they both agreed that it was difficult to explain how they felt. Watching the towers coming down on a TV screen was one thing, but actually going there to see the desolation and feel the mood of other visitors was another.

We still had a couple of hours to kill. The last thing I wanted to do was wander and the boys had nothing else in mind that was feasible, so Roo rang the limo company to ask if they could pick us up earlier. They said they could, but there would still be time for Roo and I to have a snack lunch of some kind. The boys had already eaten, so leaving them in the lobby with their laptops we found a table at 'The Bull and Bear' a typical American wood-panelled bar, with subdued lighting.

The evening news was broadcast from here for some reason and the electrical team were busy setting up the lighting and other equipment. I had no burning desire to be on the news, so quickly ordered a crab cocktail to finish before they did. I was really hungry, having missed breakfast. When it was served it looked like an enormous mound of chicken but was in fact my favourite blue crab in huge chunks with a spicy dipping sauce. Yum-yum.

Roo didn't want to eat and wasn't really 'with-it'. I'd tried to ignore his attitude, telling myself that it was my imagination but knew it wasn't. It put me right off my lunch and I couldn't finish it, so we went back to the boys who were sitting as good as gold in the lobby. I decided not to mention Roo's doldrums and luckily it was then that we were told that the car had arrived.

The driver was our lovely Drill Sergeant who whisked us off to the airport, where we had an easy check in, only to be told that there was a delay. We were offered and earlier flight but that would affect the car pickup from Heathrow so declined the offer. The prospect of a long wait wasn't so good but would have been worse had we not had the use of the Virgin Lounge, which was extremely comfortable with hostesses who were friendly and funny. What more could we ask for? The boys were fed and watered in a big way and Roo had calmed down but I still felt terribly tired. After what seemed an age, the flight to Blighty was finally called and we boarded our fifteenth plane – another 767. I had no trouble tucking up and snoozed for a while but behind me Roo was snoring so much that I was soon wide awake. I tossed and turned under my duvet until eventually, I sneeked a peek from the window. I must have slept more than I realised because just at that moment the English coast came into view – well, Cornwall actually. It was a lovely sight - all lush and green.

We landed smoothly and when the door opened onto a pleasant spring morning, I directed my hugest "Thank You" yet to the blue sky above me. We were back home safely with almost everything intact. I felt it was some sort of miracle. We hadn't been ill, or had any accidents, none of the flights were real problems, the ships had been fantastic and best of all, Roo and I were still married. That was certainly some miracle!

We were soon in the terminal and it was time to say goodbye to Harry, who was going straight back to Bristol. He would have a wash and brush up in the Virgin Revivals Lounge and then be taken home. I was determined not to cry, but it was a close thing and even Lukey hung on to him for much longer than usual.

Dennis was waiting for us in Arrivals and somehow managed to squeeze us and our inflated luggage into the car. Roo talked for a while, Lukey slept and I watched the countryside pass us by. I did love England – in spite of all the rubbish everywhere. Everything looked so different. So twee.

The M25 turned into the M11 and then we were on familiar country lanes. Passing the village shop, I saw someone I knew and waved but they must have forgotten who I was, because they didn't return the wave. Had we been away that long? Then, our house – still with the roof on and the hedge in front bursting with greenery came into view. How I loved our house. It looked so British and solid, I could have hugged it. In spite of the fantastic time we'd had and the range of experiences, it was good to be home.

Freddie was a bit skinnier, while the other two looked just the same. Moje barely looked up at us but I don't suppose he knew we'd been away for so long and didn't realise he should have welcomed us home. The sheep in our field definitely seemed to be "baa'ing" in a welcoming way and my English dickies fluttered around on the bird table, as if I'd personally fed them every day for the last three months. A family of sparrows had moved into the wooden house on the study wall and as usual, the worker bees were already being busy processing in and out of the red brick of the pantry wall.

Sitting next to the lovely vase of flowers that Lisa had thoughtfully left us was a mountain of post, but I assured Roo that most of it would be junk and persuaded him to have a few hours' sleep before tackling it and that's what both of us did. With a contented sigh, I closed my eyes as soon as my head hit the pillow. But my contentment was short-lived. Suddenly, I sat bolt upright and shouted, "*The Duty Free – it's still on the plane!*" Sure enough, that's where it was – well, by that time of course, it had been taken off.

The money we'd saved would be eaten up with the cost of postage but if that was the only thing to go wrong we couldn't complain.

I truly believe we were watched over by a Guardian Angel. Look out for yours'.

"How I deal with Sadness"

Living with a depressive and getting through each day without jeopardising your own sanity is a tricky one. To begin with, I went round and round in circles beating myself up about it because I was convinced that I was responsible somehow.

He was my 'Knight in Shining Armour' when we first met. He saved me from the desperate life-situation I found myself in at the time and I felt I had to repay that kindness by rescuing him when it was his turn. When I realised that I didn't have the answers he needed to set his mind free, I felt as though I'd failed him.

I'm no Saint. I often have difficulty containing myself. I believe I'm entitled to express my feelings and think it's important that I do. My exasperation sometimes reaches boiling point and I erupt with all the force of a typical Taurean, especially when Roo puts on a brave face for others and the assumption is that I've 'exaggerated' his condition. I find that so frustrating and unfair.

Asked to give advice to the partner of a depressive, the first thing I'd say is believe that depression is a real illness. Expecting them to 'pull themselves together' is not an option. For some people medication is the answer but if like Roo they have a liver which can't take it (literally) then there's nothing you can do except tackle every day 'cold turkey' and find an alternative way of handling the symptoms.

Try to find someone to lean on, someone you can confide in and trust. Someone who genuinely cares but won't pass judgement. It may look as if everyone else is having a fantastic, carefree life but you'd be surprised how many people out there could relate to your particular problems; especially if they're also the partner of a depressive. By swapping notes, you'd know that you're not alone and might come to realise that other people are tearing their hair out too. Depression isn't choosy – it will affect anyone, so I don't know why so much stigma is attached to it. Shoving it under the carpet, pretending it doesn't exist won't work. I'm afraid it has to be faced head on. The words, 'Repression' and 'Depression' are exactly the same, apart from the first letter.

But having said all this, dealing with it as well as trying to live your own life can be torture, exspecially if you can't see a light at the end of the tunnel. I admit I was guilty of attempting to conceal Roo's illness from the boys in the beginning, but they were much younger then and I suppose it was my motherly instincts protecting them from something nasty.

Finding the right balance to suit you and all those affected is the key to managing this miserable illness. Now that I'm retired, it's easy for me to drop everything and give Roo the time he needs, but it wasn't always like that. So many times, having just walked into work, I'd have to listen to him howling down the telephone begging me to go home. The worst of these times was when I was visiting my biological father who was three hours' drive away and in the last stages of a terminal illness. I'd just arrived when Roo calmy told me over the 'phone that he was going to kill himself. That situation was unusual, but I had to make a choice and decided that if he was going to do it, I wouldn't be able to get back in time to stop him anyway and concentrated on my dad instead.

So when I hear others saying they don't know who to give priority to – the depressive, elderly relatives, the kids, their work AND be expected to stay healthy themselves at the same time, I can totally empathise because I know positive planning is impossible when depression is so unpredictable.

I would suggest that partners try to respond to the problem each time without getting cross. This will be really difficult sometimes, but take a deep breath and count to ten because if a depressive thinks no one cares about them, they'll quickly sink deeper into despair and clam-up. Then neither of you will know what's going on. Ask them how they're feeling You might wish you hadn't asked and have to run for the bus or get the next train, but by giving them a bit of your time when they really need it can make a huge difference – even if it's only for a few minutes.

I'm no therapist, but it seems that by doing this in the same way each time is a form of cognitive therapy. If the worst moments are at the start of the day – as Roo's usually are, attempt to shake them off by asking them to explain exactly how they feel. Having had all night to brood during fitful sleep or rising early with no one else awake to bounce their feelings off, it's no wonder they're in such a state first thing in the morning when they're convinced that it's the start of yet another hopeless day.

There are a ton of websites with suggestions for self-help, information on treatments and support groups and from what I've read – especially from forums on the internet, there are thousands of partners trying to cope. I'm told some GP's are sympathetic, some aren't. Personally, the last thing I wanted was my own medication to help me help Roo and as I wasn't looking for a counsellor either I've never spoken to my GP about all this. But for most people it's the right place to start – even if it's simply to talk to a captured audience and hopefully be pointed in the right direction.

Believe that things will improve even if you have your doubts. Make sure you remember the good bits inbetween the bad bits and think of ways to make MORE good bits so you have something to look forward to. Fill the empty moments with something – *anything* – even if it's simply going out for a walk together.

I made Roo buy a bike but his excuse not to use it was that he didn't want to go out alone. I don't do bikes. You really need two proper knees to cycle on two wheels and there would be rumours of whale sightings if I was caught wearing Lycra. However, thinking of both him and the possibility of losing some of my blubber, I bought a tricycle rather than a bicycle because Roo said I wouldn't be quite so unbalanced. (I'm sure he was talking about using three wheels). I do look like an overgrown toddler but my trike has a big basket, which is handy for shopping and will be even more handy should I need an oxygen cylinder at a later date.

Once again, you think I'm not being serious but this illness can be so distressing it's important to reflect on at least some parts of your life with a little humour. But my biggest tip is not to wait until you're at breaking point to find whatever help or support you both need. Call for the Cavalry. Surround yourself with anything and everything you think might work for you and begin a process of elimination. Summon up your own God – *the outcome may surprise you.*

PS:

Why did I keep this journal?

It was a combination of two things.

For Roo and I to remember every little detail from a trip as big as this without writing it down would have been impossible. So I promised myself that I would keep a diary of everything we'd done and write the descriptions of every place we'd visited. Some days I wrote two, or three times to make sure I hadn't left anything out. Often, I'd scribbled headings or a funny quip on a restaurant menu. A few times, I used loo roll to jot down my thoughts and when my notepad ran out on one of the flights, I wrote on two airline sick bags. (Who was that novelist who wrote the basis for a whole book on a cigarette packet?) All the finer details - the silly, funny things, the mood of the moment, a true picture of the despondency that depression brings would have disappered forever – especially with Roo having trouble recalling what he had for lunch.

The other reason, was to log Roo's illness. If I'm honest, I thought I might see a pattern, or recognise some sort of trigger and find a cure for his depression. I realise now that there isn't going to be a breakthough and that we may never discover the reason for his illness but writing my feelings down on paper and reading it back has helped me and that in turn, must surely have helped him. We've struggled with his uncontrollable need to self-destruct for nearly twenty years now, five them of them without sufficient medication to prop him up so he's a bit of a hero in that respect.

After the call to Virgin Atlantic about the Duty Free, we settled down again but my sleepiness had gone and I laid in bed reflecting on our trip around the world in seventy-five days. (Or was it seventy-six by crossing the Dateline?)

I must have gained at least 100 pounds but in the process been enriched with the sights, sounds and smells of faraway lands I never expected to see so it was worth every pound. I'd tasted strange food, marvelled at culinary expertise and saw how naïve we are about what is actually edible. I'll never forget the love I felt cuddling Orion, the Koala or the novelty of feeding a Kangaroo or the magic of standing quietly beside an upside down Panda so's not to wake her and the shock of coming face to face with a 9` shark. I never expected to see another Angel, be attacked by a pterodactyl or witness the beauty of Milford Sound. At Easter Services from now on, I'll always drift back to the one we attended in Tahiti and to find a meeting place as amazing as the Opera House will be tough. I'd followed a whale and was proud of myself for actually firing a machine gun at a terrorist – even if he WAS made of paper. Washing my hair, I'll often be reminded of my silly dance on the beach at Bali Hai and every now and then, I'll frighten the boys by saying, *"Let's walk the sky!"*.

If you are suffering the effects of this horrible illness, don't be scared, because you are not alone.There are many more people than you could possibly imagine trying to cope with exactly the same thing. You may never discover the reason for being like this, but remember - it's not madness, it isn't a weakness and it isn't your fault. Hope is everything and I would encourage you to find the strength to walk the sky with optimism and not give in to the demon we call depression. If you are the partner of a depressive, give them all the love you can.